SOCIOLOGY AND SOCIAL POLICY

Sociology and Social Policy

ESSAYS ON COMMUNITY, ECONOMY, AND SOCIETY

Herbert J. Gans

Columbia University Press
New York

Columbia University Press
Publishers Since 1893
New York Chichester, West Sussex
cup.columbia.edu

ISBN 978-0-231-18304-8 (cloth : alk. paper) |
ISBN 978-0-231-18305-5 (pbk. : alk. paper) |
ISBN 978-0-231-54509-9 (e-book)

Library of Congress Control Number: 2016957470

Columbia University Press books are printed on permanent
and durable acid-free paper.
Printed in the United States of America

Cover design: Jordan Wannemacher

For Louise, David, Consuelo, and Jacob

Contents

Preface and Acknowledgments

This collection brings together some of my essays on a number of current social conditions, issues, and problems. While many of the essays are wholly analytic, those dealing with social problems also propose solutions. They illustrate what I believe sociology can contribute to social policy. Unlike the other social sciences, which emphasize public policy, social policy also covers the nongovernmental sectors of society.

The book is at the same time a plug for policy-oriented sociology, for social research that answers the empirical questions raised by social policy analysts and policy makers. It can also aid them in developing policies that deal with social conditions and problems.

In addition, policy-oriented research can identify many of the likely consequences of alternative policies, including who will be benefitted, hurt, or otherwise affected by each of these policies. Such analyses should help the policy makers—and the politicians—who must choose the best policy.

Sociology is particularly well suited to playing this policy-oriented role. My conception of the discipline is fairly simple; it studies what people and their institutions and other social structures (including economic, political, and cultural ones) do with, for, to, and against each other. Putting it this way emphasizes the fact that at its best sociology is thoroughly empirical and employs grounded theories and concepts.

Sociology has other advantages. Less restricted by arbitrary intellectual boundaries than some of the other social sciences, sociologists conduct sociological research on economic, political, cultural, and historical subjects and whatever others policy-oriented studies demand.

Sociologists' qualitative methods, especially fieldwork and in-depth interviewing methods, can observe what people actually do and talk with them about issues and problems that matter to them—and to those charged with policy making.

Sociological analysis can also investigate the social structures in which people are embedded, including those that help explain their behavior and that cause the problems policy makers, politicians—and citizens—must try to fix.

The discipline's quantitative research methods can provide the numbers that policy makers and politicians always need to justify their decisions and actions.

This collection is a sequel to my 1992 collection *People, Plans, and Policies*, published by Columbia University Press, which is itself a sequel to a 1968 collection *People and Plans*, published by Basic Books.

The title of the new book substitutes social policy for planning mainly because I long ago moved out of the city-planning and social-planning fields in which I began my career.

Social policy is not very different from social planning, except that it generally operates in and on the present, whereas planning more often concerns itself with the future.

However, many of the social policies discussed or advocated in this book are not immediately practical. Being an academic, I take advantage of the academic's freedom to propose pushing the envelope beyond the currently acceptable. We can therefore advocate policies that could solve problems better than other policies but that are now politically or otherwise impractical.

When I am being impractical, I do it with the hope that some of the resulting suggestions will also be made by and supported by others and, in the longer run, will enter the national policy conversation. If and when the political and other kinds of time are ripe, the suggestions might even become politically and otherwise practical.

Because the last version of this preface is being written shortly after Donald Trump's election and the virtual Republican takeover of all branches of federal and state governments, it is very clear that the times are not ripe. Consequently, my policy and other proposals are now largely wishes and hopes.

However, this is even more reason to enter the national policy conversation with proposals for creating a more egalitarian and otherwise humane country. These proposals must also be discussed widely so that they can be transformed into feasible policies. The policies and the political strategies to bring them about need to be available the moment all the times are ripe.

The five parts into which I have divided this book are similar to the parts of its 1992 predecessor, but the essays themselves are somewhat different.

Part 1, on the city, is mostly devoted to critical analyses of contemporary urban sociology. I have been especially concerned with an increasing tendency to emphasize the causal role of space and place in urban studies, thereby downplaying the social, economic, and political forces and agents that better explain the urban condition.

This spatial bias too often leads to ineffective or undesirable social policies, because it tries to change the so-called physical environment rather than the human forces and agents that need to be altered.

Part 2, about poverty, is now a much researched field. Perhaps for that reason, I have focused on questions that I think still need to be explored further, particularly about the poorest of the poor and about multigenerational poverty, to complement current research on intergenerational poverty.

However, my recent writing about poverty has more often emphasized unemployment and other job-related issues that increasingly affect a much larger population and threaten to drive them into poverty as well.

Part 3 therefore consists of essays on jobs and the political economy. The latter is included because today's private economy can no longer provide sufficient decently paying and reasonably secure jobs to all who need them.

Consequently, government must step in with jobs, income, and other means of support to the country's many unemployed, underemployed, and underpaid people. This being politically improbable in today's polity, I have also been looking for feasible strategies for political change, including in this part's last essay, to educate students about the economy into which they are graduating.

Part 4, about race and class, is dominated by two underlying ideas. One, announced in its title, is that race and racism must almost always be seen, and studied, in connection with class and its forms of discrimination. The other is a yet-unsolved American puzzle: why the country and especially its white population have never stopped demonizing and discriminating against African Americans, notably poor ones.

For African Americans, racial difference is a near-permanent obstacle, while for other races, it is not. Other races benefit from the fact that definitions of race, and perceptions of skin color as well as other racial characteristics, change with the times.

Chapter 14 tells how the poor Southern and Eastern European immigrants who came here between 1870 and 1924 were then seen as dark or "swarthy" races. Once their descendants became American and middle class, they were redefined as white and described as ethnic groups.

The final essay in part 4 updates my long-standing critique of the blaming systems that are used to demonize the poor, especially the black poor. That essay, my second look at the Moynihan Report of 1965, can be read as a case study of these systems.

Part 5 is based on my equally longstanding curiosity about whether and how ethnic groups finally disappear into one or another American mainstream. The two essays in this part revisit the descendants of the above-mentioned European immigrants and suggest how what remains of their ethnic distinctiveness is disappearing—and may finally disappear altogether.

The last section of chapter 15 notes that the religious institutions that these immigrants brought with them also Americanized, and most have already disappeared. However, many of the mainstream religions are also losing worshippers, and perhaps religion generally may be heading in a direction similar to that of ethnicity.

I have appended an academic autobiography that describes my overall research career, especially how I became interested in the fields in which I have written, including those making up this collection. The appendix may therefore provide some context for the essays, and for those who are interested, in their author.

Finally, I should underline that many of the articles in this book are essays and that most were written because I was intrigued by an idea, a hunch, or a current domestic policy issue. As essays, they omit literature reviews and are short on bibliographies, thereby slighting the people whose ideas and findings I drew on.

Also, I have not updated these articles. Everyone's writings are time bound, even those that become classics, and any updating would soon be out of date as well.

Because most social science journals will not publish essays, I am especially grateful to the editors who published mine.

They are: Lawrence Bobo, editor of the *DuBois Review*; Martin Bulmer and John Solimos, co-editors of *Ethnic and Racial Studies*; Jeffrey Madrick, editor of *Challenge*; and Anthony Orum, then editor of *City and Community*.

I am also grateful to their staff members who helped, or stood in for me, in my regularly failed attempts to meet the complicated demands of publishers' computers.

They are Sara Bruya of the *DuBois Review*; Amanda Eastell–Bleakley of *Ethnic and Racial Studies*; and Debra Solis and Joanne Reider of *Challenge*.

SOCIOLOGY AND SOCIAL POLICY

PART ONE

THE CITY

My introduction to urban sociology began with my doing several community studies both in urban neighborhoods and in suburbs. As one result, I began to wonder whether and how cities and suburbs—as well as small towns and villages—actually differed from one another, which then got me interested in what urban sociology was studying and what it should be studying.

I also became curious about two specific issues, the first being whether there is really such a thing as *the city*, and if not, how one conceptualizes the variety of cities.

Today's U.S. urban sociology is mostly Big City sociology, but actually existing cities may be huge, big, average, and small. They can also be distinguished in other ways, such as global cities, national political and cultural capitals, regional centers, and industrial and market cities.

Suburbs, small towns, and villages are diverse as well, but chapter 1 offers a solution: to give up all the different names for types of places and instead begin by calling them all settlements.

If they were all called settlements, specific studies could focus on their social, economic, political, cultural, spatial, and other characteristics. Thus, a study of settlements that compared poorer with more affluent settlements could help us understand how these are similar and different, regardless of whether they are called cities or suburbs.

Describing all types of localities as settlements may also open up new questions for research. *Settlements* emphasizes the people and groups doing the settling, rather than the geographic, legal, political, and administrative characteristics of the communities in which they have settled.

To further stimulate new research, the chapter suggests that urban sociology could be divided into four fields, one of which would be the sociology of the city. Another could be called spatial sociology—a name that leads directly to my second issue.

It asks whether and how what planners used to call the physical environment determines social life and structures in the settlements in which people live.

These days urban sociologists write not about the physical environment but about space and place. I view space as dirt, or more politely, as the surface of the earth to which gravity has attached us since we came out of the trees.

Space becomes place when humans and the social structures in which they are embedded occupy the space, divide it into bounded lots, build on it or dig into it, live or work or play in it, or buy and sell it.

The prime empirical question should be a causal one: do space and its transformation into place cause the social structures of settlements, or do these structures determine how space is turned into place?

The best answer to this question is both, but chapter 2 argues that, more often than not, the social shapes the spatial. I wrote it mainly because I felt that, in recent years, urban sociology has paid too much attention to how space shapes place, underplaying the social, economic, and political forces and agents that determine what happens to space.

Chapters 3 and 4 can be read as case studies shedding further light on the analysis in chapter 2. Thus, chapter 3 argues against seeing the *ghetto* mainly as spatially different from other neighborhoods. In fact, it is usually an ordinary neighborhood about which the racially dominant population, i.e. whites, has decided that other people, distinguished mainly by their darker skin, must live there and only there.

Social policy cannot do away with *ghettos* by treating them as space. They can be made more livable, but they can be eliminated only through policies that put an end to racial discrimination and segregation.

Chapter 4 applies this causal argument to a critical analysis of a currently highly influential spatial approach: the concentration of poverty. It argues that poverty is concentrated when 40 percent of a neighborhood consists of people whose income is below the poverty line.

Much of concentrated poverty research is devoted to identifying neighborhood effects. Such effects include many of the problems traditionally associated with poverty, as well as the likelihood of passing these on to the next generation.

However, the concentration researchers do not sufficiently consider the possibility that many of the effects they ascribe to the neighborhood may be primarily caused by poverty. But poverty is mainly created by national and local institutions and not by neighborhoods.

The causal issues in concentration effects research might be illuminated if researchers also studied the high degree of residential concentration among the rich, but no one has yet carried out such studies.

Nonetheless, neighborhood effects research has been used to justify tearing down public housing projects, and to disperse a small number of the concentrated poor to other neighborhoods. These policies omit making available to the poor the jobs and income supports that are crucial to reducing poverty significantly.

Since concentration research spans urban and poverty issues, chapter 4 can also be read to introduce part 2 of the book, and because the research has been undertaken principally in *ghetto* neighborhoods, the chapter is also relevant to part 4 of the book.

CHAPTER 1

Some Problems of and Futures for Urban Sociology

Toward a Sociology of Settlements

I n 1968, Manuel Castells asked, "Is there an urban sociology?" and answered his question by noting that "after fifty years existence, only one subject for research in urban sociology remains untackled: its subject matter" (Castells, 1976, p. 59). Castells was commenting on European as well as American urban sociology, and a few years later, he wrote a book about what was now the urban question, in which he added that "from the point of view of scientific vocabulary, I could well do without . . . certain terms . . . 'urban,' 'city,' 'region,' 'space,' etc." (Castells, 1977, p. 441; see also Gottdiener, 1985).

Castells' skepticism was belied by the massive amount of analytic work he devoted to his questions, the terms he dismissed, and the related questions he eventually answered. Now forty years have passed, and the kinds of questions he raised then still deserve to be considered.[1] My article is narrower in scope than Castells' articles; moreover, it is limited to American urban sociology. Also, my analysis is not intended to do away with the field but to propose some intellectual reorganizing to encourage needed research and suggest a few new research questions.

Some Problems

Although American cities have long been diverse in many characteristics, in 1938, Louis Wirth unintentionally covered up that diversity by an all-embracing definition of cities as large, dense, and socially heterogeneous (Wirth, 1938).[2] That definition also implied a definition of the rural areas to which he compared cities as lacking this trio of characteristics, but strangely enough, Wirth failed to refer to other major kinds of communities, for example, towns and suburbs.[3]

Today, a majority of Americans live in the suburbs and a growing number of these are becoming larger, denser, and more heterogeneous than many cities, while truly rural communities are few and far between (Gans, 1962). In any case, Wirth's still widely used definition and the comparison that accompanies it have lost their usefulness.

More important, today most American research in urban sociology focuses on cities, mainly very large ones. Actually, the significant portion of that research deals not with cities *per se* but with topics, topical issues, and problems that are located *in* cities, currently, for example, around race and class. However, topic- and problem-centered urban sociology is as old as the hills.

Park's (1915) essay "The City," which is said to have initiated empirical urban sociology in America, is actually not an analysis of the city but a survey of general sociological topics, especially of course the immigration and ethnic (or "race relations") questions in which Park and his colleagues were especially interested.[4] Many of these topics showed up again as chapter heads in the introductory text that Park wrote with Ernest Burgess a few years later (Park and Burgess, 1921)—a text that, incidentally, did not include a chapter on the city. However, the ecologically inclined among Park's colleagues were interested in cities, or at least in urban growth and in the competition for space.

Interestingly enough, a couple of generations later, when ecology had long since lost its dominance in the field and the neo-Marxists had moved urban sociology toward studying the urban economy, growth was still on the agenda. Indeed, the growth machine (Molotch, 1976) continues to be a much cited concept in the field.

Park and his colleagues wrote about a Chicago that was growing rapidly, with most of the growth coming from, by WASP standards, strange immigrants. The neo-Marxist approach to the urban economy coincided with the urban financial crisis. It should thus not be surprising why today's urban sociology is particularly concerned with issues of race and class and more recently also with spatial sociology, which reflects in part a political concern with privatization and the disappearance of urban public space (e.g., Mitchell, 2003; Kohn, 2004).[5] Thus, I think it is fair to say that the field called urban sociology is really problem- and issue-oriented sociology in and about American cities.

Needless to say, this is all to the good, partly because it keeps sociology publicly relevant and useful, although one must add that urban sociologists do not study these topics in very many cities. Ever since its beginnings, American urban sociology has concentrated on Chicago—and especially its *ghetto* (Small, 2007), as well as a few other, mostly large cities, including New York, Los Angeles, and at the moment, post-Katrina New Orleans. Conversely, the field has paid virtually no attention to the suburbs, as well as the small towns and rural areas (America's villages) that remain culturally and politically significant even if their past demographic domination has ended.

Although part of the explanation for the field's concentration on a few cities must be the government's and the foundations' interest in them, one can only speculate about some of the other causes. For one thing, other fields conduct specific studies in the suburbs, small towns, and rural areas, especially those easily accessible to busy scholars. For example, an immigration researcher and his urban sociologist colleague were the first to look at the suburbanization of brand new immigrants (Alba and Logan, 1991).

Furthermore, a field that studies the entire range of communities in which Americans live and work may be logistically and otherwise unworkable. Communities, whether they are big cities or villages, are immensely complicated agglomerations of primary and secondary groups and networks, as well as an array of economic, political, religious, cultural, and many other institutions and structures, most of them organized hierarchically. These are, in addition, connected ecologically and in other ways to a set of yet other interrelated hierarchies that often extend far beyond the official boundaries of the community. Urban sociologists have not fully acknowledged the extent to which their research has simplified the empirical reality with which the field is concerned.

Urban Sociology's Illogical Typology

One form of simplification results from what I think of as the field's four-item naming system: city, suburb, town, and rural area. This is, in addition, an illogical typology. Thus, cities and suburbs are distinguished literally by their location on other sides of the "city limits," whereas towns are distinguished from cities and from each other mainly by their size, and rural areas refer to communities attached to a practically obsolete type of agricultural economy.

All of these communities are defined by their boundaries, which often began as cow paths or in other random ways but now have a variety of political, financial, and other functions. However, these are only the official boundaries. Economic and other institutions inside them serve market or service areas within boundaries unrelated to the official ones. Some of the market areas are now becoming global in size. Furthermore, the people who live in these communities create their individual boundaries depending on where they work and play and where they find the goods and services they prefer and the relatives and other people they visit regularly.

Each of the four community types is burdened by other definitional and measurement problems. For example, the communities that have been or that are currently called cities range from today's versions to places once reserved for gods, priests, kings—some of them called divine—the dead, the military, and others.[6] In size, cities have ranged from minuscule, like King David's Jerusalem or the Troy of the Trojan war, to today's metropoli with populations of over 20 million (Gans, 1991).

Similarly, suburbs lie not only on the other side of city limits but may also be bedroom communities, which resemble in some respects the bedroom neighborhoods of many outer cities. Towns are sometimes politically differentiated from cities, but otherwise, there is no consensus about when they are small enough not to be called cities. A rural area without farmers seems a contradiction in terms.

In part because of their vagueness, these types have lent themselves easily to stereotyping. Thus, urban is now shorthand for very big and crowded cities, often occupied by the poor and the dark-skinned; suburban usually refers to low-density bedroom communities.

In reality, each of these community types is itself immensely diverse, and the within-type variations may well exceed the between-type ones. How does one compare a suburb of mass-produced tract houses like Levittown with one consisting of architecturally designed and individually built mansions—or a very rich one like Scarsdale, New York, with an extremely poor one, such as Robbins, Illinois. What is to be done with Stamford, Connecticut, a city in Connecticut that is also a suburb for commuters from New York City and other nearby workplaces? And how can one compare rural areas dominated by the weekend and summer homes of affluent urban residents with those occupied by industrial-size farms and the migrant laborers that tend the fields?

One of the ways urban sociology has dealt with these complications is by ignoring them; another is by inventing adjectives to deal with at least some of the variations. There have long been central, inner, and outer cities, but there are now also inner and outer suburbs; edge, edgeless, satellite, and global cities, as well as metropoli and megacities. Suburbs are subdivided among other things into streetcar, commuter, industrial, tract, and bedroom suburbs, as well as exurbs and that leftover from the ecological era: the urban-rural fringe. But some researchers argue that many Americans actually live in metropolitan and micropolitan areas and polynucleated regions, without much attention to city limits or other official boundaries.

Some of the field's typological concepts also have normative associations that influence empirical analyses. Urban sociology has often celebrated the city, even if the Chicago ecologists and others denigrated the urban poor. The urban celebration is ancient, which should not be surprising because the city has often welcomed scholars, especially free-thinking ones, when other communities have been hostile. In addition, the city has long been a surrogate and proxy for a variety of values treasured by intellectuals, among them modernity, high culture, urbanity, cosmopolitanism, and democracy.[7] Conversely, the suburbs still evoke, including in some urban sociology texts, the stigmatizing images of sterility, conformity, and homogeneity that they acquired in the 1950s.

A Sociology of Settlements

Most other sociological fields are burdened with similarly problematic typologies and other handicaps, and more thought needs to be given to reducing or eliminating them. In the case of urban sociology, doing away with the typology might encourage and perhaps even force urban sociologists to find a single term to delineate what they study. The word that immediately comes to mind and that I have already used here is community, but it has given rise to so many definitions—and sentimental associations—that another term is needed.

My first choice would be settlement but aggregation would do, too, for in a way the term itself does not matter. A single term might encourage a focus on what all settlements have in common as well as on how they differ, which in turn should encourage more attention to the entire range of con-current activities and processes to be found inside every settlement. Such a frame would in turn encourage new distinctions between settlements as well as raise empirical and theoretical questions that probably would not come up when settlements are from the outset classified as urban, suburban, town, or rural. Indeed, in a world beset by energy shortages and global warming crises, distinctions based on the distance people live from their workplaces and mass transit are far more relevant than whether they live on this or that side of the city limits.

Furthermore, as long as race and class remain such important issues, set-tlements should be compared in terms of their racial and class composition and segregation; a comparison that should precede such variables as size. For example, there may be patterns that distinguish mono-, duo-, and multi-racial settlements.

Given the importance of local economies, settlements with predomi-nantly labor-intensive economies can be compared to those that are capital-intensive. The term settlement itself suggests that there are places in which a majority of groups and institutions are settled and those in which various portions or segments are transient or in other kinds of flux.

The shift to the settlement does not rule out traditional topics, however. Size and density are still relevant research topics, although a perhaps more relevant spatial analysis would examine whether and how settlements use urban design, street plans, highway location, and other devices to separate land uses and classes or isolate racial minorities.

Perhaps, it is even time to end the long preoccupation with boundaries and bounded communities. If a widget maker somewhere in Long Island ships its products largely to California and Europe but the social service agency a few blocks away finds that most of its clients come from within a two-mile radius, why does it matter that both are located in a settlement with the same boundaries? True, the widget maker pays taxes and the service agency is funded by some of these taxes, but in most other respects, their boundary sharing is irrelevant.

Perhaps a study of boundaries could determine whether and how settlements are bounded, separating official boundaries from the unof-ficial and informal ones that various groups and institutions create for themselves or are created out of competition. Then, one could look at the effects of the various kinds of boundaries on different people, institu-tions, and interests.

Currently topical issues can also stay on the research agenda, but analyzing them in settlements may encourage looking at today's "urban" topics in other places. For example, what is concentrated poverty like in a small settlement; what kinds of growth machines, if any, operate in the settlements in which industrial agriculture is pursued; and what happens to neighborhood effects in settlements composed of only two or three official or unofficial neighborhoods? At the other end of the spatial scale, the time is more than ripe to determine how multinational corporations operate in diverse settlements, from metropoli to tiny localities.

Overall, a focus on settlements would suggest examining and comparing the interactions, routine and unusual, peaceful and conflict ridden, and competitive and cooperative among and between all the various groups and institutions without concern as to whether they were urban or not but without losing sight of the fact that they are settlements. One likely result would be a much larger set of categories by which to classify settlements and a more logical array of typologies. That might encourage urban sociologists to study some of each of the kinds of settlements in which most Americans live, work, and play.

Once the intellectual borders in which the current typology has trapped the field are opened, researchers now called urban sociologists can take their concepts from all over the disciplinary map. In fact, because every last one of the structures, processes, cultures, and other phenomena that are studied in sociology's many fields take place in one or another kind of settlement, the concepts that are applied in all these fields can be used by settlement sociologists as well.

Other Possibilities

In theory, the concepts that scientists use do not have to reflect those of the lay world. Thus, theoretical physicists can work with string theory and dark matter but are not required to conduct studies of heaven or even the sky. However, social scientists, and sociologists especially, cannot distance themselves quite as casually from lay concepts.

Thus, replacing the urban-suburban-town-rural area typology with a unitary concept like settlement would not be easy. Indeed, sociologists themselves will be hard put to look at settlements and not see them as cities or suburbs or small towns. Giving up the long-standing typology for a new concept would require the concurrent elimination not just of a traditional frame but of an equally long-standing mindset. Even the term urban evokes so many images, social processes, and structures that it is as difficult to drop from everyday discourse as from the field's conceptual repertoire.

Being realistic, the old typology will not soon disappear from sociological thought. However, in that case urban sociologists should begin to further develop and systematize the field's basic typology or formulate typologies that connect with the research questions being studied.

There is at least one other possibility: to divide what is now a single field into four. One field would essentially continue today's urban sociology for those whose interest is limited to cities. However, that field should then be renamed the sociology of the city. The second field would be the sociology of settlements I have outlined above.

A third field, which is especially necessary to grasp the complexity of settlements, would be devoted to community studies, a genre that has always been related to urban sociology but cuts across and is useful to other fields in the discipline. Qualitative community studies are particularly necessary, whether they involve participant observation or interviewing or both, because they can grasp the richness of social processes, structures, and cultures in ways other research methods cannot. They also permit thick descriptions of the everyday lives of people, groups, and institutions.[8]

The fourth field is spatial sociology, which needs to be separated from urban sociology because spatial analyses should be undertaken in virtually all fields of the discipline. As long as life on this planet is tied down by gravity, the humans studied by sociology must occupy "natural" or "physical" *space*, using the social and cultural tools available to them to make it into *place*—as well as built and unbuilt environments (Gans, 2002).[9] Whether it be a family, a governmental agency, or a corporate firm, it "sits" on space and creates the place from and in which it plays its roles in the larger society. Why spatial analysis has surfaced in and has been restricted to urban sociology as much as it has is therefore puzzling.

The separate field is needed for another reason; spatial analysis deviates too much from the other ways of doing urban sociology. Whatever the differences in their missions and underlying ideologies, ecology and neo-Marxist analyses are basically compatible because they have both studied the use, competition, exchange, and regulation of land, and the various social structures involved in these processes. Community studies investigate these and other social structures, and the "cultural turn," when not seeking to replace structure *per se*, adds meaning, values, symbols, and other mainly noneconomic and non-political concepts to structural and other analyses of settlements.

However, one of the dominant forms of spatial analysis has a very different agenda, to show that space and place have independent social effects that can shape a variety of aspects of social life prior to social intervention. Moreover, this spatial analysis takes such effects for granted and thus only needs to describe them rather than discover them by empirical study. Such "physical" determinism may facilitate architectural thought but it is not a sociological analysis.

Whether space and place have social effects and, if so, what kinds of effects, are worthwhile questions for empirical analysis. However, that analysis must also consider the likelihood that these effects are themselves socially caused. Consequently, the analysis must trace the causal processes by which settlement structures and institutions turn space into place, and then see what social effects follow. As long as turning space into place and a built environment costs money, one major social cause is generally to be found in the settlement economy and its distribution of capital and income.

For example, while high dwelling-unit density, that is, the number of people per room, undoubtedly has social effects, these are themselves the effects of such social causes as the land values and building costs of the dwelling unit as well as the occupants' poverty or involuntary segregation that force them to live at such density. Thus, looking at the social effects of space and of place making is the last stage in a long causal analysis. Spatial research that incorporates this or similar models would be a useful field in any future urban sociology.

Coda

One of these days, the sociology of settlements, whatever it is called, will expand to cover virtual settlements. When more people spend a larger part of their lives on the web or its successors so that the places they create and the environments they build will be located in and on virtual space, the social effects and other complexities of physical space and place may become clearer.[10] Although corporate and other power holders that dominate physical space and place also seem to be influential in their virtual equivalents, there are many differences in the two kinds of spaces and places. The comparative study of physical and virtual settlements should be productive for our understanding of both.

Acknowledgments

I am grateful to Talja Blokland and to Leon Deben, Claude Fischer, and Harvey Molotch for comments on an earlier draft, and as always to Tony Orum for his comments and other support.

Notes

Reprinted from *City and Community*, vol. 8, no. 3, 2009, by permission of John Wiley & Sons Ltd.

1. Castells has done so himself recently (Castells, 2002). He is now less skeptical about the field, but his discussion of its future concentrates on the themes and research questions he has pursued in his own work.

2. Actually, the definition seems to have originated earlier in the circle around Robert Park, for he discussed the three characteristics a decade earlier in a presentation to the American Sociological Society (Burgess, 1926, p. 4).

3. Wirth did not explain the omission, but as many readers of his essay have noted, Wirth, like Simmel before him (Simmel, 1908), was also, or actually, comparing *Gesellschaften* with *Gemeinschaften*. Moreover, according to Lannoy (2004, p. 51), Park and his colleagues were making the urban-rural comparison to put the then fledgling urban sociology on an equal footing with the already large and well-established field of rural sociology.

4. The topics Park discussed in the essay included, among others, work and industrial organization, mobility, primary and secondary groups, social control, deviance, and the mass media.

The same lack of interest in the city *per se* can be found in Simmel's 1908 essay about Berlin that is said to have influenced Park. Simmel paid virtually no attention to that city but dealt with urbanity, cosmopolitanism, and other "mental" effects of the metropolis on intellectuals.

Although Ernest Burgess is immortal because of his portraits of Chicago's concentric zones (1925/1967), a close look at the zones themselves display less interest in ecology than in the distribution of socioeconomic classes and ethnic neighborhoods.

5. Perhaps there is also a connection with the Marxist analysis of space (e.g., Gottdiener, 1985; Lefebvre, 1991), although its main agenda seems to have been a debate with Louis Althusser and his supporters about the Marxist analysis of capitalism.

6. One should note, however, that most of these functions involved people holding power, and often absolute power. Mumford (1961) described some of the ancient cities as control centers.

7. It is worth noting that when Wirth was writing "Urbanism as a Way of Life," many of America's most influential intellectuals were still living in New England small towns and villages. A number of them expressed the bitterly antiurban ideology that Jefferson and others already voiced at the country's beginnings.

8. However, community studies conducted solely by participant observation are probably incapable of understanding large- or even medium-sized settlements unless conducted by teams (e.g., Warner and Lunt, 1941). However, individual researchers can analyze neighborhoods in large settlements.

9. Although spatial sociologists, geographers, and others are still debating definitions of space and place (Hubbard, Kitchin, and Valentine, 2004), I choose to call the clusters of dirt to which gravity attaches us space and reserve place for the end product of what "society" and we do to put boundaries, a price, and uses on the clusters.

10. They will be even clearer when the analysis considers the fact that all those participating in the virtual community are working on computers or their successors that, like they, sit on or are otherwise attached to physical space.

References

Alba, R., and Logan, J. 1991. "Variations on Two Themes: Racial and Ethnic Patterns in the Attainment of Suburban Residence," *Demography* 28, 431–453.

Burgess, E. 1925. "The Growth of the City: Introduction to a Research Project," in R. Park, E. Burgess, and R. McKenzie (eds.), *The City*, pp. 47–62. Chicago, IL: University of Chicago Press, 1925, 1967.

Burgess, E. 1926. *The Urban Community*. Chicago, IL: University of Chicago Press.

Castells, M. 1976. "Is There an Urban Sociology?" in C. Pickvance (ed.), *Urban Sociology: Critical Essays*, pp. 33–59. London: Methuen.

Castells, M. 1977. *The Urban Question: A Marxist Approach*. Cambridge, MA: MIT Press.

Castells, M. 2002. "Conclusion: Urban Sociology in the Twenty-First Century," in I. Susser (ed.), *The Castells Reader on Cities and Social Theory*, pp. 390–406. Malden, MA: Blackwell.

Gans, H. 1962. "Urbanism and Suburbanism as a Way of Life: A Re-Evaluation of Definitions," in A. Rose (ed.), *Human Behavior and Social Processes*, pp. 625–648. Boston, MA: Houghton-Mifflin.

Gans, H. 1992. "The Historical Comparison of Cities: Some Conceptual, Methodological and Value Problems," in H. Gans (ed.), *People, Plans and Policies*, pp. 99–109. New York: Columbia University Press.

Gans, H. 2002. "The Sociology of Space: A User-Centered View," *City & Community*. 1, 329–339.

Gottdiener, M. 1985. *The Social Production of Urban Space*. Austin, TX: University of Texas Press.

Hubbard, P., Kitchin, R., and Valentine, G. (eds.). 2004. *Key Thinkers on Space and Place*. London: Sage.

Kohn, M. 2004. *Brave New Neighborhoods: The Privatization of Public Space*. New York: Routledge.

Lannoy, P. 2004 "When Robert Park Was (Re)writing 'The City': Biography, the Social Survey and the Science of Sociology," *American Sociologist* 35, 34–62.

Lefebvre, H. 1991. *The Production of Space*. Oxford, UK: Blackwell.

Mitchell, D. 2003. *The Right to the City: Social Justice and the Fight for Public Space*. New York: Guilford Press.

Molotch, H. 1976. "The City as a Growth Machine," *American Journal of Sociology* 82, 309–330.

Mumford, L. 1961. *The City in History: Its Origins, Its Transformations and Its Prospects*. New York: Harcourt, Brace and World.

Park, R. 1915. "The City: Suggestions for the Investigation of Human Behavior in the Urban Environment," *American Journal of Sociology* 20, 577–612.

Park, R., and Burgess, E. 1921. *Introduction to the Science of Sociology*. Chicago, IL: University of Chicago Press.

Simmel, G. 1908. (1950). "The Metropolis and Mental Life," in K. Wolff (ed.), *The Sociology of Georg Simmel*. Glencoe, IL: Free Press.

Small, M. 2007. "Is There Such a Thing as 'the Ghetto'?" *City* 11, 413–423.

Warner, L., and Lunt, P. 1941. *The Social Life of a Modern Community*. New Haven: Yale University Press.

Wirth, L. 1938. "Urbanism as a Way of Life," *American Journal of Sociology* 44, 1–24.

CHAPTER 2

The Sociology of Space

A Use-Centered View

B ack in the 1960s, I was once asked to speak to a meeting of young architects about planning for societal betterment, only to discover that my audience was solely interested in how they could reform America through architecture and design. I should not have been surprised. Being in the space business, they were spatial determinists who believed that by redesigning space, they could change society.[1]

Sociologists who study space are not architects, but now that spatial sociology is reemerging from a long hibernation, the field needs to think about where it stands on the relation between space and society. This is important for two reasons. First, since all social life is "emplaced," as Thomas Gieryn (2000, p. 466) puts it in his pioneering essay, spatial sociologists must protect against the danger of reconceptualizing the obvious: doing studies to show that all social life exists in space. Second, they must resist the temptation of reifying space, a danger for any new field that seeks to call attention to itself and the concepts it wants to introduce.

Because humans are attached by gravity to the surface of the planet, they exist on natural space. Natural space is a presocial notion, so that sociologically, at least, it is literally air over dirt, or as Gieryn (2000, p. 465) calls it, "stuff."[2] Natural space becomes a social phenomenon, or social space, once people begin to use it, boundaries are put on it, and meanings (including ownership, price, etc.) are attached to it. Then the air-over-dirt becomes a lot or a plot, and if residential users obtain control over the bounded space, it becomes their place.[3]

Spatial sociologists study how society, i.e., individuals and collectivities, transform natural into social space, how they use and exchange it, what social, economic, and other processes and forces come into play in these uses and exchanges, and how both kinds of space affect individuals, collectivities, and social processes and forces.

I find it helpful to look at space and society through a causal lens, asking two questions. First, do both natural and social space have causal power, creating social effects, and, if so, when, how, and why? The second question reverses the causal arrow: Do individuals and collectivities exert causal power, creating effects on both kinds of space, and, if so, when, how, and why?

Although the answer to both questions is yes, the second is the most important for the sociology of space. I would argue that individuals and collectivities shape natural and social space by how they *use* these, although each kind of space, and particularly the social, will also have effects on them.

Spatial determinists may believe that space always has social effects, but such effects are not automatic and are indirect. The presence of gold "under" natural space has considerable economic effects, but only in societies in which gold is valued. Similarly, when homeless people must raise families in a dilapidated motel room, the social space they live in has behavioral effects, but only because welfare agency benefits are too meager to enable recipients to afford livable dwellings. Thus, space almost never has total and direct causal power, and then functions as an intervening causal variable.

In the above, I emphasize the term "use" intentionally, for I believe that a central concept of spatial sociology should be land use. *Use* is defined broadly here, meaning not only how individuals and organizations live and work in space, but what else they do to and with it. Elaborating the traditional dichotomy of use value and exchange value (Logan and Molotch, 1987), use also covers production and reproduction, buying and selling, speculation, allocation, distribution, competition, as well as control, exploitation, theft, and destruction of space. Indeed, use is about everything that emplaced humans do as space users.

The Use-Centered Approach to Space

This causally flavored use- and user-centered way of looking at space and spatial sociology can be illustrated by applying it to several concepts and issues that are relevant to the field, including land use, location, density, propinquity, public space, neighborhood, community, and political economy. In each case, my intent is to show that the users and uses involved determine what happens to the natural or social space, and that its effects on them are brought about by social agents and their actions. Consequently, the direct effects of space on society are limited.

Land Use

Land use is, as already noted, a central concept because all social life is emplaced. Although I have defined use very broadly indeed, how people use the social spaces they build on (or dig in) and occupy has received surprisingly little study. A half century ago, the sociology of housing appeared to take off as a research field, but it never did. Today, little is known about how people live in their homes, for example, how parents and children compete for the available space, or what neighbors fight over. We know as little about what affluent people do with all the interior space in today's "McMansions" as about whether poor people are endangered by living in deteriorated houses. In a period in which drastic housing shortages and zero vacancy rates in some cities force not only the poor but many others to spend half their incomes on rent, the question of how space indirectly shapes family budgets and thus lifestyles—including the decision not to have children—becomes relevant.

The Sociology of Space

Journalists periodically provide data on how the White House pecking order is reflected in office assignments, but we do not know whether and how workplace hierarchies are expressed in office and other workplace design. Organizational sociologists have not yet done enough work on how offices with windows and other spatial perks are assigned—and fought over.

Governments usually have the power to regulate land uses. How and why planning and zoning agencies, building inspectors, landmark preservationists, and others affect land uses the way they do and on what grounds deserves further study than it has received from sociologists.

Many other interesting research questions could be asked about land use, beginning with those studied earlier by the so-called Chicago School ecologists and ethnographers. Some of their questions deserve restudy because of the drastic changes in cities, suburbs, and metropolitan areas over the last 75 years. Ernest Burgess's concentric zones model (Burgess, 1925) and Homer Hoyt's sector theory (Hoyt, 1939) may be obsolete, but class hierarchies and racial exclusion still structure residential land use.[4]

With tourism becoming a major industry in many American cities, the question of which land uses are added to the existing supply of tourist locations, and who chooses and rejects them, is also a way of looking at the social construction of cities. In New York, tourist demand for gospel music has helped turn some Harlem churches into tourist attractions, and I have a hunch that as European whites have to learn to live with people of darker skin color, American *ghettos* themselves have become a more popular tourist destination.

Land Values

Land use (and exchange) give value to land, and that value in turn helps to determine literal use. Social stratification structures land use, but land values play a major role in determining which classes choose and are chosen to go where they do. How land use determines land prices and rents and vice versa is still worth studying, as are the roles different users play in land value determination: not only renters and owners, but also builders, realtors, bankers, and speculators, as well as other spatial venture capitalists and growth machine operators. Indeed, land speculation is a significant activity in many communities but the subject is rarely even mentioned in the sociological literature.

Economists attached to the Chicago School looked at land values as indicators of urban growth, and that analysis is still useful. Their land value "gradients" (Hoyt, 1933) were developed when mass transit largely determined where people lived and worked, but gradients (or other models) based on the dominance of the automobile should be developed.

Location

In one of its meanings, location is a relational concept; it refers to social spaces that make connections between users or uses. All other things being equal, the most highly valued connections obtain the most convenient locations, and studying which users decide what uses are most valuable, as well as who or what determines convenience, will tell us a lot about location. In presuburban American cities, central location as defined by the convergence of transportation lines was the indicator of convenience, and students of land values and realtors identified "100 percent blocks" where values were highest. More often than not, department stores could be found on these blocks. Evidently, shopping was as central in land value determination as in people's communal lives. It would be useful to find the equivalents of the old 100 percent blocks; they are probably the most popular sections of the most popular malls in suburban and exurban areas. Political centrality may have changed less than economic; city halls usually remain where they are when central business districts move or disappear—and palaces stay in use when monarchies become republics.

Density

Density is a particularly important concept in spatial sociology, for how much actual and potential social space is available per capita helps determine how much living space people can afford and the dwelling-unit density at which they live, just as employers decide at what densities their various employees will work, and restaurant owners at what densities their diners will eat. How people with disposable income decide how much living space they want deserves more study, as does my previously asked question of how they cope with the shortage of living space in high rent cities.[5]

A related subject is whether and how governments decide the square footage at which people are crowded in their dwelling unit (dwelling-unit density) and how much of its lot a residential building can cover, which helps determine areal density. Even so, the most urgent density questions are still those about social and other effects, i.e., if and when densities become harmful.

A half century ago, a good deal of housing research was devoted to "crowding studies" (e.g., Freedman, 1975). However, the researchers often failed to find the expected negative effects of crowding. For example, no one was ever able to prove that the school difficulties of poor children could be explained by insufficient space and insulation from noise for doing homework, and negative health effects were often much smaller than expected (e.g., Wilner et al., 1962).

Some of the harmful effects of crowding were eliminated when public health measures were instituted starting in the nineteenth century. Before then, high areal and dwelling-unit density almost guaranteed epidemics among the poor, which then often spread to the more affluent. Today, however, poverty and inequality, as well as the stresses accompanying them, are thought to be more significant causes of ill health (Wilkinson, 1996). True, crowding has declined significantly even among the poor, but the children of the affluent seem able to bring their school sicknesses home to their parents even at the lowest densities. However, in agricultural societies, areal density can become critical; land shortages can lead to starvation and emigration.

Questions about the social and emotional effects of high density could not be answered in part because the effects were hard to discover, but also because societies varied in what dwelling-unit densities people considered desirable and tolerable. Some people seem to need—or even want—less privacy than others, and in all cultures, people have mechanisms for maintaining personal privacy even when space is at a minimum. New Yorkers regularly apply these mechanisms when they ride the subways during rush hours.[6]

Areal density is different from dwelling-unit density. New York's Park Avenue apartment dwellers live at higher areal densities than most poor New Yorkers, but they live at low dwelling-unit density and many also own weekend and summer homes on large lots. Poor people, who cannot "go away" on weekends, therefore live more of their lives in the streets, and in parks when these are available. However, they also inhabit darker and less airy buildings, although not much is known about the effects of these conditions on health and morale.

Propinquity

Students of propinquity and neighboring look at the effects of residential adjacency; the classic studies are Festinger, Schachter, and Back (1950) and Merton (1947). While it was once believed that the low amount of space between houses encourages friendly social contact or conflict, neighboring skills, as well as the demographic homogeneities in a population that spell compatibility, are more important than the lack of space between dwelling units (Gans, 1968, ch. 12). Neighbors with children of the same age may establish social relations; incompatible neighbors usually learn how to ignore each other if only to avoid conflict. To be sure, to some extent the problem is solved by the organization of the housing market. The fact that neighborhoods, and thus adjacent dwelling units, are usually similar in price encourages some homogeneity among neighbors.

However, lack of physical space between neighbors can have negative effects on felt personal and familial privacy. Occupants of rowhouses and apartments with thin walls, or with between-dwelling unit vents that let in conversation or noise, or single-family houses close enough to each other to make family fights public often experience such intrusions. Even five feet of space between houses seems to be enough to minimize such intrusion, one reason why the preference for the detached single-family house remains as strong as ever even if fewer and fewer home buyers can afford it.

Nonresidential propinquity has not received much attention, other than from zoning experts and planners who try to prevent what they deem to be incompatible land users from becoming next door neighbors. Definitions of and judgments about incompatibility have not been studied sufficiently, however. Whether adjacent office buildings, and the people in them, are even neighbors is worth asking, if only to find out if any kind of neighboring takes place.

Public Space

Public space is an almost sacred concept in some left and liberal circles, as if places that are open for public meetings had built-in political advantages. Totalitarian polities may deny people the opportunity to meet, but the availability of public space does not guarantee democratic politics. Hitler was a master at using public space, and other dictators of the right and the left have likewise created attention-getting political spectacles. The attention resulted from the spectacles themselves, however, not from having the space, except that their ability to command huge spaces once in power also enabled them to put on humongous spectacles that attracted attention in part because of their size.

Dictators can force people to come to their meetings, but in democratic societies, public space obtains political significance only when people are willing to attend.[7] Sometimes, they are attracted by causes; sometimes, by free food and drink or by entertainment provided with the politics. Whatever the motives of the attenders, however, public-space-using organizations may obtain visibility, attract some new supporters, and create a mobilizing bond among existing members if people respond to what is happening. Still, the public space itself has only limited causal power, and nothing is more debilitating organizationally than a small attendance in a large public space.

Actually most public space is used for recreational purposes most of the time, and who uses various kinds of public space how much for these and other purposes is an important research topic. Whether and how people use parks, playgrounds, pools, and beaches is not only relevant to the sociology of leisure but it is also of importance to government, particularly since budgets for such spaces are usually the first to be cut when tax receipts decline. In low-density communities, the major users of public recreational space are probably people who cannot afford to buy or rent homes with private outdoor space.

Neighborhood Effects

The notion of the spatially bounded neighborhood has had a powerful effect in American intellectual life. For much of the last century, city planners have laid out new communities with clearly defined and bounded neighborhoods, in part to instill a "sense of community" in and encourage social life among their residents.

Among sociologists, somewhat the same spatial notion has taken the form of looking for "neighborhood effects." In this field of study, the neighborhood is conceived to have good or bad effects because of what it does for or to people, particularly the poor (Brooks-Gunn, Duncan, and Aber, 1997). Neighborhood effects studies tend to be quantitative and therefore able to produce correlations; consequently, they can also identify neighborhoods in which particularly negative or positive social patterns can be found. Although neighborhood effects researchers are working with a spatial concept, they do not always define neighborhood or report who and what in the neighborhood actually produces effects.[8] Moreover, quantitative researchers too often use census tracts as proxies, as if a Bureau of the Census statistical artifact could have good or bad effects.

Even if neighborhood is properly defined, it is still only a bounded area, not a collectivity—such as a political district—with resources, power, or even neighborhoodwide support systems that can influence what people do or what happens to them.[9] Neighborhood agencies may do something to help or hurt the poor, but then the cause is the agencies and their staffs, not the neighborhood. Similarly, the number of slum buildings, drug dealers, taverns, or whorehouses in the neighborhood may correlate with the residents' level of poverty, but what goes on in these land uses will affect people's welfare or their behavior. Even if it were possible to prove that the combined efforts of all agencies and facilities inside a neighborhood had an effect on the residents, the cause remains in the agencies and whatever political and other efforts made their combination effective.

The shortcomings of the neighborhood concept do not apply to neighbors, i.e., fellow residents, if, for example, they are able and willing to help jobless neighbors get jobs. Poor people rarely have access to extra jobs, however, and, like their more fortunate peers, may not want to be helpful to strangers or to people unlike themselves. If large numbers of people in a bounded area helped each other in important ways and did so because of feelings about the area itself, one could perhaps consider this phenomenon as a neighborhood effect. Still, even then, the effects must be ascribed to the people involved and their relations, and not to the neighborhood.

Community Models

A use-centered approach to space will be useful in the understanding of what actually happens in and distinguishes cities from suburbs and other community types, enriching and transcending the ideal types and models used to understand for the standard forms of settlements. Many American cities are surprisingly similar and not very different from typical suburbs; both are primarily homeownership communities in which density levels are approximately the same, and by now many suburbs are virtually as heterogeneous in age and socioeconomic distribution of residents as cities.

If researchers look at what land users actually do in and with space in both kinds of places, they will find a considerable degree of similarity. Poor suburbs are obviously far more like poor urban neighborhoods than like rich suburbs, density differences notwithstanding. Probably the major difference between cities and suburbs is population skin color, there being no completely lily white cities, and that variation has some significant class and other consequences.

Suburbs now also have industry, and since heavy industry has either left America or resettled in rural areas, an old cause of urban-suburban variation has also been eroded. Shopping malls may already be bigger than cities' central business districts. Although urban housing is generally older than suburban, age of housing often does not affect housing use. Of course, very large cities and global cities differ in many respects from smaller ones, although even they have many areas in which land users and use patterns are quite similar. The truly global sections of New York or London are ultimately not very large.

On the whole, cities still have a greater variety of land uses, but partly because their citizens lack the power to exclude land uses they do not want. In addition, cities remain at the center of older transportation networks, thus attracting a variety of land uses that need to be central to as many urban neighborhoods, suburbs, and other communities as possible. Whether still-vital cities will lose their monopoly on centrality depends in part on the future amount of highway building and congestion.

Looking directly at what space users do with space should enhance the understanding of how communities actually function. For example, empirical studies should be able to clear up the disagreement generated by surveys about what has actually happened to voluntary associational life, organizational participation, and civic engagement.

A user-centered approach will also shed a somewhat different light on sociology's models of urban form. These models look at cities from hypothetical and outside standpoints, similar to views from the air, but the users of cities do not see concentric or polycentric models and, besides, they often ignore the boundaries that researchers see and draw. Even when the Chicago sociologists were writing, many of the city's residents never got to the Loop. They stayed in the shopping streets and satellite business districts that supplied the stores they could afford and the goods they preferred, as well as storekeepers who spoke their language, literally and figuratively. Indeed, urban theorists need to ask themselves for whom the central business district was and is central.

When one looks at what I think of as the lived city as mapped by its users who do the living, the differences between cities seen by model makers begin to shrink a bit. To be sure, 1920s Chicago is not 2000s Los Angeles, but if one were to hold time constant and flatten out Los Angeles to make it comparable to Chicago, the lived Chicago region is much the same jumble of land uses and oddly placed satellite shopping and other districts as is Dear's Los Angeles region (Dear, 2002).

In the urban part of Chicago, land users must reach their destinations via a grid system, and in Los Angeles, they have to cope with canyons, but the suburban counties of Chicago and of every large American city do not look very different from the Los Angeles area anymore. Still, the question to study is how significant spatial differences between Chicago and Los Angeles are for their users. Most likely, the economies and polities of the two areas, not to mention the locations of relatives, friends, and often-used facilities, are of far more significance than the features observed by spatial researchers.

Moreover, once language and concept variations are set aside, the two models are not as different as they have been depicted. Indeed, Daphne Spain pointed out how comprehensively both models ignored genders other than male (Spain, 2002). Chicago's huge immigrant population brought globalization to the city in the nineteenth century, and constant economic restructuring took place in Chicago as well, making it as dual, hybrid, and now cyber (Dear, 2002, p. 24) as any other big city, even if the Chicago School sociologists never used or heard such words. Although the Los Angeles model is labeled postmodern and postindustrial, the region has ethnic areas of first and second settlement and experiences "invasion and succession" just like older cities, even if the old Chicago terminology is no longer in use. Racial steering takes place whatever the model, and I am not sure tipping points vary drastically either between the two kinds of cities or between cities and suburbs when all other relevant variables are held constant.

I do not mean here to quarrel with either the Los Angeles or Chicago model, but to urge some hesitation in objectifying and reifying any model, to put more weight on street-level empirical findings, and to understand from what angles and with what agendas the models and their makers view the city. Every model focuses on some features of the city and ignores others; and all model makers come at their analysis with ideologies. Dear's analysis is of and on the left, while the Chicagoans, apparently unaware of their politics, clearly saw government as an unnatural intervener in ecological processes. In addition, they analyzed the city as if they were in the real estate business on the side.

Political economy

An important chapter in postecological sociological thinking about space was the emergence of the neo-Marxian combination of spatial analysis and political economy that was begun by Henri Lefebvre (1991). (The development of neo-Marxist urban sociology by Manuel Castells, David Harvey, and others was a further but, in significant respects, a separate chapter in this story.) Although Lefebvre also analyzed cities, he used spatial analysis for his critical analysis of modern capitalism.

Rereading this analysis after the demise of the state socialism (or was it state capitalism?) of Eastern Europe and China, as well as the currently virtual quiescence of socialist thought, obviously invalidates some old issues and raises some new ones in the spatial analysis of the political economy. For example, is the Lefevbrian spatial analysis still relevant to the analysis and critique of capitalism? Does any kind of spatial analysis draw attention away from more urgent problems of and with capitalism?

Despite the insights that Lefebvre contributed, he defined space so all inclusively that he sometimes framed capitalism as an evil form of land use. Moreover, he could not anticipate modern global varieties of capitalism, both in core and peripheral parts of the planet. For example, the development and continued spread of giant conglomerate and multinational corporations calls for new critical analyses. These firms are so large that their major decision-makers limit their spatial decisions to countries or regions; local managers or subcontracters are given responsibility for smaller-area spatial decisions.

In addition, organizational structures and actual manufacturing or service-providing facilities are rarely in the same place. American corporations incorporate in Delaware or Bermuda, put their headquarters elsewhere, and operate in yet other places. The places in which they make their money can be all over the world. The economic power and the political influence that go with increased organizational size and multinational or global scope may also enable firms to evade government regulations about space use, even if a small firm can bribe politicians more easily than a larger and therefore more visible one. But when jobs are scarce, governments, and especially elected officials, may relax land use regulations in order to attract employers, especially big employers.

The industrial firms that dominated the American economy when Lefebvre wrote have been supplemented by various kinds of service firms.

Also, firms must now be distinguished by whether they are capital-or labor-intensive, and with hospitals, universities, and other nonprofits becoming privatized, capitalism is constantly diversifying.

Outside the United States there are formerly state socialist economies—and capitalist ones, too—in which state control over the economy is nonetheless still prominent. The ease with which the managers of state-owned socialist firms became capitalist entrepreneurs is a sign that broad comparisons may be useful. Whether all the kinds of capitalist organizations use space in significantly different ways remains to be seen, but capitalism can no longer be analyzed as an ideal type.

Furthermore, many firms, even those that are not part of a conglomerate or multinational, are now so footloose that they can go where they choose or where they receive the most subsidy from competing communities. Footlooseness also forces a whole new set of questions on spatial studies and plays havoc with traditional location theory; even so, the location decisions of footloose firms are more structured than the term implies.

The Power of Space

I do not want to downplay the economic, emotional, health, and other effects of space on people. Social space often has such effects, and a great deal of research must be done because the same space does not always have similar effects on everyone. The same building can impact people in various ways, and it may have no effect at all on others. When Mies van der Rohe's Lake Shore Drive apartments in Chicago were unveiled in the early 1950s, their floor-to-ceiling windows facing Lake Michigan thrilled many visitors but generated enough suicidal panic among others that ceiling-to-floor curtains had to be hung on all the windows. However, if the cost of a new city hall vastly exceeds the original budget, all poor taxpayers will be penalized proportionally more than affluent ones. Despite the ambiguous findings of crowding studies, sheer lack of space can have major harmful effects, particularly in agrarian societies. If family plots are too small, people will starve, but if the plots are too small because land is unequally distributed, the cause is to be found in the class hierarchy, not in spatial factors.

In modern and affluent societies, industrial agriculture can cope with space shortages—as well as other spatial problems, such as soil inadequacies, flooding, or drought. The corporations that carry on such agriculture have the political clout, which family farmers lack, to ameliorate flooding and drought and to protect their land and its productivity.

Natural space produces effects less often than social space, but these effects are more likely to touch everyone. When a volcano blows, it may kill everyone in the immediate vicinity. There are other examples of the power of natural space to shape and, especially, to damage, society, but increasingly, the final stages of the process are caused by individuals and collectivities. A large part of southern Louisiana, including New Orleans, is slowly sinking beneath sea level thanks in part to industrial and other institutional decisions made without attention to long-range negative effects.

Once upon a time, hills were used by countries, communities, and elites to defend themselves against their enemies. Now, rich people will pay large amounts of money for such space.[10] In poor countries, the same hills may be relegated to the poor, as in South and Central American favelas. Once upon a time, low lying and swampy shores were also left to the poor, but now the rich are more likely to claim such space, with governments protecting their shorelines against flooding.

The most easily demonstrated causal power of natural space in our day is the aforementioned volcano or the earthquake-prone fault that can destroy entire communities. Of course, people who live near them often come back and rebuild, thus overcoming the limits of natural space. Indeed, spatial sociologists could do more studies of why communities are so often rebuilt in dangerous locations.

The other form of causally significant natural space is land with valuable subsurface material, such as coal, oil, natural gas, and precious and other metals. Economic institutions and forces determine which subsurface resources will be exploited, while political ones now have to look for unpoliticized sites in which to bury nuclear and other toxic wastes.

Spatial Research and Policy

My focus on uses and effects is well suited to future research. Studies of the uses and effects of social space offer another framework for virtually all the topics that sociologists study. Equally important, both kinds of research are relevant to policy research and policy itself. Knowing how people use space can contribute to user-friendly architectural design and spatial planning. Despite the difficulties of effects research, understanding

how and why spatial decisions result in harmful effects can guide reme-
dial public policy. Searching for the causes of spatial effects helps identify
the responsible agents and forces, as well as policy that can change or
redirect them.

Spatial sociology can also be useful to show when spatial policy is not
appropriate. Tearing down buildings in which poor people live in order
to eliminate street crime, or designing new neighborhoods to enhance
social life and civic activity, are only two examples of misguided spatial
policy. Persuasive researchers in possession of the relevant spatial research
might have helped the New Urbanism movement actually be both new
and urbanistic.

Notes

Reprinted from *City and Community*, vol. 1, no. 4, 2002, by permission of
John Wiley & Sons Ltd.

1. The written version of the talk can be found in Gans, 1991.

2. Needless to say, natural space also includes what is under the dirt, whether it is
a coal mine or a volcano. Indeed, without water somewhere under the dirt, natural
space may never become social.

3. Like all dichotomies, the natural-social space distinction is imperfect, but I
think of the former as space that individuals and collectivities are unwilling or
unable to control. There are still areas of the planet that no human being has ever
seen or visited; likewise, there is inaccessible space in American wildernesses that no
one can visit or even see, except perhaps by flyover.

The side of Mount Everest that professionals and now tourists in large numbers
are climbing is clearly social space, but whenever snow and windstorms, avalanches,
and other disasters occur, humans lose control, and Everest temporarily becomes
natural space once more.

4. Informal zones now develop in many American cities in which middle-class
interracial (black-white) families feel comfortable. Not coincidentally, these zones
are frequently located in or near university campuses.

5. Knowing how people who live in crowded circumstances, by American standards, would rank having more space in comparison with other goods and services
of equal cost would be useful, but the same question ought to be asked in other
countries where all dwelling units are smaller.

6. I trust that at least one spatial sociologist is doing empirical work on the practices of cell phone users, and on the current debates and conflicts over how much
they can invade the aural privacy of others.

7. Actually, having to use public space is sometimes a sign of political weakness; powerful groups can afford to meet in private space.

8. This is made more complicated by the fact that people tend to define their own neighborhood for themselves, and their definitions may vary from those of their neighbors. People with limited mobility construct and use very small neighborhoods; adolescents may define the neighborhood as that area from which they escape to obtain privacy for their peer-group activities. People who can jump easily into cars may not even be able to identify the spatial boundaries of their neighborhood.

9. In some cities, neighborhood boundaries are also the boundaries of political districts. If the local districts have any political say over the allocation of resources, they can literally have neighborhood effects, although these are apt to support first and foremost the politically connected residents.

10. This article was written on a hill that was once a Revolutionary War battle site but is now the location of an Ivy League university.

References

Brooks-Gunn, J. D., Duncan, G. J., and Aber, J. L. (eds.). 1997. *Neighborhood Poverty*, Vols. 1 and 2. New York: Russell Sage.

Burgess, E. W. 1925. "The Growth of the City," in R. E. Park, E. W. Burgess, and R. McKenzie, *The City: Suggestions of Investigation of Human Behavior in the Urban Environment,* pp. 47–62. Chicago, IL: University of Chicago Press.

Dear, M. 2002. "Los Angeles and the Chicago School: Invitation to a Debate," *City & Community,* 1, 5–32.

Festinger, L., Schachter, S., and Back, K. 1950. *Social Pressures in Informal Groups.* New York: Harper & Bros.

Freedman, J. L. 1975. *Crowding and Behavior.* San Francisco, CA: W.H. Freeman.

Gans, H. J. 1968. "Planning and Social Life," in H. J. Gans, *People and Plans,* ch. 12. New York: Basic Books.

Gans, H. J. 1991. "Toward a Human Architecture," in H. J. Gans, *People, Plans and Policies.* ch. 1. New York: Columbia University Press.

Gieryn, T. F. 2000. "A Space for Place in Sociology," *Annual Review of Sociology,* 26, 463–496.

Hoyt, H. 1933. *One Hundred Years of Land Values in Chicago.* Chicago, IL: University of Chicago Press.

Hoyt, H. 1939. *The Structure and Growth of Residential Neighborhoods in American Cities.* Washington, DC: U.S. Federal Housing Administration.

Lefebvre, H. 1991. *The Production of Space.* Oxford: Blackwell.

Logan, J. R., and Molotch, H. L. 1987. *Urban Fortunes: The Political Economy of Place.* Berkeley, CA: University of California Press.

Merton, R. K. 1947. "The Social Psychology of Housing," in W. Dennis (ed.), *Current Trends in Social Psychology,* pp. 163–217. Pittsburgh, PA: University of Pittsburgh Press.

Spain, D. 2002. "What Happened to Gender Relations on the Way from Chicago to Los Angeles?" *City & Community,* 1, 155–167.

Wilkinson, R. G. 1996. *Unhealthy Societies.* London: Routledge.

Wilner, D., Walkley, R., Pinkerton, T., and Tayback, M. 1962, *Housing Environment and Family Life.* Baltimore, MD: Johns Hopkins University Press.

CHAPTER 3

Involuntary Segregation and the *Ghetto*

Disconnecting Process and Place

According to the dominant origin myth, the first modern *ghetto* was created by sixteenth-century Venice, which involuntarily segregated its Jewish population and locked it up at night in the neighborhood of a former iron foundry. Today, *ghetto* continues to be defined, by academics and the general public, as a place for the involuntary segregation of racial, ethnic, or other minorities, but at least two other definitions are also in use in the United States.

One might be called the race-class definition; it refers to black *ghettos* marked by extreme or concentrated poverty. The other is a residual definition, sometimes used critically or ironically, for voluntarily or self-segregated populations, such as the occupants of intellectual *ghettos*, or the affluent residents of gilded *ghettos*, Jewish and other. As often happens, one word is defined in several different ways.

I think that for researchers, definitions are tools, and they should therefore be as clear, easily operationalized, and widely agreed-to as possible. Applying these criteria, I suggest the *ghetto* is a place to which the subjects or victims of the involuntary segregation process are sent.

This definition is framed with the United States in mind, but it is also useful for comparative research. Since it has a long history, it can be used to compare past and present places and processes. In addition, the definition can be applied in cross-national and cross-cultural research, for example, to compare American black *ghettos* with those of other involuntarily segregated groups, such as Eastern Europe's Roma, the Japanese Burakumin, and Australia's aborigines.

Moreover, although in today's America only racial minorities are involuntarily segregated in *ghettos*, even here, the term does not have to be limited to racial minorities, provided it is properly qualified and preceded by an explanatory adjective. Indeed, a historical study would require distinctions between racial, ethnic, religious, and yet other *ghettos*. Moreover, very poor people, whatever their skin color, who need to find the cheapest housing, are for all practical purposes involuntarily segregated in economic *ghettos*.[1]

The term *ghetto* is also relevant for analyzing the places that housed what Erving Goffman (1961) described as total institutions, such as prisons, mental hospitals, and reservations for native Americans. However, for brevity's sake alone, this article will be limited to racial *ghettos* and omit the prefix.

Places occupied by the voluntarily or self-segregated have generally been described not as *ghettos* but as enclaves.[2] The Puerto Rican, Mexican, and other Latino "*barrios*" are usually enclaves, although many black Latinos are sentenced to the same involuntary segregation as African Americans. "Mixed neighborhoods," which are shared by involuntarily and voluntarily segregated people, are thus *ghettos* for some and enclaves for others.

Involuntary and Voluntary Segregation

The *ghetto* being a place, it cannot be understood without looking at the processes by which it comes into being and without which it cannot exist: primarily involuntary segregation and ghettoization. Understanding involuntary segregation requires an analysis of the societal Othering process: the selection of minorities who are stigmatized, discriminated against, racialized, and ghettoized. Such an analysis must also ask which minority or minorities are so selected and for what reasons, including the uses to which dominant or majority populations put them.

Enclaves are seen as places settled by racial, ethnic, religious, or other minorities that are not stigmatized by the white majority but self-segregate themselves, for example because they share a language, culture, or nationality. True, such minorities, other than very orthodox religious ones, generally do not seek total self-segregation; most especially want some neighbors from the white or non–ethnic majority.

Nonetheless, the most widespread form of voluntary segregation is economic. As long as many people, especially homeowners, at least in America, want secure and if possible rising property and status values, the building industry, real estate market, and zoning officials, among others, are ready to supply them with economic enclaves.

However, the boundaries between involuntary and voluntary (or self-) segregation are not hard and fast. People with limited incomes—even those in the middle class—are not choosing their residences entirely voluntarily, nor are people who need to live near relatives. In fact, no social being, animal or human, has completely free choice of where to live.

Sometimes the involuntarily segregated participate in their own exclusion, being unwilling to live where they are not wanted. More important, however, by enabling family and friends, as well as culturally similar and like-minded people, to live together, involuntary segregation can provide the same support system and sociability as voluntary segregation. Still, the involuntarily segregated know they can live only in places assigned to them by others. The researcher just has to know how to ask them the right way.

Furthermore, voluntary segregation may produce involuntary segregation. White flight from racially mixed neighborhoods also increased the involuntary segregation of blacks. The self-segregation of the very rich is in part influenced by fear of the involuntarily segregated poor. In many parts of the world, the rich live behind walls for fear of kidnapping; in the United States, they tend to choose gated or guarded communities, sometimes hiring private police forces who patrol for strangers who look like they belong in racial or economic *ghettos*.

In addition, the boundaries between involuntary and voluntary segregation are often hidden. Segregators generally deny their activities, and the involuntarily segregated mostly remain free to choose where in the *ghetto* they want to live. In large communities, they can choose between *ghettos*. Economic segregation is rarely seen as involuntary, because it is usually ascribed to the workings of seemingly impersonal economic forces.

Ghettoization and Deghettoization

Involuntary segregation requires *ghettos,* which are created by the ghettoization both of people and places. In America, slaves and their emancipated descendants have been ghettoized from birth, and many Afro-Caribbean immigrants undergo ghettoization when they arrive here. Conversely, European Jews were deghettoized after their arrival in America, even if a number of neighborhoods remained off-limits to them for many decades and a few still are.

Sometimes neighborhoods have been built as *ghettos*, but most started as white neighborhoods, which became *ghettos*, for example when an expanding central business district took over an adjacent *ghetto* and its residents moved into an emptying white neighborhood. Emptying Jewish neighborhoods seem to be ghettoized more often than those occupied by other white ethnics. If the latter are financially less able or for other reasons unwilling to move, they may resort to harassment of and violence against the first black arrivals, and thus discourage others from moving in.

Ironically, extensive white residential mobility, including "white flight," has enabled blacks to improve their housing condition. However, in the process, some *ghetto* areas from which they departed became depopulated and were left to the very poorest of the ghettoized. The resulting concentration of extreme poverty is often accompanied by the departure of stores, public offices, and other community facilities, resulting in the social isolation of the remaining residents (Wilson, 1987).[3]

Conversely, gentrification may lead to deghettoization, as the involuntarily segregated are replaced by more affluent white and other residents. The victims of gentrification move to other *ghettos,* and the white gentrifiers become self-segregated, although not always by choice. Some white and black gentrifiers choose to move to poor *ghettos* because they say they want to raise their children in economically and otherwise diverse areas.

The *Ghetto*

The *ghetto* is merely the place in which the involuntarily segregated are housed; it is the spatial representation of the sociopolitical process of involuntary segregation. In fact, the *ghetto* is in many respects an ordinary neighborhood, which resembles other neighborhoods similar in age, the socioeconomic level of the population, housing stock, and related features. However, like other ordinary neighborhoods, all *ghettos* are not alike (Small 2007). In addition, a *ghetto* neighborhood also differs from ordinary neighborhoods in several ways; I will only mention four.

First, *ghettos* are demographically both more homogeneous and heterogeneous than other urban or suburban neighborhoods. Unless they are changing neighborhoods turning into *ghettos,* they are likely to be monoracial or nearly so. At the same time, they are generally multiclass areas, especially in communities too small to allow the establishment of class-differentiated *ghettos.* As a result, the ghettoized classes must live together, or at least adjacent to each other.

Second, *ghettos* are apt to be more diverse in land use than other residential areas. Because of continuing discrimination, *ghettos* have to be more self-sufficient than other areas, with a fuller array of stores, public and private facilities, as well as professional offices than equivalent white neighborhoods.

Third, *ghettos* are likely to be qualitatively inferior in almost all respects to neighborhoods of similar age, class, housing stock, etc. Since the involuntarily segregated are a captive audience, they are subject to economic, political, and other kinds of exploitation, including by coethnics and coracials. *Ghetto* residents usually pay more for housing and most other goods and services than whites, although they earn far less than whites.

Even with income held constant, the *ghetto* is more crowded than other neighborhoods and has less public open space as well. Most of its stores, public and private facilities, as well as professional offices are of lower quality than those in white areas.

At the same time, the *ghetto* may contain more of the land uses and facilities that other neighborhoods do not want, for example, bus depots, sanitation facilities, and other noisy and toxic land uses. Partly as a result, *ghettos* are noted for their high asthma rates.

Fourth, the *ghetto* absorbs and reflects the varieties of marginalization, harassment, injustice, and stigma imposed on the involuntarily segregated. For example, poverty combined with discrimination by financial and other institutions leaves more of the *ghetto* economy off the books than the economy of white neighborhoods (Venkatesh, 2006).

Ghetto pathology rates are normally higher than those in white neighborhoods when class and other factors are held constant. School performance rates are lower; drug and alcohol addiction rates are higher, as are depression, stress, and stress-related diseases. Street crime is more prevalent, and thus so are police presence, harassment, and arrest rates. Having a *ghetto* address reflects and adds to the stigma borne by its residents, and can add to their difficulties in obtaining jobs.

Some of the differences between *ghettos* and other neighborhoods reflect the greater poverty of involuntarily segregated populations. Nevertheless, other characteristics associated with the *ghetto* could once be found in poor white neighborhoods. Such neighborhoods have virtually all disappeared, however, since most of today's white poor live amidst their economic betters.

Conclusion: Disconnecting Process and Place

Ghettos as commonly defined can exist only in societies that involuntarily segregate some of their members, and most of the *ghetto's* distinctive spatial features are effects of that process. Not only must the analysis of process be separated from that of place, but the causes of what takes place in the *ghetto* are found in one or another aspect of the processes that together produce involuntary segregation.

To be sure, *ghettos* are not uniform, but the differences between them often have little to do with place. Affluent *ghettos* differ from poor and middle-class ones, although these differences are the effects of class—and the same class differences associated with white neighborhoods.

Although concentrated poverty has been studied almost entirely in *ghettos,* it actually reflects patterns of class stratification that have little to do with race. In the days when many whites were poor, their neighborhoods also included areas of concentrated poverty.[4] Jacob Riis and other muckrakers assisted the twentieth-century housing reform movement by identifying such areas in a number of American cities.

Finally, the search for neighborhood effects has also been limited largely to the *ghetto,* but to my mind, researchers have not made a case that residential neighborhoods, including *ghettos,* have effects that can be attributed to the neighborhood per se. Neighborhoods are imagined communities with boundaries often determined or imposed from outside. While the boundaries sometimes generate social, economic, and political effects, most neighborhood effects stem from economically or politically powerful institutions and populations within these boundaries. Even in the very poorest areas, the deleterious effects of poverty are not caused by the neighborhood, but by institutions, most of them outside the neighborhood, that initiate or perpetuate poverty and conditions associated with it. The *ghetto* itself does not often impoverish people.

Too much emphasis on place gets in the way of antipoverty policy. Enabling the poor to escape poverty requires policies creating or strengthening the institutions that make that escape possible. Improving the places in which the poor, black or white, live will not hurt, but it will normally raise the income only of those who do the improving. Moreover, places are local, yet neither poverty nor racial segregation can be eliminated by local policies.

The disconnection of process and place is particularly necessary now that sociologists have rediscovered space and place. Whatever the virtues of spatial sociology, it can easily be infected with the spatial or physical determinism of architects and urban designers. Their professions may impel them to believe that space, place, or the built environment determines social and other processes, but sociologists must remember that these processes are causally prior. Ultimately, space and place are causally relevant mainly because gravity forces human societies to be attached to the surface of the earth.

Notes

Reprinted from *City and Community*, vol. 7, no. 4, 2008, by permission of John Wiley & Sons Ltd.

1. Thus when William J. Wilson (1987) analyzes black *ghettos* as areas of concentrated poverty, he is describing areas that are both racial and economic *ghettos*, while Pattillo (2003) views the *ghetto* as purely racial. One can, however, argue about (and study) whether economic segregation is as involuntary as racial segregation.

2. The Jewish neighborhood that Wirth (1928) studied was, despite the title of his book, an enclave.

3. Wacquant (2007) has described these areas as hyperghettos, although since their residents are no more or less ghettoized than most other blacks, they are really hyperpoor areas.

4. If researchers could gain access to the neighborhoods of the very rich, they would discover areas of concentrated affluence, which enable the very richest to maintain their distance from the lesser rich.

CHAPTER 4

Concentrated Poverty

A Critical Analysis

W hen presidential candidate Barack Obama announced his urban policy, he promised a *new* program to attack concentrated poverty—a socially harmful kind of poverty said to exist in African-American neighborhoods where at least 40 percent of the population lives below the poverty line. The concept had been circulating in the academic research and public policy worlds for the last twenty years, and several major public policy organizations had recently urged a new attack on this form of poverty, but the Obama promise raised the concept to high national visibility once more.

What candidate Obama may not have known, and what the president may still not know, is that concentrated poverty is an intellectually and empirically questionable concept that offers almost no constructive lessons for antipoverty policy. It is also a spatial concept, which raises questions of whether poverty and related inequalities can be significantly reduced by local housing, land, and other spatial policies.

Concentrating poor people in a limited area is said to increase troubled, trouble-making, and antisocial behavior among them. Such behavior would be lessened if poor people were spread out over a larger area, and perhaps even eliminated if they were sent to live in middle-class neighborhoods. However, concentration merely makes poverty more visible than spread-out poverty, calls attention to concentration, and thereby diverts attention from policies that would reduce or end poverty.

Concentrated Poverty and the Underclass

When the term "concentrated poverty" was first used in the late 1980s, the people so concentrated were being described as members of an underclass. Indeed, concentrated poverty is an offspring of the "underclass," a technical-sounding term that blamed the victims of poverty. "Underclass" was also the latest synonym for the undeserving poor that was popular with journalists, social scientists, and policy analysts from the late 1970s to the late 1990s (Gans 1995; Katz 1989).

Like some other ideas that later turned into punitive descriptions of the poor, concentrated poverty began as part of a larger and scholarly analysis. In his seminal 1987 book, *The Truly Disadvantaged*, William Julius Wilson sought to explain why poor inner-city African Americans were more disadvantaged than other poor urban residents. His theory emphasized the departure of more affluent blacks from inner-city neighborhoods and the resulting isolation of those left behind, but the term he thought best captured their condition was "concentration effects."

Wilson, too, had described this population as an underclass. Subsequently, other scholars tried to count the number of neighborhoods in which the black underclass was to be found. Needing a quantifiable definition, they decided that such areas were concentrated if, according to the U.S. Census, more than 40 percent of the population lived on incomes below the poverty line. Wilson's reference to concentration *effects* initiated a concerted search for related neighborhood effects (e.g., Briggs 1997; Sampson et al. 2002). That search still continues, accompanied by a long and lively debate about both the existence of such effects and the proper research methods for identifying them (e.g., Jencks and Mayer 1990; Sampson 2008).

The term "underclass" was sent to the terminological sidelines in the late 1990s after the end of the crack epidemic and the decline in violent street crime, as well as by the economic good times and the resulting drop in unemployment that took place during the Clinton administration.

Concentrated poverty also went into terminological decline, in part because the same good times had led to a sharp decrease in the number of such areas. Besides, concentrated poverty had never caught the fancy of journalists. It remained popular mainly with demographers and other social scientists who were still looking for areas inhabited by poor people who could not or would not live by middle-class standards.

The term reappeared in the policy literature around the turn of the new century, partly because of the deterioration of the economy and thus of the condition of the poor, but also because it could be used to justify Hope VI, the federal program to tear down public housing projects. Since only poor people lived in these projects, they were by definition areas of concentrated poverty, giving the term a new reason for existence.

Over the years, concentrated poverty inherited all the punitive "behavioral" indicators associated with the underclass, such as joblessness, unmarried motherhood, gang membership, use of hard drugs, high levels of street crime, and the several kinds of interpersonal violence often found in very poor areas. Concentrated poverty retains its black *ghetto* association as well, even though it can be found in Latino and white neighborhoods, too.

A Critique of Concentrated Poverty

The notion of concentrated poverty contains enough shortcomings that its adoption and use by social scientists, particularly as a causal concept, is hard to understand.

First, there is no persuasive empirical evidence to suggest that the level of concentration of poor people in a particular neighborhood causes their poverty-related problems and the behavior patterns that upset the larger community. Correlational studies are numerous, but they are inconclusive unless researchers can describe the causal and other processes by which concentration is said to affect the residents of these neighborhoods.

Second, there is no reason that neighborhoods per se, whether concentrated or not, should have such effects. Neighborhoods, whether demarcated officially or unofficially by their inhabitants, do not control or allocate resources and do not make policy and political decisions. They are, like other spatial aggregations, containers; and it is only the contents of these containers that can have effects on their inhabitants. A neighborhood hospital will help sick residents and a good local school will improve school performance. Their positive effects will take place in the neighborhood, but they are not neighborhood effects because their resources and policies originate elsewhere.

Wilson has always taken pains to stress that residential neighborhoods are not economic containers; they cannot create jobs or raise incomes. That he is right, and that improved economic conditions for the poor originate elsewhere, was demonstrated during the good economic times of the 1990s, when the number of concentrated-poverty neighborhoods decreased sharply. National and regional economic conditions as well as antipoverty policies determine the fate of poor people, wherever they live.

Actually, studies that count or otherwise analyze concentrated-poverty neighborhoods are not even about neighborhoods. Because researchers doing these studies need numbers, they must use whatever quantitative data are available. In this case, they end up reporting numbers for census tracts, the administrative areas into which the U.S. Census divides communities in order to facilitate its work. Even if their boundaries sometimes coincide with those of official neighborhoods, census tracts are data-gathering containers that cannot affect the lives of the people living in these tracts.

The measurement of concentration is equally problematic. It is also determined by available quantitative data—in this case U.S. Census studies on the proportion of census-tract residents below the poverty line. The census data are available for several proportions, the highest of which is 40 percent. It became the indicator used to define and identify poverty concentration. Jargowsky and Bane (1990), two of the founders of concentrated-poverty research, chose this indicator after they had toured several cities and discovered that tracts with 40 percent of poor residents were in noticeably worse condition physically and otherwise than tracts with 20 or 30 percent of poor residents.

Even so, no systematic empirical work is available to suggest that poor areas are always in worse physical shape and their occupants are more troubled or trouble-making when 40 percent are poor. Other researchers have encountered similar physical and social conditions in areas in which a lower proportion of the population was poor. Conversely, Sessoms and Wolch (2008) studied a sample of Los Angeles areas with 40 percent poverty levels and found that "they do not conform to stereotypes of concentrated poverty areas."

Admittedly, poverty concentration is very high, by definition, in public housing projects, including those that were declared to be physically and socially "distressed" and then torn down. Even so, their condition, as well as high levels of problematic behavior by some of their residents, is better explained by the residents' extreme poverty than by their concentration.

The size and density of the projects may have played a small part as well. For example, many drug dealers could be found in the big projects because enough customers were available at close hand, making both especially noticeable. Moreover, the project families included a large number of teenagers, some of whom organized drug-dealing gangs and sometimes terrorized project populations that lacked police protection (Venkatesh 2000). Poor people who do not live in huge public housing projects become drug addicts as well, but they and the drug dealers serving them are less visible.

The much publicized distress of the now-destroyed public housing projects is best explained by the decades-long withdrawal of public funds, not only for the maintenance of the buildings but also for the upkeep of those residents unable to work or to find work. The effects attributed to the concentration of poverty are therefore better assigned to generations of elected officials in Washington, DC, beginning with the Nixon administration, as well as the Real Estate Investment Trust (REIT) and other lobbyists that influence federal public housing, jobs, and welfare policy.

Third, no one has yet answered the theoretical question of why concentration per se should have any effects on people's behavior or identified the causes of such effects. The researchers studying poverty concentration apparently assume that bringing together poor residents turns them into an antisocial and sometimes dangerously mob-like critical mass. When this critical mass is reached, increases are thought to take place in joblessness, unmarried motherhood, violence, and the other shortcomings of which the concentrated poor stand accused.

Dispersing that critical mass and moving its concentrated poor people into better-off neighborhoods will, it is argued, reduce or end these practices. This will happen because the better-off and better-educated people and the services and facilities located in these neighborhoods will help, and set a good example for, the impoverished newcomers.

However, the causal processes leading to concentration remain to be identified, and whether the critical-mass hypothesis can explain anything is doubtful. A critical mass of people, poor or rich, may hasten the spread and perhaps worsen epidemics. It will also circulate and legitimate the fads and fashions that provide variety in everyday life.

But how can a critical mass cause the serious problems, the endless and often insoluble crises, and the destructive and self-destructive behavior that dog the lives of significant minorities of the poor? Can the presence of drug-addicted neighbors really lead anyone to become a drug addict? And why would living in an area marked by street fights and drive-by shootings therefore persuade anyone to commit homicidal violence?

Furthermore, if concentration causes the claimed social effects, the people so affected should be physically close and therefore living at extreme levels of density. Although residential density was high in the most distressed public housing projects, it is often low in other concentrated-poverty tracts. This is particularly true in cities in which empty buildings in poor neighborhoods are quickly torn down and vacant lots separate still occupied buildings. The residents of a concentrated-poverty tract may not even be living near each other.

In fact, most of the alleged behavioral effects of concentrated poverty have been shown to have other causes. Joblessness is, as already noted, an effect of the areal economy. Most people applied for welfare (before Bill Clinton eliminated it as an entitlement program) because they could not find steady work and needed the money, not because their neighbors were on welfare.

A high rate of single-parent-family formation is at least partly an effect of male joblessness and the consequent shortage of marriageable males. It could also reflect the youthfulness of the area population, since poor women often have children when they are young and marry later, when they or their men are economically reasonably secure (Edin and Kefalas 2005). Teenage pregnancy is frequently associated with unusually low income and is often an effect of dropping out or being pushed out of school, but unless pregnancy is contagious, it cannot be an effect of poverty concentration. The crack industry was always associated with violence, and the anger and frustrations associated with poverty play a major role in interpersonal violence. In sum, economic and social conditions are among the principal reasons for most of the ills said to be caused by poverty concentration.

Indeed, I would suggest the hypothesis that many if not most of these ills may be the direct or indirect effects of severe or extreme poverty (usually measured as an income of half the poverty line) rather than of poverty concentration (Gans 2009).

Tracts with the highest poverty concentration may also be those with the greatest number of residents living in extreme poverty. These residents were, after all, left behind in their neighborhoods when many of those who could afford to obtain better housing did so. The left-behind people, who might be called residuals, are likely to be extremely poor. I would be surprised, however, if many residuals can be found in areas of low poverty concentration, if only because the rents are often way beyond their means.

Although concentrated poverty researchers should have been concurrently looking at the effects of extreme poverty, too few have been interested in income-level data. This is true of poverty researchers in general; many have simply counted the number of people below the poverty line, failing to distinguish whether those living on half the poverty line income were undergoing the same experiences and dealing with the same problems as those earning twice as much. Perhaps economically comfortable researchers do not notice that living on $10,000 a year—approximately half the current poverty line for a family of three—creates many more problems than living on $20,000.

In retrospect, the attention given to poverty concentration is somewhat surprising, because in America, where residential areas are generally differentiated by price, a great many people live in places concentrated by income. Even so, scholars have not looked for concentration effects, good or bad, among the general population. No one has studied whether areas like New York's Park Avenue or Philadelphia's suburban Main Line concentrate the rich and therefore cause debauchery or decadence. Wall Street's concentration of bankers, speculators, and other investors cannot explain the excesses of contemporary capitalism.

This author once studied a new post–World War II suburb that, like most other new suburbs of that period, was concentrated not only by income but also by age, life cycle position, occupational status, and other characteristics (Gans 1967). While the huge number of young residents with young children created a variety of effects, from regular epidemics of childhood diseases to abnormal growth patterns in school enrollments, no one proposed tearing down the community for being overly concentrated.

Policy Implications

The concept of concentrated poverty must also be criticized for its policy implications. Three such implications especially deserve discussion: dispersion or deconcentration, localization, and distraction.

Dispersion

Poverty is logically best deconcentrated by dispersion: moving the concentrated poor out of their neighborhoods. Dispersion programs come in two kinds, those that move poor people to higher-income areas and those that send them off to find their own housing, which means that many wind up in equally poor or even poorer areas.

Dispersion programs that move poor people to better-off areas are voluntary; they recruit the households to be moved, and this policy has been tried frequently over the last quarter century (Goetz 2003). The most famous example is the so-called Gautreaux project, established following a 1976 court decision to counter the extreme racial segregation of Chicago's public housing projects.

Gautreaux helped several thousand public housing residents move to the Chicago suburbs (e.g., DeLuca and Rosenbaum 2010). These consisted of a self-selected and screened *ghetto* population, many of them presumably upwardly mobile families, including single-parent ones wanting a better life for their children.

Summarizing broadly, many of the movers adjusted to life in predominantly white middle-class suburbs without undue difficulty. Since middle-class people are not always helpful or kind to their poorer neighbors (Sanchez-Jankowski 1999), and not all whites to darker-skinned ones, those experiencing undue class or racial harassment moved back to the city. So did people financially unable to keep up with middle-class Joneses. Movers who were lonely for family friends and old support systems sometimes returned to their old neighborhoods.

The majority who stayed have improved their economic condition but only slightly, due in part to lack of needed job skills and continuing racial discrimination in hiring. Dispersion is not an antipoverty policy. Better public facilities have produced positive results for many, particularly those children who improved their school performance and went on to college. Unfortunately, no studies are yet available of the adult fate of these youngsters and of how many were able to escape poverty.

Voluntary dispersion projects, at least in America, suffer from two related and predictable defects: better-off communities rebel if they are required to welcome large numbers of people from the poorest neighborhoods in the city. Consequently, most voluntary dispersion projects are condemned to remaining small.

This is particularly true of programs that move poor people to suburban and other homeowner communities, where people worry that the arrival of too many dark-skinned newcomers of lower status will reduce their property values.

Involuntary dispersion has involved far larger numbers of people but has resulted in fewer benefits for the dispersed. The primary involuntary program has been the federal Hope VI program, which brought about the destruction of "distressed" public housing projects all over the country (Goetz 2003). In some cases, lower-density housing, mixed racially and by class, has been built on the cleared land, but usually only a small minority of the former public housing residents have obtained apartments. In other cities, the projects were torn down, but no new housing was built at all.

In effect, in several places, Hope VI turned into a sequel to the urban renewal program of the 1950s and 1960s (Bennett et al. 2006). Once more it displaced enough poor blacks to deserve being described as Negro Removal again, at least in some cities. Although both relocation programs and benefits have been more generous than they were during urban renewal, and a larger proportion of the displaced have obtained better housing in better neighborhoods, still, sometimes a majority of the displaced have ended up in other poor *ghetto* areas, including equally distressed black suburbs (e.g., Popkin et al. 2009). And once again, public policies have led to a reduction in the total supply of already scarce low-cost housing.

To be sure, dispersion, even of the involuntary kind, should not be rejected out of hand, for several of the now leveled housing projects were no longer fit for human occupancy. However, people were also separated from family, friends, and neighbors and lost other support systems. Those who had to find housing far from the city were now at an even worse disadvantage in the labor market.

Involuntary dispersion of any kind is unjustifiable. But what if project residents could have chosen new, rehabilitated, or otherwise standard housing in good neighborhoods before they lost their apartments, with moving assistance designed to undertake group relocation for those requesting it? Then, the dispersed residents would have obtained better housing and better communities, and remained near at least some family and friends.

Localization

Concentrated poverty, being a real concept, leads to local spatial policies. In some cases, this emphasis can be justified, for example when people occupy dangerous housing and neighborhoods, or when subsidized workplaces are built for employers that offer jobs to the local residents. However, spatial programs usually lack an economic component, and thus do not give poor people a chance to escape poverty. Economic improvement requires national job creation as well as income-support policies and metropolitan areawide antipoverty programs to implement these policies at the local level.

The Obama administration's program to fight concentrated poverty emphasizes two programs (Wilson 2010). One is a dispersion program called Choice Neighborhoods, which proposes to correct many of the faults of Hope VI. The second program, called Promise Neighborhoods, seeks to replicate the widely praised Harlem Children's Zone project in twenty neighborhoods around the country. Like Geoffrey Canada's Harlem program, the Promise Neighborhoods project features a large number of preschool, school, parenting, and employment retention programs to help the next generation escape poverty.

In some ways, the Harlem Children's Zone project reminds those of us active in the 1960s of the hopes placed on Head Start, a mostly school-centered program for young children. Although it improved school performance significantly, its effects were often dissipated when its graduates had to return to their neighborhoods' substandard public schools. Moreover, we discovered during that same time that individual projects, then called demonstration projects, which were begun by charismatic leaders with highly dedicated staffs, could not easily be duplicated on a larger scale and in other places. Maybe today's policy makers and program directors have learned from the experiences of the 1960s, however.

As currently formulated, the Promise Neighborhoods project appears to include few programs related to job creation or income support, although presumably such programs could still be added. Moreover, other parts of candidate Obama's urban policy proposed increases in the minimum wage and Earned Income Tax Credit (EITC) payments, job creation schemes, and a variety of other economically oriented antipoverty programs, some of which are now getting under way. Still, the current economic crisis has forced his administration to orient its economic programs to the broad swath of the population described as middle class. (Candidate Obama's antipoverty proposals are described in his Urban Policy paper at www.barackobama .com/issues/urban–policy.)

Distraction

The third shortcoming of policies against concentrated poverty is that they can distract programmatic and other attention from poverty and focus attention solely on deconcentration. In that case, economically oriented antipoverty policies may not even be considered. Fortunately, the Obama administration is not likely to let itself be so distracted.

However, conservatives in Congress and in the lobbies that seek to influence Congress could press for involuntary dispersion projects, rejecting any attempts to reduce or eliminate poverty. If unknowing liberals can be persuaded to believe that dispersion and other spatial programs will nonetheless help poor people economically, the conservatives might even succeed.

Preventing the Misuse of Concepts

Like the cultures of poverty and underclass, concentrated poverty began as a social science concept that was later turned into a blaming term accusing poor people of harmful and socially undesirable practices. Concentrated poverty is less offensive than the earlier terms because it has not achieved the same popularity as its predecessors. It is also less personalistic; it blames the aggregation of poverty on a mob-like critical mass, not the poor themselves.

Unless social scientists begin their research with political agendas, they are not responsible for how their scientific concepts are used politically. They should, however, consider possible misuses of their concepts before they put them on paper or into the computer. Another possibility is to so qualify the concepts that they are less easily toyed with. Unnecessary neologisms should be avoided and researchers encouraged to depend on older and time-tested concepts that have not been misused by policy makers and politicians.

They should also renounce concepts when they are subsequently misused, as Wilson (1991) did, for example, when he announced publicly that he would stop using the underclass concept. If public policy rests on or includes misused concepts, social scientists who have employed these concepts ought to be protesting their misuse, as well as the policies in which the misuses took place (Steinberg 2010).

This issue is not hypothetical. Hope VI and the nationwide destruction of public housing it undertook was publicly justified in part as a reduction of concentrated poverty. Whether the concept led to the federal policy or was brought in afterward to justify the policy is an empirical question that ought to be addressed by urban historians. Nonetheless, social scientists had invented the idea of concentrated poverty, and they should have criticized its use in policy making. All those active in concentrated poverty research should have identified and opposed the deficiencies of Hope VI.

Most funded antipoverty research is undertaken among the victims of poverty. Consequently antipoverty researchers should be sure also to do research on their victimizers. If studies of the poor that mainly catalogue their deviations from mainstream behavior cannot be avoided, they should be accompanied by at least some observations on similar deviations among the more fortunate classes.

Poor people do not have a monopoly on blameworthy behavior. However, being poor, they are condemned to conduct it in public and thus make it visible to others, including researchers. The drug dealers that serve affluent drug addicts deliver. "White-collar crime" is not committed on the street, and whatever misdeeds correlate with concentrated affluence take place behind closed doors.

Note

Reprinted from *Challenge*, vol. 53, no. 3, 2010, by permission of Taylor & Francis Group. My thanks to Paul Jargowski, Christopher Jencks, Hilary Silver, Stephen Steinberg, and William Julius Wilson for help with or helpful comments on an earlier draft of the article.

Further Reading

Bennett, L.J. Smith, and P. Wright, ed. 2006. *Where Are Poor People to Live?* Armonk, NY: M. E. Sharpe.

Briggs, X. 1997. "Moving Up Versus Moving Out: Neighborhood Effects in Housing Mobility Programs." *Housing Policy Debate* 8, no. 1: 195–234.

DeLuca, S., and J. Rosenbaum. 2010. "Residential Mobility, Neighborhoods and Poverty." In *The Integration Debate,* ed. C. Hartman and G. Squires, 185–97. New York: Routledge.

Edin, K., and M. Refalas. 2005. *Promises I Can Keep.* Berkeley, CA: University of California Press.

Gans, H. 1967. *The Levittowners.* New York: Pantheon Books.

_____ . 1995. *The War Against the Poor.* New York: Basic Books.

_____ . 2009. "Antipoverty Policy for the Excluded Poor." *Challenge* 52, no. 6 (November–December): 79–95.

Goetz, E. 2003. *Clearing the Way: Deconcentrating the Poor in Urban America.* Washington, DC: Urban Institute Press.

Jargowsky, P., and M. Bane. 1990. "Ghetto Poverty: Basic Questions." In *Inner City Poverty in the United States*, ed. L. Lynn and M. McGeary, 16–67. Washington, DC: National Academy Press.

Jencks, C., and S. Mayer. 1990. "The Social Consequences of Growing Up in a Poor Neighborhood." In *Inner City Poverty in the United States,* ed. L. Lynn and M. McGeary, 111–86. Washington, DC: National Academy Press.

Katz, M. 1989. *The Undeserving Poor.* New York: Pantheon Books.

Popkin, S., D. Levy, and L. Buron. 2009. "Has Hope VI Transformed Residents' Lives?" *Housing Studies* 24, no. 4 (July): 477–502.

Sampson, R. 2008. "Moving to Inequality: Neighborhood Effects and Experiments Meet Social Structure." *American Journal of Sociology* 114, no. 1 (July): 189–231.

Sampson, R.; J. Morenoff; and T. Gannon-Rowley. 2002. "Assessing 'Neighborhood Effects.'" *Annual Review of Sociology* 28: 443–78.

Sanchez-Jankowski, M. 1999. "The Concentration of African-American Poverty and the Dispersal of the Working Class." *International Journal of Urban and Regional Research* 23, no. 4 (December): 619–37.

Sessoms, N., and J. Wolch. 2008. "Measuring Concentrated Poverty in a Global Metropolis: Lessons from Los Angeles." *Professional Geographer* 60, no. 1: 1–17.

Steinberg, S. 2010. "The Myth of Concentrated Poverty." In *The Integration Debate,* ed. C. Hartman and G. Squires, 213–27. New York: Routledge.

Venkatesh, S. 2000. *American Project,* Chicago, IL: University of Chicago Press.

Wilson, W. 1987. *Truly Disadvantaged,* Chicago, IL: University of Chicago Press.

_____ . 1991. "Studying Inner-City Social Dislocations." *American Sociological Review* 56, no. 1 (February): 1–14.

_____ . 2010. "The Obama Administration's Proposals to Address Concentrated Poverty." *City & Community* 9, no. 1 (Winter): 41–49.

PART TWO

POVERTY

Researchers investigating concentrated poverty (see chapter 4) have paid too little attention to the actual income of those who live in such neighborhoods. Suspecting that many were the poorest of the poor, I became interested in finding out what was known about them, and chapter 5 reports on what I learned.

We know very little about who lives at the bottom or how they survive, but incredibly enough, they include people who live on $2 a day or less, the World Bank's global poverty line. We also know too little about their personal and social lives, which is important to know in part because mainstream America views them almost exclusively as a lazy, immoral, and even dangerous class, often calling them the undeserving poor.

Chapter 6 proposes a related but insufficiently explored hypothesis: that many of the poorest of the poor are most likely the descendants of more than two prior generations of poverty. If their ancestors were slaves, probably five or more generations. What I describe as multigenerational poverty may be cumulative, each generation leaving its descendants handicapped by additional economic and other burdens from the very start.

Chapter 7 updates one of my old, but still counterintuitive ideas: that poverty persists in part because it benefits many of the better-off sectors of society. The chapter lists what I consider to be the major benefits and beneficiaries of poverty, although empirical research to demonstrate these remains to be done.

I first explored this idea in a paper called "The Positive Functions of Poverty," which appeared in the September 1972 issue of the *American Journal of Sociology*, but the term used here, benefits, is a less technical term than functions, with broader applications.

CHAPTER 5

Studying the Bottom of American Society

Introduction

In *Challenge to Affluence* (1963), the Swedish economist Gunnar Myrdal coined the term *under-class,* which he defined as "unemployed, and gradually unemployable and underemployed persons and families at the bottom of society" (p. 38). His concept was strictly economic and said almost nothing about the demographic characteristics or skin colors of these persons and families.[1] Myrdal was writing at a time when the overall American economy was still healthy. Nonetheless, he saw that it already contained a poverty-stricken and immobile substratum "in the basement of the stately American mansion" (p. 49).

Since then, the economy has undergone frequent traumas, and the population in America's basement has grown. Although the racial makeup of that population needs more study, a sizeable proportion is African American. Moreover, many of the stereotypes with which the people at the bottom were burdened have persisted for generations, placing a further roadblock to their escape from poverty. In addition, better-off whites have sometimes used versions of the same stereotypes to harass middle-class blacks and impede their further upward mobility (Feagin and Sikes, 1994).

The fragility of today's American economy and the dismal state of the labor market are further enlarging the economic substratum about which

Myrdal was writing. At the same time, the economic and social gap between that substratum and the rest of society will widen, further distancing the bottom of American society from its higher strata, and even from fellow Americans with incomes closer to the poverty line. Judging by the consequences of the Great Recession and earlier economic crises that victimized blacks more than other groups, an ever larger proportion is likely to be black.

What Should We Know About the People at the Bottom?

Despite all the research into American poverty, amazingly little is known about the occupants of the bottom stratum. Neither demographers nor the agencies that collect income data seem to have obtained much information about them. Likewise, qualitative researchers too rarely inquire into the incomes of the poor people they have studied. Indeed, much of social science seems insensitive to the existence of several levels of poverty. Surely the distinctions between poverty levels matter, but while the very poorest people may face the same problems and crises as other poor people, these are likely to be more intense, longer lasting, and even permanent.[2]

Researchers should get to work to determine how people at the bottom exist, cope with, and suffer from their minimal income and their maximal inequality. The resulting studies should provide America with a thick description of the bottom of their society. Such studies should focus particularly on the conditions that need to be eliminated, and the policies and politics that would begin to do so. Studies of how people survive and even triumph over these conditions are also needed in order to debunk and fight the stereotypes that stigmatize them, and that can be used to oppose antipoverty policies. Although some people will always be at the bottom even in the richest society, policies to improve the conditions of those at the bottom will reduce the gap between them and the rest of society.

The remainder of the paper will report some of what little we know about the people at the bottom, but wilil concentrate largely on some of the questions that need to be asked about them. Many of these questions will be derived from the existing sociological literature on poverty.

What Do We Know?

Myrdal's basement and society's bottom are metaphors, and are not easily turned into empirically useful concepts. Perhaps one could ask people at the lowest income levels if they feel themselves to be at the bottom of society, but even if they may feel that way, they may not want to admit it. A better start is to begin with a quantitative measure of the country's bottom income level. Two such measures are already in use.

One measure, devised by the U.S. Census, is termed *deep* poverty. It is set at an income of half or less of the official poverty line income: currently about $6500 for an individual and $11,500 for a family of four per year. A second measure, developed by social scientists Kathryn Edin and Luke Shaefer, is called *extreme* poverty. It describes living at the World Bank's global definition of poverty: on $2 per individual per day or $2920 per year for a family of four (Shaefer and Edin, 2013). This figure is roughly equivalent to living at 13 percent of the official American poverty line.

The two measures permit a few basic statistics about the people at the economic bottom of society. By the Census Bureau definition, 6.6 percent of the population, or 20.4 million people, lived in deep poverty in 2011. This population made up 44 percent of all poor people in 2011 (Shierholz and Gould, 2012). Applying the Shaefer-Edin definition of extreme poverty indicates that 4.3 percent of all households with children were living on less than $3000 in 2011.[3] That percentage rose from 1.7 percent of all households with children in 1996, an increase of 159 percent (Shaefer and Edin, 2013).

Not much more is known about the populations in deep and extreme poverty themselves. The largest number are white, but proportionally more are non-white: 4.4 percent of all non-Hispanic whites, 10.5 percent of Hispanics, and 12.5 percent of blacks were living in deep poverty in 2011. Fully 23.6 percent of single parent families were living in deep poverty, about a fourth of father-headed families, but only 2.4 percent of all married couples with children were earning at that level (National Center for Law and Economic Justice 2012). Most of the states with the highest proportion of people in deep poverty in 2011 were in the Deep South and the Southwest, but the District of Columbia topped the list that year.

Shaefer and Edin report that about half of the population in extreme poverty in 2011 was white, the rest being black and Hispanic. Almost 40 percent were married, while another 50 percent were families headed by single mothers. These kinds of data and impressionistic evidence from a range of sociological and journalistic sources suggest that the people at the bottom can be divided into the following overlapping types:

1. *The Unemployables*:
Households in which people who would otherwise be working are victims of chronic physical, emotional, or cognitive impairment, and/ or old age but for a variety of reasons are not receiving any or insufficient retirement or disability payments. This category also includes ex-felons, the imprisoned, and people with arrest records that make them unemployable in many states.

2. *The Long-term Unemployed and Severely Underemployed*:
People in the mostly rural but also urban pockets of deep and extreme poverty, including Appalachia, the Deep South, and America's biggest cities. This population also includes young men who are family or household heads, probably mostly black and Latino, who have never found full-time employment. It also includes previously poor people who lost their jobs during and after the Great Recession and have been made even poorer by long-term joblessness, and old people without Social Security.

3. *The Severely Underpaid*:
People employed at jobs below minimum wage and in the so-called underground economy; also those ineligible or otherwise unable or unwilling to obtain monetary and other material benefits to which they are entitled, notably disability payments, TANF benefits, food stamps, childcare credits, etc.

4. *The Casualties of Poverty*:
People who are not disabled but have been overcome by the catastrophes of poverty and also lack access to informal support systems and formal helping facilities. A significant number are likely to be multigenerationals, people mired in deep or extreme poverty for two or more generations who can now no longer get out (Gans 2011; Sharkey 2012).

If and when the labor market is restored to good enough health so that the unemployment and underemployment rates will decline and the labor participation rates will rise again, some of the recent arrivals at the bottom and old timers may be able to leave. Blacks, but also other darker-skinned people, will, however, be held back by racism even if they are able-bodied and otherwise qualified to move out of the basement. Moreover, at this level of society, racism is not the laissez faire form of middle-class society (Bobo and Smith, 1998), but a brutally overt variety that further penalizes people fighting for their survival. Blacks are probably always the most vulnerable, and I would not be surprised if a number of rural black families (and even some urban ones) have endured deep poverty for many generations. There must also be some who have been living in extreme poverty for that long, but it is hard to imagine that many families at such a low economic level could have survived over this time span. A significant proportion must have been too disabled or too defeated to establish a family that could raise children, and premature deaths among adults and children were undoubtedly very frequent.

What Else Must We Learn?

Obtaining data about the people at the bottom of society requires agreement on one or more measures of income levels, which could be current measures of deep and extreme poverty. It would require the U.S. Census and other agencies to collect and report at least the basic economic, social, and other data about them that it already reports about other population categories.[4] Once agreement is reached on quantitative measures of bottom-level poverty and the needed data are gathered, they should be analyzed and reported by census tract or other local area so that researchers seeking more detailed data can focus on these areas and their populations in various communities across the country. Even before such data are available, researchers can look for areas and people likely to be in dire straits. Although some such areas have already been studied, they tend to be of special and visible populations of the very poorest, such as the homeless, the people on Skid Row, and occupants of the remaining public housing projects. Now researchers must look for the more typical areas housing people with bottom-level incomes.

When such areas are identified, interviewers and ethnographers can make contact with residents who live in deep and extreme poverty. Studying them is not easy, since many may be hard to reach for one or another reason. Others may not want to cooperate with researchers, and some will surely make researchers uncomfortable. Also, the areas in which they live are some-times dangerous and frequently unhospitable to outsiders. Intrepid qualitative researchers will find ways of establishing research rapport in these areas. Then interviewers should collect family and life histories, including work, income, residential, medical, and other histories. The interviews should tell us how people obtain and live on minimal incomes, how they spend, and what they must forgo, especially in the triage situations they surely face all the time.

In addition, interviewers should obtain data about people's social and community lives and the networks, both formal and informal organizations and institutions, in which these lives are taking place. The life histories will enable researchers to understand the periods of security and insecurity these households have experienced over time. Interviewers can also obtain data on the major problems, crises, and catastrophes that their interviewees have endured, which ones they have overcome, and how, and what they are doing to deal with still existing problems.

Generational histories must be sought as well so that adults in deep or extreme poverty for at least two generations can be interviewed about what they know of the lives of earlier ancestors. Perhaps the researchers can even discover when, how, why, and which ancestors of theirs first hit bottom and found themselves living in extreme poverty. Interviews will provide some basic information, but much of the needed data about life at the bottom of society must be collected ethnographically. The best method may be an open-ended and broadly framed community study that yields descrip-tions and explanations of everyday community, social, work, and familial life. Ethnographers can be on the spot to see typical and atypical events for themselves and can study what people do and not just what they say they do.

Thus, researchers can observe the routines and habits people develop for the ups and downs they face at society's bottom as well as the sources of pain and the opportunities for satisfaction and enjoyment.

Particular Areas of Inquiry for Interviewers and Ethnographers

GENERAL COMMUNITY LIFE

The first task is to discover whether the basic formal and informal institu-tions, organizations, and agencies found in poor communities with incomes closer to the poverty level exist or are absent among the people at the bottom of society. Whether and how they connect with the population they are intended to serve (and control), and whether and how that population connects with them or fails to should be looked at as well.

Further, researchers should ask whether and how the very poorest constitute a spatial community, or whether they are scattered among poorer people of somewhat higher income. Such a study can also test the notion of concentrated poverty, determining whether and what negative—and positive—effects follow from living in deep or extreme poverty as well as high levels of spatial concentration (Wilson 1987). Such a study is most needed in white areas at the bottom of society, for the existence of concentrated white poverty would show that it is not a black phenomenon. That in turn might reduce the use of concentrated poverty as a term for blaming poor blacks for not always living up to middle-class standards of behavior.

ECONOMIC LIFE

The workplaces and other income sources at the bottom of society are undoubtedly very different from those available to people near to and above the official poverty line. People in deep poverty may be in the most underpaid sectors of the working poor population, many of them in the informal economy (Venkatesh 2006). However, the most urgent economic question is how people in extreme poverty obtain their daily $2 income and how they can survive on it.

FAMILIAL LIFE

Ethnographers need to look intensively at familial life and how it is structured, as well as what kind of support, security, and stability it provides or withholds from its members. Given the importance of respect and self-respect, especially among poor males, the ways in which families are able and willing, as well as unable and unwilling, to supply it is crucial. Researchers need to look especially for reasonably happy and well functioning families, and how they manage to achieve such a state on a very limited income. However, researchers must also explore family life when parents and single parents, and even multi-parent families are stressed out or otherwise diverted from fulfilling minimally necessary parental roles, and how children and adolescents deal with the effects.

Do children at various stages of childhood and adolescence search for parental substitutes, or can they and their peers find substitutes especially in their own informal groups without much adult participation? Perhaps even more important, researchers will need to see how single adults, especially older ones, many of whom probably many suffer from the very worst poverty, survive or fail to survive.

PROBLEMS, CRISES, AND CATASTROPHES

Ethnographers can observe how different problems develop and are dealt with, both by people with and without familial and other informal as well as formal social supports. Such studies should focus especially on the varying levels of the problems, particularly on catastrophes—permanent crises for which there are no solutions. Especially important are cumulative crises that result in part from preceding ones and lead to yet others. A typical example, faced frequently by single mothers, are crises initiated by a child's illness, the mother's job loss resulting from her absence from work, and the subsequent economic and other crises, including possibly eviction. Which crises terminate in catastrophes that put an end to, at least to what counts as, a normal existence at the bottom of society?

More needs to be learned as well about the effects on physical and emotional health of lives rarely free of problems, crises, and catastrophes. Special emphasis should be placed on levels of stress and clinical depression and how they are dealt with, as well as on periodic or chronic stress disorders. If these occur, do they resemble post-traumatic stress disorders suffered in natural and manmade disasters and in combat? Does anyone survive such disorders and extreme poverty *sui generis* without permanent physical, social, emotional, or cognitive damage?

COPING

Another question calling for answers is whether and how people cope with and survive deep and extreme poverty. What solutions, if any, have they found, for example, to deal with regularly occurring and cumulative crises. What sources of satisfaction can be found in the face of constant problems and crises? Are people able to develop daily or other routines that offer some stability and security, and when is the search for excitement a more satisfying solution?[5] What sources of diversion, entertainment, and escape are most readily available at the bottom of society?

Do the very poorest people, especially those in extreme poverty, obtain or invent distinctive cultural toolkits and tools (Swidler 1986) that help them cope, and, if so, how? Can effective coping tools be identified, and, if so, could they help inspire or guide policies that would provide relief from some of the noneconomic problems of deep and extreme poverty for a larger population? One would also want to know how successful coping affects response to opportunities for upward mobility, even if only to incomes at the official poverty line. Does coping help or hurt seeking to escape from the bottom of society? For example, if lowered expectations enable people to cope with problems and crises, do they also operate to interfere with upward mobility?[6]

Ethnographers must attempt to discover whether people are aware of their position at society's bottom, how they react to that awareness, and with what levels of resistance, protest, anger, and resignation, if any. Above all, the researchers should observe whether people try to move up in the socioeconomic pecking order and, if so, how—and someone ought to find and interview those who have been successful.

CRIME AND VIOLENCE

Criminologists have been studying street crime among the poor for decades, but more needs to be known about whether and how such crime differs at the bottom of society. The same is true of the study of criminal and violent gangs, which is currently undergoing another revival (Goffman 2014; Papachristos 2007; Rios 2011; Venkatesh 2000). Such studies must include nonviolent gangs, those that do not sell drugs or engage in other money making enterprises—normal adolescent peer groups that are called gangs only because its members are poor. However, the majority of adolescents in society's basement who do not belong to any such groups should be given the most attention. Researchers should examine their community, and other aspects of their social lives.

Since gangs seem to have flourished for generations, in some cases similar ones with much the same structures, more needs to be known about what functions these gangs perform for their members. Do they help compensate for the absence of other social supports, including familial ones; do they aid young people to develop self respect and learn how to deal with disrespect? Do they offer members a chance to be and feel useful? And what equivalent groups, if any exist at the different stages of adulthood? The current media and other publicity given to interpersonal violence in poor *ghetto* neighborhoods suggest that the incidents of such violence and the contexts in which they occur should receive special attention.

The constant police shadowing, frequent police violence, as well as the criminalization and incarceration of young black and Latino males is now being studied (Black 2009; Goffman 2014; Rios 2011; Wacquant 2009), but further research is required at the bottom of society and especially among poor whites. Poor communities in which these police actions do not take place must be identified as well.

THE RACIAL HIERARCHY AT THE BOTTOM

Three conflicting hypotheses deserve testing. The first proposes that the very poorest people must so concentrate on survival that ranking other people or discriminating against them by phenotype is of very low priority. The second is that people at the bottom engage in the same ranking as everyone else, and are perhaps looking even more intensely than the more fortunate for people who are socially, morally, and otherwise inferior to them. A third and related hypothesis suggests that the bottom of society is embedded in the same racial hierarchy as its better-off strata: one in which whites are at the top and blacks at the bottom, except in areas where Latino income is significantly below black income. In that case, one would want to know whether deeply and extremely poor whites, Latinos, and other non-blacks act in concert to keep blacks at the bottom and also increase the income and status gap between themselves and blacks.

COMPARATIVE RESEARCH

When more is known about the extremely poor, comparative research should be done to identify the similarities and differences of populations at the various levels of poverty. How are areas in which poverty is deep or extreme socially different from those in which most people have incomes closer to the poverty line? And are these areas treated differently by institutions and organizations ostensibly established to help, such as welfare agencies and charities?

Looking at income variations among the poor also provides another opportunity to test the concentrated poverty hypothesis; whether the poverty-related behavior patterns considered problematic or in violation of mainstream norms are better explained by the concentration of poverty than by levels of poverty (Gans 2010). If concentration, as measured by percent poor in a designated area is the significant causal variable, these behavior patterns should be the same whether people's income is near the poverty line, or at deep or extreme poverty levels. If these patterns increase or worsen as income declines, then poverty itself is clearly the major causal variable, with all the policy implications this suggests. Since most current research in poor communities is taking place in black and Latino areas, studies of poor white areas are essential to determine similarities and differences caused by race.

Policies Against Deep and Extreme Poverty

Perhaps the very first step of the policy-oriented part of the proposed research is the creation of a more dramatic vocabulary, for example by calling the two kinds of poverty desperate and catastrophic. Concurrently, policy-oriented researchers should revive the now almost forgotten connection between war and poverty. However, they should use it to insist that the victims of deep and extreme poverty are the most serious casualties of the class warfare that takes place in all hierarchically organized economies. Then they can argue that these casualties deserve benefits that resemble those granted to casualties of other wars.

The next step is to acquaint better-off Americans with the bottom of their society and what life is like there. Ethnographies are particularly useful in such an enterprise since their narrative approach may gain them a public audience beyond the academy. Researchers can identify the structural and cultural forces and agents that operate in and shape life at the bottom of society, thereby demonstrating also that the bottom is at the same time a basement of the larger structure that is society. A related research question that also shows the extent to which bottom and higher strata are connected would examine whether and when people at the bottom accept mainstream values and treat them as ideals to be pursued.[7]

Such research should also lay out the reasons why people cannot gain access to the monetary, cultural, and other tools needed to achieve these values.

Policy-oriented researchers would then be able to ask what kind of supports would enable people to pursue mainstream values now and in the future. Data on the extent to which the very poorest Americans strive and even achieve these values are important for policy making. These data may help policy-oriented researchers attack some of the blaming terms and punitive legislation with which people at the bottom are held down and which conservatives and others use to sabotage antipoverty policies.

Whether research that describes the lives, problems, and triumphs of the people at the bottom of society will encourage political support for anti-poverty policies is, however, another matter, and itself an empirical question. Bottom-of-society research may come up with some policies tailored to distinctive conditions in that part of society, but the best policy to help its population is a universal antipoverty one that decreases the huge and ever-increasing economic gaps between the nonpoor and the poor. Specific policies include creating new jobs in the country's physical and social infrastructures for those who can work, including supported work positions for people who have been out of the labor force for too long. Raising the minimum wage and providing nearly equivalent income support to those who cannot work or find work is essential.

Temporary and permanent disability payments to the many unemployable people at the bottom of society—including healthy ones who have become permanent economic victims of a dysfunctional labor market—would relieve some of their pain and suffering. Housing subsidies and other supports to make the lives of the defeated poor reasonably comfortable should be provided as well. The long-standing interest in eliminating childhood poverty and the current interest in early childhood education should be used to determine how to help children move out of the bottom of society. Policies that can be implemented both with and without the aid of parents or other guardians are needed, but without taking the children away even from unsupportive families.

Current experiments with community and school programs such as the Harlem Children's Zone and others should be adapted for the special conditions at the bottom of society. The most important goal: to enable not only the most talented and ambitious children, but also the academically and otherwise average ones to escape from the bottom. That escape may have to be supported until and even beyond the last year of education, to try to make sure that the program graduates are not forced to return to the bottom of society. Education alone cannot and never could eliminate poverty.

The multigenerationally poor may need even more specialized aid, and more than a generation may be required before the children of multigenerationals can move very far above the bottom of society.

Political Concern About Deep and Extreme Poverty

Needless to say, the likelihood of these or any other supportive policies being enacted is currently minuscule. The polity almost never helps people who lack economic and political power and will be even less helpful when the economy is as unequal as it is presently.

Then too, some better-off people seem to obtain special satisfaction in imposing additional pain and suffering on the people at the bottom of society. Others may gain that satisfaction by imagining the very poorest people to lack the moral qualities that enabled them to be better off. Others cannot see that the poor lack access to the mainstream routes of upward mobility, and yet others believe they live in a zero-sum society and fear that the poor will obtain public funds that should go to the better-off.

Whatever their motives for making sure that the people at the bottom of society remain there, the better-off also help to perpetuate the blaming language and injurious images used to stereotype and stigmatize people at the bottom. Blaming them for their failure to improve their position in society can then be used to block policies that would do so. As I noted earlier, however, the same blame game is also used to block better-off racialized minorities from improving their position in society. For that reason alone, members of such minorities are sometimes in the same boat as their poorest co-racials. As a result, they should have a direct interest in improving economic and other living conditions at the bottom of society.

Notes

Reprinted from *Du Bois Review*, vol. 11, no. 2, 2014, by permission of Cambridge University Press.

1. About a decade later, Myrdal's hyphen had disappeared and "underclass" had turned into a racialized blaming term. Although some social scientists used it as such, many more rejected it (Katz 2013; O'Connor 2001). Others avoided Myrdal's term and the stratum about which he was writing.

2. We know now that inequality has social and emotional effects in addition to those resulting from deprivation (Wilkinson and Pickett, 2009), and perhaps being at the bottom or feeling oneself to be there has similar additional effects.

3. Luke Shaefer and Kathryn Edin also propose two other measures more in tune with American conditions: one is adding food stamps as income, the second is also adding tax credits and subsidized housing. These reduce the percentage of household in extreme poverty to 2.2 percent and 1.6 percent, respectively.

4. Why demographic data-collecting agencies do not do so already is itself an empirical question. Judging by the opposition to some U.S. Census questions, the business community may not be interested in learning more about people who lack disposable income to buy its wares, and political conservatives may object to counting and identifying people having to live below subsistence levels of income.

5. I refer here to the distinction between security and excitement (Sanchez-Jankowski 2008) and my similar one between routine seeking and action seeking (Gans 1962).

6. This would make possible an empirical test of Oscar Lewis's (1968) notion of the culture of poverty, which, he claimed, prevented poor people from escaping poverty.

7. A revival of Hyman Rodman's (1963) concept of value stretch, which suggested that poor people's values include both aspirations which they share with the mainstream and pragmatic norms to guide everyday behavior under conditions in which mainstream values are irrelevant.

References

Black, Timothy. 2009. *When A Heart Turns Rock Solid: The Lives of Three Brothers On and Off the Streets.* New York: Pantheon.

Bobo, Lawrence D. and Ryan A. Smith (1998). "Jim Crow Racism to Laissez Faire Racism: The Transformation of Racial Attitudes in America." In *Essays on the Conception of Groups and Group Identities in America*, edited by Wendy Katkin, Ned Landsman, and Andrea Tyree, 182–220. Urbana, IL: University of Illinois Press.

Feagin, Joe R. and Melvin P Sikes (1994). *Living With Racism: The Black Middle Class Experience.* Boston, MA: Beacon Press.

Gans, Herbert J. (1962). *The Urban Villagers: Group and Class in the Life of Italian-Americans.* Glencoe, IL: Free Press.

Gans, Herbert J. (2010). Concentrated Poverty: A Critical Analysis. *Challenge,* 53(4): 82–96.

Gans, Herbert J. (2011). The Challenge of Multigenerational Poverty. *Challenge,* 54(1): 71–80.

Goffman, Alice (2014). *On the Run: Fugitive Life in an American City.* Chicago, IL: University of Chicago Press.

Katz, Michael B. (2013). *The Undeserving Poor: America's Enduring Confrontation with Poverty.* New York: Oxford University Press. Second Edition.

Lewis, Oscar (1968). The Culture of Poverty. In Daniel P. Moynihan (Ed.), *On Understanding Poverty: Perspectives from the Social Sciences,* pp. 187–200. New York: Basic Books.

Myrdal, Gunnar (1963). *Challenge to Affluence.* New York: Pantheon.

National Center for Law and Economic Justice (2012). *Poverty in the United States: A Snapshot.* New York: National Center for Law and Economic Justice.

O'Connor, Alice (2001). *Poverty Knowledge: Social Science, Social Policy and the Poor in Twentieth Century U.S. History.* Princeton, NJ: Princeton University Press.

Papachristos, Andrew V. (2007). Murder by Structure: A Network Theory of Gang Homicide. PhD Dissertation, Department of Sociology, University of Chicago.

Rios, Victor M. (2011). *Punished: Policing the Lives of Black and Latino Boys.* New York: New York University Press.

Rodman, Hyman (1963). The Lower-Class Value Stretch, *Social Forces,* 42(2): 205–215.

Sanchez-Jankowski, Martin (2008). *Cracks in the Pavement: Social Change and Resilience in Poor Neighborhoods.* Berkeley, CA: University of California Press.

Shaefer, H. Luke and Kathryn Edin (2013). Rising Extreme Poverty in the United States and the Response of Federal Means-Tested Transfer Programs. *Social Service Review,* 87(2): 250–268.

Sharkey, Patrick (2012). *Stuck in Place: Urban Neighborhoods and the End of Progress Toward Racial Equality.* Chicago, IL: University of Chicago Press.

Shierholz, Heidi and Elise Gould (2012). *Already More than A Lost Decade: Poverty and Income Trends Continue to Paint a Bleak Picture.* Washington, DC: Economic Policy Institute.

Swidler, Ann (1986). Culture in Action: Symbols and Strategies. *American Sociological Review,* 51(2): 273–285.

Venkatesh, Sudhir A. (2000). *American Project: The Rise and Fall of a Modern Ghetto.* Chicago, IL: University of Chicago Press.

Venkatesh, Sudhir A. (2006). *Off the Books: The Underground Economy of the Urban Poor.* Cambridge, MA: Harvard University Press.

Wacquant, Loic (2009). *Punishing the Poor: The Neoliberal Government of Social Insecurity.* Durham, NC: Duke University Press.

Wilkinson, Richard G. and Kate Pickett (2009). *The Spirit Level: Why Greater Equality Makes Societies Stronger.* New York: Bloomsbury Press.

Wilson, William J. (1987) *The Truly Disadvantaged: The Inner City, the Underclass and Public Policy.* Chicago, IL: University of Chicago Press.

CHAPTER 6

The Challenge of Multigenerational Poverty

I n America, poverty is generally perceived as a temporary economic state, thanks in part to the American dream of permanent upward mobility.

Nonetheless, many people are poor for many years, others for most if not all of their lives, and some may have been poor for generations. Since no one seems to have looked for or at them, this paper explores what I call multigenerational poverty, asks whether it exists, suggests what we need to find out about it, and discusses some implications for antipoverty policy.

The paper also considers two corollary hypotheses. The first is that the most serious and intractable American poverty is multigenerational and that the people who have been poor for two or more generations experience a disproportionate share of all poverty-related problems, their own and the country's.

The second hypothesis suggests that most if not almost all of the multigenerationally poor are also severely poor—earning less than half the poverty-line income of $22,000 in 2008. I described the severely poor in my 2009 *Challenge* article (Gans 2009), and this article is in some respects a sequel about very long-term, severe poverty.

Admittedly, it is possible that multigenerational poverty is numerically insignificant, but it seems unlikely. America still contains a number of subregional "pockets of poverty" as well as poor rural communities, small towns, and urban neighborhoods that have been poor for a long time.

In addition, today's poverty can sow the seeds of multigenerational poverty. We know that extensive spells of unemployment and underemployment often result in many years of subsequent employment at low wages even when good times return. This type of downward economic mobility can leave its marks on the next generation, beginning with children's poor school performance and other problems that could have longer-term economic effects (Oreopolous et al. 2005). Likewise, a number of illnesses and other problems associated with current poverty are frequently passed on to future generations.

For example, abused children can, as adults, abuse their own children and thereby effectively hinder them from escaping poverty. In fact, as I suggested in the earlier article, poverty probably causes traumatic stress disorders as well as post-traumatic ones in some people, and the effects of these disorders may hold down future generations.

Obviously, multigenerational poverty should have been looked into long ago, and not only for scholarly reasons. Since at least the end of the 1960s' War on Poverty, American antipoverty policy has "creamed"; that is, many of its programs have been targeted to the working poor and to others who can be helped comparatively easily and in large numbers with the minimal budgets usually allotted to antipoverty programs.

However, the multigenerationally poor, like other severely poor people, need help the most. Providing such help could also lift the political fortunes of antipoverty policy, for mainstream America might then feel more kindly toward the poor people it now stigmatizes as undeserving.

Programs to shrink the number of multigenerationals would produce another positive effect: a reduction in the size of America's economically excluded population that Myrdal (1963) called the underclass. Since that underclass is heavily nonwhite, it is also an undercaste, much like gypsies and the indigenous and aborigine populations found in countries all over the globe.

Research Questions About Multigenerational Poverty

What, then, do we need to know about multigenerational poverty? I suggest that three sets of questions are most urgently in need of answer.

First, we have to find out how many of the currently poor are descendants of one or more generations of poor ancestors. Information must be compiled on their incomes, including how many are living in severe poverty. We must also know whether they are held back economically more by the severity of their current poverty or by its intergenerational duration, and whether relieving them from severe poverty might end its multigenerational effects.

Their sources of income should be determined; so should their place of residence. Do they live in pockets of poverty; in rural, small town, urban or suburban areas, and does geographic location affect their poverty and related ways of life? Are multigenerational rural and urban poverty different, and in what ways?

Second, the roles and functions that generation plays in their lives have to be understood. The concept of multigenerational poverty hypothesizes that poverty can be passed on directly and indirectly to the next generation and that it could worsen with every generation that people remain in poverty. However, more specific knowledge is also needed: Which conditions, factors, and processes, economic and other, take place during and between generations that create the persistence of poverty?

One might expect, or at least hypothesize, that, all other things being equal, later-generation poor people will be worse off than earlier-generation ones, because each has inherited some of the problems passed on by earlier ones. However, this might not be true automatically, and particularly in a growing economy. In that case, a number of later-generation poor people could manage to move out of poverty if they have not been permanently damaged by their heritage and are in the right place at the right time.

In theory it is even possible that in some pockets of poverty, people reach an intergenerational stasis: an unchanging economic environment and a modicum of social stability enable them to develop coping patterns, including low expectations for the future, that allow them to live relatively normal lives without traumatic problems for themselves and others.

I should point out that generational patterns can be identified among other populations as well: the third- and later-generation rich differ in some respects from the so-called new rich; and people whose great-grandparents graduated from college will more often be found among the country's elite than equally talented people who are the first college graduates in their families.

Likewise, immigration research indicates that second generations differ from their immigrant parents in some uniform ways, and third and later generations do so as well. However, immigration researchers study the effects of a set of closely related changes, not of a multifaceted economic, social, and political condition like poverty.

Comparative generational research might indicate that some general patterns of change between generations can be discovered. If so, and if such research applies to the study of multigenerational poverty, it may be possible to identify a general cumulation process from the first generation in poverty to later ones. Perhaps particular problems and behavior patterns arise in one generation, exerting a cumulative effect as they reach later generations.

Then one can ask what effects, positive or negative, does each low-income generation experience; what conditions, problems, as well as survival skills and coping patterns, are passed on from generation to generation and how? Are multigenerationally poor people better able to cope than those newly confronted with the same degree of poverty? Or does generation become irrelevant if and when the economy in which the poor are embedded changes between and during generations?

Third, the generational effects of the various problems and crises that might be associated with poverty need to be identified. These problems can be divided into the following:

1. *Hereditary and transmitted diseases and similar incapacities.* Although some chronic illnesses and physiological handicaps are passed on, others, including addictions, may be transmitted from one generation to the next. They are passed on either because they influence child rearing or because similar socioeconomic conditions affect the next generation similarly, for example, by producing a new cohort of addicts.

If two generations suffer from the same severe poverty, it is reasonable to assume that each generation might independently turn to alcohol, drugs, or some other form of escape and oblivion. And is this pattern also applicable to the stress-related illnesses, such as some kinds of mental illness, heart disease, strokes, and the like, from which poor people suffer at higher rates?

As I noted above, abusing parents may transmit the abusing pattern to the next generation, and the same process may apply to other intrafamilial forms of violence. If a fragile self-respect is transmitted, the interpersonal violence sometimes generated by such fragility may continue for another generation as well.

2. *Poverty-related situational crises.* Poor people experience many more crises of various kinds than the better off, a number of which may have

reverberations that can last into the next generation and beyond. I suggested previously that various forms of downward occupational mobility can set processes into motion that have negative consequences for children's school performance and later life. Similar losses, whether of jobs, welfare benefits, or access to low-cost housing, could produce the same or worse effects among the poor.

Many other troubles can have intergenerational consequences. Ex-felons are especially disadvantaged in the job market, and even an arrest record, a common handicap for poor males, can sometimes hold back their children. In small towns and neighborhoods where "everyone knows everyone else," the descendants of stigmatized people, for example "ne'er-do-wells" and "welfare dependents," may inherit the parental stigmas.

3. "*Vulnerabilities.*" All of us vary in the degree to which we are vulnerable to problems and crises. Poor people do not differ in this respect, except that they face many more problems and crises without the material and other resources to deal with them that are available to the better off. It is, however, possible that the continuing barrage of problems and crises that they encounter enable some to develop survival skills of a kind that better-off people do not need.

Whether vulnerability, resilience, and survival skills increase or decrease over the generations is also a relevant empirical question. Individuals presumably vary most in this respect, but among the poor particularly, the family, however structured, is both the most vulnerable institution and the first line of defense. It is the initial target of economic adversity and the social and other problems that follow, but it must also initiate defensive and other responses.

Families are figuratively and regularly battered by poverty, and when family members lack the resilience, skills—and support groups—they often batter each other literally. Intrafamily abuse and family breakup are among the typical outcomes, but so is the single-parent family that becomes a preemptive solution for women who choose it in part to forestall familial conflict, spousal and child abuse, and other emotional hardships.

Poor single-parent families generally have lower incomes than poor two-parent families, making it harder for them to escape poverty or to enable their children to do so. The daughters of single parents are at risk of becoming single parents themselves, thus increasing the possibility that family poverty will be passed on. Moreover, the higher rate of family breakup that accompanies poverty means that two-parent families can also suddenly be damaged by economic and other crises that then affect the next generation.

Because rates of abuse and single parenthood have been rising over the past several decades, a hypothesis that family vulnerability increases in each generation seems justified. Similar hypotheses about heightened vulnerability should be considered for other important social relationships. One could ask, for example, whether the ability to make and hold friends, or to participate in informal and formal groups, such as religious ones, declines with each generation in poverty

4. *Racial and class factors.* Many of the country's multigenerational poor are African American and from other nonwhite populations. Racial stigmatization, discrimination, and segregation not only are continuing obstacles for the nonwhite poor, but also often continue to shackle future generations.

Moreover, a sizable proportion of multigenerationals are the descendants of Southern, Caribbean, and Latin American slaves. Consequently, one must ask whether slavery—and the long-term social and economic restrictions imposed on ex-slaves after emancipation—has enduring effects (Patterson 1998). Stereotypes deployed during slavery have persisted to this day. Thus, one must ask what other components of slavery have survived, and whether they have perpetuated or worsened poverty beyond that experienced by poor people whose ancestors were not enslaved.

Patterson also argues that African-American familial vulnerability is in part a result of slave owners' breaking up of slave families by selling individual members, as well as forcing the wives of slaves to become their involuntary sex partners. Such effects may differ with the varieties of slave-owner practices across the Western Hemisphere and may explain the apparently somewhat lower familial vulnerability of poor Latino immigrants and their descendants (Telles and Ortiz 2008).

Conversely, rates of family breakup were high among poor European immigrants during periods of economic depression, although variations may exist among those whose ancestors endured various forms of peonage. Yet other variables must be considered, such as the particularly punitive forms of racial discrimination especially aimed at poor African Americans.

Race plays another role for poor whites. Since the majority of whites, at least those not living in poor white communities or poverty pockets, have escaped poverty over the past half-century, many of the remaining poor ones, particularly in the cities, may suffer from a variety of handicaps that have immobilized them for generations.

Class needs to be considered as a social as well as economic factor. Social inequality creates negative effects that are independent of economic inequality, adding to lack of self-respect, stress, depression, and all their consequences (Wilkinson and Pickett 2010). If multigenerationals are (or are in danger of being) located in an economic underclass, they will in addition suffer more severely from inequality than other poor people.

5. *Coping patterns.* Not all generational effects are negative, and some may enable poor people to cope with multigenerational poverty. Empirical research among the multigenerational poor will have to identify these patterns, but they are likely to be habitual practices and routines as well as social relationships and institutional ties that may have been handed down from past generations. These patterns and habits may themselves become multigenerational because they have proven successful, not only for ensuring sheer survival but for creating some stability. They are also a significant source of the satisfaction and pleasure that very poor people can enjoy and may help them maintain hope for a better future.

Some of these coping patterns resemble those practiced by better-off people, but many are probably very different. The crucial empirical question is which of these patterns, if any, can help people leave poverty when economic conditions improve, and which, if any, prevent them from doing so and continue to keep them poor.

I use the term "coping pattern" for three reasons. First, it accurately describes how poor people deal with frequently occurring problems and crises. Second, it is an alternative term for "culture." It may therefore encourage researchers to avoid the term "culture of poverty," which has been used to blame the poor for their own poverty and has aided conservatives in opposing antipoverty programs.

Third, coping patterns lend themselves far more easily to empirical study than culture does. Thus, studying them would help us determine which have good, bad, or neutral consequences, and which are passed on to the next generation.

The coping patterns that could help poor people to exit poverty cannot be identified until the appropriate economic opportunities appear available. However, during past world wars, when everyone able to work was put to work, many poor people suddenly stopped being poor. They obviously knew how to cope.

Some Policy Implications

Antipoverty policy to deal with multigenerational poverty cannot be intelligently formulated until we learn from the now invisible multigenerationals themselves and from research about and among them. Actually, the first step must make them visible, to acquaint policy makers and politicians with their problems and to generate "political will" to aid them.

Some of the needed programs will resemble those I have described for reducing severe poverty (Gans 2009). These have to begin with jobs programs, but many of the poor have little to offer in the labor market. Consequently, income supports will be as urgent as jobs programs. However, elected officials and voters will probably need to be persuaded that multigenerational poverty is a societally caused and historically generated disability before they will assent to disability-related income support programs.

The multigenerational poor will also need medical and other programs to counter chronic illnesses, including those inherited from past generations. Support systems to help people overcome and prevent crises will be needed as well. The coping patterns that multigenerationals have used for such purposes will provide some guidelines and models for such systems.

Children must be distanced from ancestral economic and other conditions that made familial poverty multigenerational but without separating them from their families. The many preschool educational programs now operating in low-income neighborhoods may provide clues for some of what needs to be done. Even so, many young people will need post-school help in the labor market.

Nonetheless, the greatest challenge is offering the right help to the adults living with the traumas of generations of severe poverty. Some may be able to leave poverty, but those unable to work or find work must be helped to make as useful and satisfying a life as possible by other means.

Aiding the multigenerational poor could be politically risky. Making them visible also exposes them to the possibility of becoming the newest incarnation of the undeserving poor. Indeed, if the country is not soon restored to economic good health, some of its most politically alienated citizens may go looking for new low-income scapegoats for America's economic and political problems.

Researching Multigenerational Poverty

Studying multigenerational poverty is not going to be easy. Poor people do not usually keep family records or create family histories. They may also have lost track of their ancestors more frequently than better-off people have.

Consequently, databases with multigenerational samples of poor people will have to be found, and new ones developed. Some genealogical research among poor people should be possible as municipal and other local archives are digitized. Moreover, existing databases, including the historical U.S. Census, the Panel Study of Income Dynamics, and others can be mined for data about least a couple of generations.

The literatures of intergenerational research, mainly produced by economists (e.g., Bowles et al. 2005) as well as similar literatures in developmental psychology will be particularly useful for identifying findings that can then be studied among multigenerational samples. Life course studies that extend beyond one generation (e.g., Elder 1999) may be similarly useful. Historical works on poverty that contain family biographies can be reanalyzed, and novels about multigenerational characters and communities that are based on some empirical research should at least provide ideas for future research.

Then there are occasional surprise discoveries, frequently in old files and records stored in back offices and attics. Thus Telles and Ortiz (2008) gained access to the interviews of a 1965 study of Mexican immigrants and could reinterview the respondents and interview their descendants three decades later. They were thus able to obtain some data for four generations of the same families.

Three other kinds of research ought to be undertaken as well. First, ethnographers should move into and study poor neighborhoods and communities in order to identify multigenerationals, focusing especially on three-generation households, the longest-term residents as well as the lowest-status ones. The latter are apt to include people who are often treated as outcasts by the rest of the community and who may be the descendants of earlier outcasts.

An ironic precedent exists for such research—the late-nineteenth-century "family studies" conducted by eugenicists to prove that crime and other kinds of deviant behavior among the poor were genetic in origin (e.g., Rafter 1988). College psychology texts still sometimes discuss the "Jukes" and the

"Kallikaks," households or families that were accused of being retarded and the descendants of a long line of similarly damaged ancestors.

The "studies" were methodologically suspect, and their findings were not credible, but they probably identified severely poor rural people who had been rejected by their communities for generations and were never given a chance to hold normal jobs and act like normal people. They also suffered from a variety of poverty-related diseases, including alcoholism, and since many were illiterate, they could therefore easily be labeled as "morons" by ideologically programmed and untrained interviewers.

Second, poor three-generation households and families, as well as samples of grandparents, should be interviewed about their family histories, with questions about both prior generations and changes during and between generations. Studies have already been conducted among such households (e.g., Burton and Sorensen 1993) and can be expanded to explore multi-generational issues.

Third, some long-term panel studies should be organized, beginning among poor three-generation households and continuing among their descendants. As in other panel studies, participants would be interviewed regularly about their economic status, their problems, and ways of coping with them, as well as about successful and unsuccessful attempts to exit poverty.

In years to come, social scientists will then be able to understand what multigenerational poverty is all about and how it can be eliminated.

Note

Reprinted from *Challenge*, vol. 54, no. 1, 2011, by permission of Taylor & Francis Group. I received helpful comments on an earlier draft of the article from Tim Black, S.M. Miller, Patrick Sharkey, and Hilary Silver. The idea for the article resulted from a conversation with Harriet Liebow, the widow of Elliott Liebow, in which she reported that the descendants of the poor African American men whom Liebow had studied for his 1967 book *Tally's Corner* were leading even more problematic and crisis-ridden lives.

Further Reading

Bowles, S., H. Gintis, and M. Osborne. 2005. *Unequal Chances*. Princeton, NJ: Princeton University Press.

Burton, L., and S. Sorensen. 1993. "Temporal Dimensions of Intergenerational Care-giving in African-American Multigeneration Families." In *Caregiving Systems,* ed. S. Zarit, L. Pearlin, and K. Schaie, 47–66. Hillsdale, NJ: Erlbaum Associates.

Elder, G. 1999. *Children of the Great Depression.* Boulder, CO: Westview Press.

Gans, H. 2009. "Antipoverty Policy for the Excluded Poor." *Challenge* 52, no. 6 (November-December): 79–95.

Liebow, E. 1967. *Tally's Corner.* Boston, MA: Little, Brown.

Myrdal, G. 1963. *Challenge to Affluence.* New York: Pantheon Books.

Oreopolous, P., M. Page, and A. Stevens. 2005. "The Intergenerational Effects of Worker Displacement." NBER working paper 11587, August. National Bureau of Economic Research, Cambridge, MA.

Patterson, O. 1998. *Rituals of Blood.* Washington, DC: Civitas/Counterpoint.

Rafter, N. 1988. *White Trash.* Boston, MA: Northeastern University Press.

Telles, E., and V. Ortiz. 2008. *Generations of Exclusion.* New York: Russell Sage Foundation.

Wilkinson, R., and K. Pickett. 2010. *Spirit Level.* New York: Bloomsbury Press.

CHAPTER 7

The Benefits of Poverty

This article proceeds from the familiar notion that all human endeavors have benefits and costs, material and nonmaterial—and that most such endeavors have benefits for some people and groups and costs for others. Even some of the most costly social evils benefit someone. Poverty is a good example of such an evil—and the article argues that it mostly benefits the more fortunate members of society.

To be sure, the poor also benefit from those of us who are better off; we pay for antipoverty and unemployment programs as well as food stamps, not to mention Medicaid, which had a budget of nearly $300 billion in 2010. We also help fund emergency clinics, shelters, and other rescue facilities—and experiment with endless other programs to help young people escape from poverty.

Nonetheless, the poor are not merely a burden on the rest of society; they also provide a variety of benefits for it. The better-off are largely unaware that they obtain such benefits, for many are not very visible. Consequently, shining some light on them may help us more clearly understand how and why poverty is useful and why it persists. For example, fortunate Americans probably do not realize that the poverty of other Americans helps to make them better off, and that if incomes, wealth, and other resources were redistributed more equally so as to reduce poverty, they would end up with a smaller share of these resources.

Very few people deliberately encourage policies to preserve or increase poverty. Even conservatives who oppose antipoverty policy on ideological grounds are not in favor of poverty, even though they oppose policies that help the poor escape it.

Even so, the benefits of poverty are all around us. They are identifiable by looking for and at the consequences of poverty and then tracing those people, firms, and institutions that gain from these consequences.

To choose a prominent example, poverty reinforces the pervasive conservatism of American politics. Since the poor vote less often than the more fortunate, they lack the power to demand fuller employment, progressive tax reform, a more comprehensive welfare state, and the liberal legislators who would support such measures. Consequently, when the poor are unable to make such demands, government economic and other policies remain more conservative.

The benefits that poverty produces for the rest of society are not sufficient to sustain its existence in that society. Larger and more impersonal economic and political forces are responsible for its persistence, even though institutional and other group and individual agents assist these forces. So, in fact, do some of the ablest poor. Those who are sent to elite schools and then are recruited to join the better-off may contribute to the country's continuing conservatism.

The remainder of the article describes the principal economic, political, social, and cultural benefits of poverty. Since poverty research has looked only at the costs of poverty, empirical evidence about its benefits is scarce, and what follows might sometimes seem counterintuitive. Occasionally, the article might sound cynical, although this not the author's intent. The discussion is meant to be empirical, although most of its assertions are hypotheses rather than findings.

The Economic Benefits

Beyond their involuntary contribution to the incomes of the more affluent, the poor provide them with other economic benefits. The abundant availability of poor people ensures that society's dirty work is done cheaply. The poor not only do most of such work—cleaning our toilets, for example— but carry out a significant portion of the most dangerous jobs, in mines, in meatpacking plants, and wherever dangerous chemicals are being used.

They do the illegal and disreputable work as well, selling drugs on the street and their bodies in automobiles.

In addition, the poor play a significant role in fighting America's wars. In the past, when wars were largely labor-intensive and fought by infantries, the unskilled poor provided much of the manpower. If they died in battle, the number of poor people was reduced, thereby sparing the better-off taxpayers from having to fund antipoverty programs for them. Today, the military wants better-educated recruits, but when enlistments sag, the army still returns to its previous source of bodies. That currently half the veterans of the Iraq and Afghanistan wars are jobless and many are fast sinking into poverty suggests that reducing the size of the country's military may increase the number of poor veterans.

Actually, some jobs that are dirty, dangerous, or disreputable are not considered such because they are performed by people who are better off. Surgeons are rarely viewed as doing dirty or dangerous work, the drug sellers who supply the rich can remain invisible, and the paid escorts who "date" them sometimes become celebrities. The poor themselves do not always have time or money to do their own dirty work, which allows the better-off to criticize them for being dirty.

Our dependence on the poor to do the dirty work cannot be overestimated. In the days before Clinton ended "welfare as we know it," Southern states stopped paying benefits during the summer so that poor mothers would be forced to pick cotton. The firms that supply us with fresh fruits and vegetables would make us pay more for them if they paid illegal immigrants a living wage.

The low pay of the working poor functions as an indirect subsidy—and benefit—to the affluent. Domestics, nannies, and home-care workers subsidize the professional classes by enabling them to combine parenting, careers, civic activities, and the like.

In states where the poor pay a higher proportion of their income in sales and other taxes than the more affluent, they even subsidize whatever government activities benefit them.

More important, the poor indirectly benefit the better-off through the creation of professional jobs that serve, service, control, and seek to uplift and reform them.

The low-income sick and injured provide regular clients for emergency clinics and jobs for the medical staffs, as well as for the medical, mental health, and social workers who treat poor drug addicts, the victims of domestic violence, and those suffering from the high stress levels and mental illnesses found among the poor.

Equivalent benefits accrue to demographers, economists, sociologists, other researchers, investigative reporters, and documentary film makers who study and in other ways keep track of the poor.

In addition, a long list of businesses might not exist if poverty were reduced. Some of the small groceries that now serve poverty-stricken areas could not survive if supermarkets did not avoid such areas. Farmers are beneficiaries of the food stamp and other food-support programs for the poor, and these programs might lose their current political support if they did not also benefit farmers.

Other businesses that benefit from the existence of poverty include sellers of used goods, makers and sellers of cheap alcohol and other low-cost addictive products, as well as pawnshops, predatory lenders and other loan sharks, the "numbers racket," and diverse gambling establishments. Faith healers, fortune tellers, and even places of worship that exploit their worshipers financially could also be added to this list.

Many others make a living by serving the poor. They include immigrant doctors who help to staff emergency clinics while still learning English, as well as some otherwise unemployable people that no one else will hire but who provide care and other services to the poor.

In the past, the poor also provided what Marxists called a reserve army of labor, which could step in when strike breakers or "replacement workers" were needed. At the same time, this army maintained indirect pressure on wages to help keep them low. Computerization and outsourcing of jobs, the weakening of unions, and the easy availability of illegal immigrant workers have, however, reduced and perhaps even eliminated the need for a reserve army, at least for the moment.

Instead, some of its previous recruits are now part of the country's large prison population. Indeed, the prison industry, mental hospitals, and similar institutions exist in part to house the surplus poor population the economy no longer needs and the rest of society no longer wants to support. A number of these men—and they have long been mostly men—may be the modern equivalents of the men who once upon a time were killed off in huge numbers by the wars fought with infantries and sailor-filled warships.

Political Benefits

As already noted, the political powerlessness of the poor results in an overall polity more conservative than it would otherwise be. It benefits the nonpoor further because much of the power that the poor lack goes to or is taken by higher-income interest groups and citizens, further enabling them to obtain a greater share of government budgets, tax reductions, and the like.

Yet even the voting poor must cede much of their influence to the better-off. Since poor and moderate-income voters generally support the Democratic Party, the Republican Party can ignore them. Actually, so can the Democrats, since such voters have nowhere else to go. They can threaten to stay home, but so many do so already that the threat is not always effective.

Further, the poor have so few influential lobbies and other organizations to speak for them that they are unable to fight current efforts in many states that restrict their voting rights.

Yet it is also possible that if the poor had more political influence, the nonpoor would call off some of their intra- and interclass conflicts and come together to vote against the poor.

Currently the ranks of the powerless poor are joined by a number of the newly jobless, foreclosed homeowners, and otherwise downwardly mobile victims of the Great Recession who are sometimes too dispirited even to vote. Ironically enough, some of the angriest victims seem to have joined the Tea Party, thereby providing further support to the corporate interests and politicians who are adding to the number and plight of the poor.

The indirect gains that the poor supply the better-off extend to local government as well. For example, poor neighborhoods often receive less adequate garbage removal and other sanitation programs than better-off ones do, the savings presumably being diverted to the latter. Higher-income school districts regularly attract the best teachers originally hired for schools serving the poor.

In addition, the poor benefit their economic betters by letting themselves be ushered out of the way when these betters want to replace them. Cities have historically torn down poor neighborhoods to provide highways for commuting suburbanites. In the 1950s and 1960s, the federal government supplied funds that enabled cities to clear such neighborhoods for more-affluent urban residents.

In the 1990s, many cities tore down the public housing projects built during and after the New Deal period and replaced them with mixed-income projects that enable better-off residents to live closer to downtown. Public housing could be torn down because it is government property, but eminent domain gives governments the power to take privately owned land and to transfer lands used by the poor to politically and economically stronger users.

Gentrification is a wholly private process by which the more fortunate can replace the less fortunate, although once this process is under way, local governments help not the poor displacees but the newcomers, most often by improving municipal services in the area. Of course, the new residents raise land values and thus community tax receipts, but these rarely go back to the neighborhoods that now house the displaced poor.

In some cities, the destruction of public housing, other land takings in low-income neighborhoods, and gentrification are currently driving the poor to the outer edges of the metropolitan area, where many are too far away to compete in the urban labor market but are also less visible to their betters if they become homeless or must resort to begging.

When governments encounter budget problems, programs that serve the poor are almost always cut first, even when governments are in liberal hands. Programs that serve the better-off, who are more likely to protest budget cuts, suffer less.

In Republican eras, programs for the poor are even cut back in favor of tax reductions to the wealthy, on the dubious grounds that they will invest their tax savings to create jobs. Even when jobs are actually created, not many go to the poor who were the victims of the initial budget cuts.

The better-off derive further benefits from poverty because poor people who do not live up to the behavioral standards of the higher classes can be labeled undeserving and declared ineligible for public aid. The more standards they can be found to violate, the larger the savings to the higher-class citizens who would otherwise have to help them. Some of these citizens may be violating the same standards, but they are not deemed to be or punished for being undeserving.

Once publicly marked as undeserving or dangerous, the poor may unwittingly provide political benefits to conservative politicians and organizations, at least if they drive people who are fearful of the poor toward conservative political forces.

Status and Other Social Benefits

Just as the poor help to maintain the American political order, so do they for the social order, especially its hierarchical structure or pecking order. Every pecking order needs a base of people who can be pecked by everyone better off in some way, and the poor provide that base by definition.

In this instance, working-class and moderate-income people benefit for once from poverty, for the various forces that keep down the poor reduce their chances of sinking to the bottom of the pecking order, at least in good economic times. Undoubtedly, many victims of the Great Recession and the jobless recovery worry about this aspect of downward economic mobility, and some oppose antipoverty programs for this reason. Others have apparently joined up with the Tea Party.

The unfortunates at the bottom of the pecking order create yet another benefit for the more fortunate population, for they are often chosen to serve as scapegoats. The poor, and especially the undeserving ones, can be assigned blame when no other targets are available. At the moment, poor illegal immigrants seem to be used most frequently as scapegoats, at least for the country's economic troubles.

To be sure, even in an economically and socially more egalitarian society, someone will be at the bottom, at least if people want or need a pecking order that allows them to make distinctions between people or social positions. Since the better-off population plays a major role in determining the specific distinctions, it also creates the markers that signify inferiority and superiority. Still, poverty seems to have been used as a marker of inferiority more often than other criteria, and even in communist societies, the poor have remained at the bottom of the pecking order.

At the same time, the low-income population can enable others to achieve upward mobility. Because the higher social and business classes believe that selling to the poor would lower their social status, petty entrepreneurs from lower-status groups can take their place. Immigrants have frequently moved up in the pecking order by being storekeepers to the poor.

Defenders of American exceptionalism can point to a sizable number of business success stories, including contemporary multinational corporations that began as mom-and-pop stores in low-income neighborhoods. The American movie industry was started by a handful of poor entrepreneurs, most of them Jewish immigrants, who opened movie theaters in slum storefronts but became rich when mainstream seekers of entertainment wanted to see their movies as well.

The poor offer social-status benefits even to the rich who take part in charitable activities. Not so long ago, some ladies from high society ministered personally to the poor, who thus helped these women maintain their social usefulness. Today both old and new monied individuals have moved on and up to "civic" and related activities that do not require direct contact with the poor. Still, the large foundations and liberally inclined small ones continue to donate to institutions that help the deserving poor.

Nonetheless, even the undeserving poor do their bit for the more fortunate members of society, for in the process of determining what behaviors are markers of undeservingness, the fortunate ones are also establishing the markers of deservingness—and these define themselves as being deserving.

Behavior patterns that poor people use to cope with and survive poverty serve the same purpose. For example, people who have only enough money to live on a week-by-week basis and must always be ready to deal with new crises cannot easily plan ahead. Likewise, they enjoy themselves when opportunities to do so appear, since they may not come again soon. Yet the inability to plan ahead or to delay enjoyment and other gratification are employed as indicators of undeservingness, enabling the more fortunate to celebrate their foresight, planning skills, and ability to put off having fun for more productive endeavors.

The markers of undeservingness can also be altered when it benefits more affluent Americans. Many years ago, poor women who moved from partner to partner in the never-ending search for stable male breadwinners were accused of "serial monogamy." However, when the sexual liberation and other movements made this practice respectable among better-off people not impelled by economic motives, poor women were then condemned for being single parents. In the process, they helped to reinforce the norms that defined the normal family as consisting of two parents. Now that single parenthood has spread beyond the poor, an undeserving family structure is likely to be redefined once more.

Still, the most important benefit that the undeserving poor provide to the more affluent parts of society is to cast doubt on the desirability of antipoverty efforts. As long as enough of the poor can be described as morally unworthy, they thereby reduce the moral imperative to reduce poverty. If enough people condemned to long-term joblessness by the Great

Recession are charged with laziness and an unwillingness to work, they can then be considered undeserving of continuing unemployment insurance. Some Republican politicians have so argued; beginning in 2010 and in 2011, a number of states have decimated state unemployment benefits. Once more the poor benefit the pocketbooks of their economic betters.

Cultural Benefits

Poverty is even beneficial to culture, for over the centuries, poor people have supplied an inordinate amount of entertainment, athletics, and arts, and the resulting diversion and aesthetic satisfaction to the better-off. Today's television comedies still show traces of the vaudeville and burlesque shows that entertained poor Americans in the nineteenth and early twentieth centuries, and the beginnings of the American movie industry on New York's Lower East Side were, in effect, a continuation of that pattern.

Museums and affluent collectors exhibit the art and artifacts of pre-industrial and peasant "folk," the pictures of poor people created by Depression-era artists and photographers funded by the Works Progress Administration, and more recently, the photographs, videos, and other visual and graphic portrayals of black *ghettos* and immigrant neighborhoods and among the homeless.

However, the music of the poor may have provided the most benefits. Over the decades, American audiences have listened to the blues, spirituals, and jazz that came out of southern poverty. In our time they have heard the soul music, rap, and varieties of hip-hop that began in the low-income *ghettos* of New York and elsewhere. We forget that the Beatles began their career in the slums of Liverpool.

Poor characters serve as heroic figures for America's entertainment—for example, the cowboy, the hobo, the hipster, and the prostitute with a heart of gold—but they also supply their share of villains. Most of the bad guys in crime dramas have until recently come from the underworld and drug-selling street gangs.

To some, the poor offer vicarious participation in the impulsive sexual, partying, and other uninhibited behavior they are alleged to practice and that they are sometimes thought to enjoy more than better-off Americans. Whether a higher proportion of poor people actually behave in this way or obtain special pleasure from doing so is highly questionable, but as long as nonpoor people believe it, they can imagine they are joining in. Further psychological benefits are available to those who subsequently condemn the poor for being immoral, thereby elevating their own moral stature.

At various times, other material and nonmaterial artifacts used by the poor become attractive to the better-off. Some of today's snacks and fast foods can be traced back to the easily stored meals that peasants, farm laborers, and slaves took with them to the fields; and at the moment, imagined and real male prison garb is fashionable among young people.

Some Policy Implications

I have spelled out only the most general benefits of poverty, but for policy purposes, more specific information is necessary—for example, how much and how the different socioeconomic strata actually gain from poverty. In addition, which of these benefits accrue to individuals and households, which go to private enterprise and public agencies, and which contribute to the public welfare of the larger society has to be determined. Identifying the benefits that are highly valued by others and those making major contributions to the public welfare will enable makers of antipoverty policy to design programs around these benefits. They can also come up with alternatives for protecting these benefits that would not burden the poor.

Learning that, and how they benefit from poverty, will not persuade the economically and influential sectors of society to support a more generous antipoverty policy. Guilt rarely moves anyone to political action. But anti-poverty programs that further increase the benefits to the better-off, such as society-wide economic growth that begins among the poor, have not yet been invented.

Low-income populations are well aware of the local people and organizations that profit directly from their poverty, since they see them or their representatives in the neighborhood. They may also sense that others benefit from their poverty. Such knowledge persuades some poor people that they must become politically more active on their own behalf, but it seems mostly to add to the resignation, cynicism, and anger of others. However, judging by the history of the last half century, even more intense and widespread anger is not likely to result in effective political action by or for the poor.

In the short run, they must depend on the powers that be for a more generous antipoverty policy. Obama was able to sneak some benefit increases into his 2009 stimulus package—a better strategy these days than talking about poverty and proposing antipoverty programs. However, more explicit antipoverty action may be politically possible and even necessary if "middle-class" (read middle- and working-class) poverty rates rise significantly and a large number of "new poor" appear.

Actually, if these rate rises turn out to be long-lasting, antipoverty programs for the new poor could become a standard budget item. Even private enterprise may endorse them, because it needs the consumer demand that will be generated by the monies paid out by these programs.

The newly poor recipients of such antipoverty programs will also vote more often than the old poor, and politicians will therefore look more favorably on providing money for these programs.

Undoubtedly someone will then propose to fold the traditional antipoverty programs for the old poor into those established for the new ones. One can only hope that if and when this proposal surfaces, the country's decision makers, including those inside the Beltway, will have learned how much the old poor have been benefiting the rest of us.

Note

Reprinted from *Challenge*, vol. 55, no. 1, 2012, by permission of Taylor & Francis Group.

PART THREE

JOBS AND THE POLITICAL ECONOMY

The major cause of poverty continues to be unemployment, under-employment and underpayment. Indeed, the most depressing feature of the current American economy is the growing number of minimum-wage and otherwise bad jobs. And that includes even those jobs that now or will eventually pay the $15 an hour minimum wage currently being demanded by the Fight for 15 movement.

For this and other reasons, all the essays in this part worry about a possible future in which there may not be enough decent jobs. In that case, a significant number of citizens, perhaps even a plurality, could someday be forced to live in permanent poverty and near poverty. Even some of the better-off workers might have to endure permanent wage and salary stagnation.

The power holders in an economically highly unequal society may have no incentive to prevent this possibility. Consequently, the victims of poverty and their allies will have to resort to political means to achieve a humane standard of living.

I begin again with a too rarely considered fact and probably centuries old truth: that there were never enough jobs for everyone needing or wanting to work. Much of Chapter 8, about the nearly permanent existence of economically superfluous people, describes what has been done and still is being done to keep them alive or to get rid of them.

Chapters 9 and 10 discuss two often-proposed policies to deal with joblessness and superfluousness. Both are currently politically unfeasible, and the two chapters therefore explore now more feasible versions of both policies.

Chapter 9 discusses the proposal to reduce the standard 40-hour work week and creating new jobs out of the work hours that become available as a result.

Unfortunately, creating new jobs through work time reduction is better in theory than in practice, at least as long as management remains free to deal with the reduction by means other than new hires.

Chapter 10 considers another long-standing proposal: providing everyone with a minimal basic income. Although it has never been adopted anywhere around the world, the policy is now being raised in the so-called national conversation of many countries, including our own.

While the basic income idea has often been advocated as a universal entitlement for all citizens, I think of it more as a way of reducing and even eliminating poverty.

Consequently, I use the chapter also to consider existing and politically realistic future policies that can be a de facto basic income program for those needing it most.

Chapter 11 joins the political to the economic, suggesting that government will have to intervene more and more in the economy. Moreover, it may have to do so on behalf of the victims of a stagnant economy.

Since today's poor and much of the working class lack the political power to get government more fully on their side, the chapter proposes how that might be made to happen.

In the chapter's political scenario, I try hard to be realistic enough to give it a chance of succeeding, and without depending significantly on the long hoped for protest and other political movements to bring about more economic, political, racial, and other equalities.

The chapter was written in 2014, before Bernie Sanders began to promise a political revolution, and also before the Fight for 15 and other movements to improve working conditions among the underpaid and other exploited workers. Since then, Donald Trump's movement of angry white working-class voters is said to have helped him win the 2016 presidential election. Even so, the experts believe that Trump cannot bring back the well-paying manufacturing and other blue-collar jobs he promised them.

What these voters will do if the jobs fail to materialize remains to be seen. Many will probably resign themselves to the downward mobility they have already experienced although they might become yet angrier at the politicians who have disappointed them. Others could turn to a yet more aggressive Far Right, hoping that the threat of violent action will improve their economic condition.

Still, perhaps enough of these working class voters will support a movement that combines ideas from the Sanders revolution with policies and programs that meet their economic needs and wants. They must also be presented in a manner and with language that appeals to these voters.

Nonetheless, such a movement can get off the ground only if it can obtain active support from nonwhite working-class voters, as well as middle-class people of all skin colors fearing a further decline in the jobs they are seeking.

Moreover, that movement must eventually coalesce with voters and politicians worried about America becoming an oligarchy ruled by the donor class. Once together, they must then persuade the Democratic party or a powerful third party to campaign and fight to turn the country into a truly representative democracy.

This party has to control federal and state governments long enough to overturn the undemocratic provisions built into the Constitution by the founding fathers.

Even then, economic power holders will always have more political clout than the rest of the citizens, which also means that they must learn enough about the workings of the economy and the polity to effectively confront the power holders.

I suggest in Chapter 11 that this learning must begin no later than high school, and Chapter 12 was originally intended to investigate what kind of economic education, if any, high school students were now receiving. Finding no reliable data, I decided to look instead at the textbooks used in high school economics.

What I learned is that the texts teach students almost nothing about the workings of the actually existing economy. Instead, they mainly instruct students how to become economists. Worse yet, they will be trained to study an idealized market economy which bears little resemblance to the economy that they must be able to understand if they are to wrest some economic and political power from those now holding it.

CHAPTER 8

Superfluous Workers

The Labor Market's Invisible Discards

Except during the extremely rare periods of truly full employment, there are always more workers than jobs. When the worker-to-jobs ratio becomes too skewed, societies and their sociopolitical structures create superfluous workers: able-bodied people who are permanently removed from the economy. Superfluous workers have probably existed ever since organized economies were invented, and they can be found today in modern as well as third-world countries.

Hard economic times produce more jobless workers who will never find jobs again. If anyone was counting them, we might discover that significant numbers of them are well on the way to becoming superfluous. In the United States, currently, more than five people are available for every job, and in some especially hard-hit communities, hundreds are applying for a handful of positions. The average jobless worker has now been out of work for three quarters of a year; and some long-term jobless are being told they are unemployable—the clearest sign that they will most likely become superfluous.

Although the economy is showing some signs of new economic growth, Dean Baker, Paul Krugman, and others have suggested that the current level of minimal job creation could continue for a decade or more. In fact, the number of superfluous workers could increase even if economic growth speeds up, for example if employers continue to move their firms overseas, outsource jobs to foreign firms, or hire more robots. And global capitalism could invent yet other methods of job destruction in the future.

Consequently, unemployment analysts must figure out how to identify already superfluous workers, as well as potential and likely ones. Concurrently, job creators must come up with new ideas for bringing such workers back into the economy, or else the country must find other ways of enabling superfluous workers to survive.

Dealing with Superfluity

Superfluous workers are not a new problem, but in the past, societies found methods, many of them cruel, to get rid of them. Although some are still practiced, such methods are no longer acceptable, which is why constructive and supportive alternatives must be developed.

We know very little about what hunter-gatherer and agrarian economies did with superfluous workers, or even if they had any. During the medieval period and the beginnings of the industrial economy, brutal working conditions, epidemics, and poverty seem to have killed or permanently injured enough people to keep the superfluous within limits. Prisons and lunatic asylums removed others from the labor market.

The European colonial countries could ship potentially superfluous workers to their colonies, and penal colonies helped further. Other countries sold the superfluous as slaves. Neither prisons, colonies, nor slavery were invented to deal with discarded workers, but they proved useful for that purpose nevertheless.

Wars syphon off superfluous workers, too, and when wars were labor-intensive, infantries, cavalries, and warships put many of them to work outside the regular labor force. The fact that many were killed or incapacitated ensured that the number of superfluous workers would not increase after the wars ended.

Improved working conditions and the welfare state sharply reduced the perils of industrial work, and both slavery and colonialism have been abolished in most modern economies. Wars are becoming capital-intensive, and the more they are fought with drones and robots, the higher the likelihood that some of the people who previously served in the military could become superfluous someday. Those who came out of combat with permanent cases of post-traumatic stress disorders might become superfluous immediately, even if they are also described as disabled.

Yet other ways of keeping the potentially superfluous out of the labor force remain. One is the continuing increase in minimal educational requirements. The two-year college certificate will soon replace high school graduation as the minimum for most jobs, and in the long run, more and more jobs might require college and post-collegiate degrees. Even periods of unpaid or underpaid interning may become common. Educating people for the jobs likely to be available benefits them and the economy even as it takes them off the labor market.

One of the remaining cruel ways of coping with superfluity is incarceration. Mostly used against poor young and darker-skinned men, the prisons replace the colonies to which some European countries once sent their convicts. While many banished to the colonies eventually wound up in colonial economies, today's convicts spend long years in prison that keep them out of the economy. When employers refuse to hire them because they are ex-convicts, those who do not return to criminal activity and those who cannot find work in the underground economy stand a good chance of becoming superfluous.

Imprisoning people is expensive, and financially strapped state economies are now sending some of their prisoners home early. Courts and legislatures may follow by reducing sentences and decriminalizing victimless crimes. In the process, they will, however, raise the number of potentially superfluous workers.

If and when the Great Job Recession finally ends, pent-up consumer demand will result in new jobs, at least for a while. Expected as well as unexpected, and perhaps even currently unimaginable, technological innovation will create further jobs. So will the new products and services they spin off. Rising Asian wages and declining American ones, as well as relevant tax law reforms, may bring some long-departed American manufacturing home, too.

Still, even if Chinese and Indian wages rise significantly, both countries have huge low-wage populations that need work, as do yet other countries in Asia, Africa, and the Western Hemisphere. Thus, new waves of outsourcing could eventually eliminate many of the American jobs initially accompanying technological and marketing innovations. Continuing worker productivity increases, as well as further advances in the computerization and robotization of work, are likely to take place also. Consequently, recruits for superfluity might become more numerous, especially if jobless recoveries continue to lengthen.

Indeed, a number of today's employers have already indicated that they will not hire the long-term jobless, often on the grounds that they are no longer up-to-date in terms of skills. Some employers may believe the long-term jobless bear some responsibility for their condition, and perhaps enough suffer from lack of self-confidence to contribute to that belief. In any case, most employers have so many applicants that they can reduce their number by arbitrarily and immediately excluding the long-term unemployed.

Types of Superfluous Workers

Strictly speaking, no one can ever be identified or counted as superfluous, for an economic miracle, or more realistically a world war, could put all but the actually unemployable people back to work. Consequently, superfluity is an ex post facto judgment, made with certainty only after jobless workers have been rejected so firmly so often that they know it is useless to keep on trying.

Still, superfluous workers need to be identified, and even if they cannot be counted with certainty, their number can be estimated. They can also be described and classified as already superfluous and potentially or likely superfluous. At least six types of the formerly employed are candidates for one or another category of superfluity:

1. the long-term jobless
2. the unemployables
3. the permanently discouraged workers
4. the damaged or disabled jobless
5. the involuntarily retired
6. the never hired

Probably the largest number of potential superfluous workers are those who have been left jobless so long that their chance of being rehired is low and continues to decline. Empirical studies should show the length of this period under different economic conditions, and the organizations that measure unemployment would have to decide when the superfluous designation should be applied.

Most likely, the long-term jobless who keep applying for jobs are eventually told, or decide for themselves, that they are unemployable and that the economy has discarded them permanently.

Many are actually victims of technological and other changes in the economy, trained in no-longer-wanted skills. They are at the same time victims of structural unemployment, although that concept blames them for obsolescent skills instead of blaming the economic and political decision makers who fail to create alternative jobs.

Others may become discouraged workers and after a while probably consider themselves permanently discouraged. The federal government does not make a temporal distinction between the two, and perhaps no one is willing to admit or officially count those who have in effect given up the job search. When and how people become discouraged, as well as permanently so, can in fact be studied, and those who have given up the job search are on the way to becoming superfluous.

However, some who have lost hope of ever finding another job are probably invisible, living so far under or outside the social structures reached by the government that they cannot be counted. Yet others have undoubtedly moved into criminal work and do not want to be counted.

A related category consists of the long-term jobless who have been emotionally and socially damaged and even disabled as a result of their job losses and other disappointments in the labor market. We have long known that unemployment itself can cause or worsen depression, mental and chronic physical illness, and other traumatic reactions that could leave people too damaged or disabled to work (e.g., Catalano 2009; Kessler, Turner, and House 1988). They are almost certain to become superfluous.

The involuntarily retired fall into two categories—those who are both discouraged and old enough to retire earlier than planned, and those who cope with their being discarded by interpreting it as retirement. The former may only experience a lowering of living standards, but the latter probably suffer some of the same pain as the damaged or disabled jobless.

The last type of superfluous worker is in some respects the most tragic—the young adults who have not yet found a full-time job and may never do so. They could be sentenced to a lifetime of odd jobs, involuntary part-time ones, and long periods of joblessness in between. Although classifying young people as superfluous workers would be irresponsible, they must be considered (for policy purposes at least) very likely candidates for superfluity.

Some youngsters may decide to avoid this fate, never applying for a lawful job and thereby avoiding the pain of rejection. The more fortunate among them will find steady or part-time work in the underground economy; others in the criminal parts of that economy, notably in petty drug selling. Some poor young people, particularly those associated with drug-selling gangs, may find steady work in that economy before they even look for work in the more law-abiding economy.

Undoubtedly, some not yet hired young adults and even adults can already be found in the country's poorer urban and rural communities. Studies of their job searches should enable policy analysts to discover at what point the likelihood of never being hired sets in, and what people do then. Ethnographic studies in very poor communities would probably even turn up older adults who were unable ever to get a full-time job.

All the suggested studies must include one other topic: the permanence of the unemployability and superfluity judgments and decisions made by employers and the jobless, respectively. Even more important, researchers must find out what economic and other conditions are necessary to reverse them.

Defining and Measuring Superfluity

The first step in dealing with superfluity is to define and measure the condition, not only to understand the nature and extent of the problem, but also to make it publicly visible. Governments are rarely eager to report rising joblessness, and improvements in counting the jobless that could have this result must be lobbied for, sometimes for a long time.

The very notion of unemployment was not invented until the 1880s (Garrity 1978). Data on long-term unemployment, discouraged workers, and involuntary part-timers was first reported only in 1994—and interestingly enough, not by the Bureau of Labor Statistics but by the Current Population Survey.

The first task is to discover empirically the periods after which long-term joblessness leads to declarations of unemployability, permanent discouragement, disability, or involuntary retirement. Subsequently, policy analysts and policy makers need to agree what lengths of joblessness justify the designation of potential, likely, and already existing superfluity.

Until categories and measures of the kinds I have suggested are produced, already available data on long-term unemployment will have to do. Studies of past periods of joblessness and their effects on the variety of job seekers, including discouraged ones, should help government determine when serious labor market conditions become crises, when unemployment insurance and other conventional supports are no longer sufficient, and when emergency action is urgently required.

In an economy that daily reports minute details about the ups and downs of thousands of stocks, the government and private enterprise should be required to offer detailed measures of long-term joblessness and related information, including its effects, at least once a month.

As noted previously, such measures make unemployment itself politically more visible. This is particularly necessary since the already and potentially superfluous are among the politically least well represented.

Some Possible Policies

Many of the potential, likely, and already superfluous workers I have identified are low in skills, and some are too young or not young enough. Consequently, most will need special kinds of jobs, others require only income support, yet others will require additional kinds of help. Unless private enterprise reforms, the government has to get serious about becoming the employer of last resort.

Although many appropriate jobs for unskilled and semiskilled workers can be found in infrastructure repair and modernization projects, the construction unions will have first call on them. Other such projects can be easily conceived if they are not already on someone's list. For example, a permanently functioning national pothole repair corps is badly needed in the many parts of the country with highly variable seasonal climates.

Another solution is community service jobs that provide support to professionals and semiprofessionals in health and other helping facilities, public agencies, and even private ones that now pay insufficient attention to the community (Gans 2011). Teaching assistantships in public schools, especially those with large classes, would be another option.

The toughest challenge may be to find work for people who have never worked. A modernized revival of President Franklin Roosevelt's Civilian Conservation Corps is a natural for younger people, especially if it can be accompanied by opportunities for people to continue their education, including in the trades and other fields that do not require further academic training. Undoubtedly some people with the right talents who are in the right place at the right time can still be helped to make careers, for example in teaching, nursing, and similar helping and other professions.

Many of the already superfluous and some of the likely ones will probably never go back to work even under optimum conditions. The older ones may need a new preretirement social security program. The totally discouraged and truly unemployable deserve unstigmatized forms of disability pay and social support, although job opportunities should always be near at hand in all nonwork programs.

Needless to say, such policies are currently not politically feasible, and probably will not become feasible until the existence of superfluous workers is perceived and documented as a national problem. Even then, this kind of policy may not be achievable until all branches of the federal government are controlled by economic liberals, or by politicians who need the votes of the jobless.

If the consumer economy is in dire enough straits, its politically influential firms might demand that the government give the long-term jobless enough income support to shore up that economy.

Superfluity and the Longer Future

If capitalism is going to be destroying jobs in the long term, drastic changes in the world of work will have to be considered. Part-time, at home, independent contractor, and freelance work are already at hand, but in the future, jobs may have to be rationed. In addition, full-time employment may have to be defined as thirty or even twenty-four hours, with workers obtaining partial employment insurance benefits to support their families.

Observers of the social scene and social critics have worried about the future of work before, and others, especially Utopian writers, have advocated less work and more play—and education—for centuries (e.g., Bellamy 1888).

Utopian voices are starting to be heard again and once more propose to fill the free time with education and culture, as well as communal and political activity, but many people would probably find yet other ways to fill that time.

They would also have to find substitutes for the social and psychological roles that work plays in modern society, for example in determining social usefulness and self-respect and in establishing class, prestige, and other social positions.

Conclusion

Whatever the terminology, an economy and society in which large numbers of workers are superfluous or in danger of becoming so is unimaginable. People who are socially declared to be useless will sicken emotionally and physically and before long begin to hurt their families and their communities. Eventually, some will also sicken or attack other and larger institutions, including political ones. Whatever damage they do will be complemented by the damage that society's forces of law and order inflict in defending itself from such attacks.

Even if the former workers were compensated with modest substitute incomes, they would be economically far worse off than the employed. Socially, they would probably be placed below the working poor, and likely to be discriminated against as dependent and undeserving. That too many are likely to have dark skin will only worsen the situation.

Creating a permanent class of superfluous workers must be avoided at all costs.

Note

Reprinted from *Challenge*, vol. 55, no. 4, 2012, by permission of Taylor & Francis Group. The article is a greatly expanded revision of an op-ed, "The Age of the Superfluous Worker," *New York Times*, November 25, 2011.

Further Reading

Bellamy, E. 1888. *Looking Backward 2000–1887.* Boston, MA: Ticknor.
Catalano, R. 2009. "Health, Medical Care and Economic Crisis." *New England Journal of Medicine* 360 (February 19): 749–51.
Gans, H. 2011. "Long-Range Policies for the U.S. Economy." *Challenge* 54, no. 3 (May–June): 80–94.
Garrity, J. 1978. *Unemployment as History.* New York: Harper & Row.
Kessler, R., J. Turner, and J. House. 1988. "Effects of Unemployment on Health in a Community Survey." *Journal of Social Issues* 44, no. 4: 69–85.

CHAPTER 9

Work–Time Reduction

Possibilities and Problems

Since time immemorial, Utopian thinkers have been predicting that someday, workers would be freed from long and arduous hours of daily toil to devote more of their waking hours to leisure, culture, community, and other pursuits. Liberating workers from laborious work and long hours would also be beneficial to their physical, mental, and familial wellness. However, in our time, work-time reduction has been proposed more often as a method of job creation: sharing the total societal workload to increase the number of jobs.

So far, the rates of unemployment and underemployment are not high enough to make it politically realistic to propose work-time reduction (WTR). Still, given the possibly dismal future of the labor market, it may become economically and politically relevant one of these days. If WTR can also contribute to individual and familial health and welfare, now is the right time to start discussing the policy's possibilities and problems.

Work–Time Reduction as Liberation

Thomas More (1516/1965) may have been the first known Utopian writer to propose the eventual reduction of human toil, but John Maynard Keynes might one day be best remembered for predicting that by 2030, people would be working only fifteen hours a week.

Keynes made the prediction in his 1930 essay "Economic Possibilities for Our Grandchildren," in which he promised not only liberation from long work hours a century hence but also a four- to eightfold increase in the standard of living (Keynes 1968).

Interest in Keynes's essay has been revived in recent years, thanks in part to Robert Skidelsky, his most recent biographer (Skidelsky and Skidelsky 2012, but see also Pecci and Piga 2008 and Sharpe 2013). Keynes was actually less worried about the workings of WTR than about how his fellow Britons would cope with the extra leisure time; the Skidelskys are concerned about people consuming too many goods that they do not really need.

More recently, the British think tank New Economics Foundation has conceived WTR as also an environmental policy and recommended a twenty-one-hour week, arguing that less work would produce a concurrent reduction in global warming (Coote, Simms, and Franklin 2010). Along with others, the foundation has also pointed out WTR's effects on worker health and familial wellness.

WTR as Job Creation

The first labor unions in the United States began to advocate WTR in the late nineteenth century. Samuel Gompers is now best remembered for demanding the eight-hour day, both to create more jobs and to improve the quality of life of his workers and their families.

The most important early step toward WTR as job creation was taken in the Black-Connery Bill of 1933, in which Senator Hugo Black (D-AL) and Representative William Connery (D-MA) called for a thirty-hour workweek to reduce the high unemployment of the Great Depression. At first President Franklin Roosevelt supported the bill, but he changed his mind (or had it changed by business community pressure). Subsequently, he helped to prevent its coming to a vote in the House. However, Roosevelt later returned to his original support for the short workweek, using the Fair Labor Standards Act to require overtime pay after forty hours and thereby bringing the forty-hour week into being (Hunnicut 1988).

World War II, which provided the full employment of that period, and the postwar affluence ended interest in WTR, but when Europe encountered rising joblessness in the 1980s, several west European welfare states cut the workweek in the hope of creating more jobs (Gans 1990).

However, although some extra employment seems to have been created by reducing the workweek by two to three hours, most countries had restored the forty-hour workweek by the end of the century (Bosch and Lehndorff 2001).

What has worked, both in Europe and in a significant number of American states, is a temporary policy called short-time work reduction, in which all workers agree to a reduction in work hours so that no one is laid off. However, the short-time policy has been successful only when the loss in wages is made up by unemployment insurance payments that replace all or most of the lost wages.

Currently, the continuation of the Great Recession, at least in the U.S. labor market, has produced involuntary workweek reductions accompanied by equivalent wage/salary reductions. The current average workweek outside manufacturing is about thirty-five hours.

Proposals for and discussions of adding jobs by shrinking work time are beginning to be made (e.g., Baker 2011, Hunnicutt 2013, Huntington 2012), and more may be expected if short workweeks and increases in involuntary part-time and temp work continue. Someday it may be noteworthy that, in 2012, President Barack Obama directed that a thirty-hour workweek be temporarily defined as full time to establish worker eligibility for health benefits.

Implementing Work-Time Reduction

WTR and its assumption that the total number of jobs may be increased by reducing employee work time seems to make logical sense, but in an actual economy, it is accompanied by a variety of economic and political problems. Consequently, it is for now best seen as supplementary to direct job creation or as an emergency solution if and when new jobs cannot be created.

WTR's main problem is that it will be acceptable to workers only if those giving up work time do not lose pay; otherwise, it becomes just another way of turning full-time jobs into involuntary part-time work and at a lower wage. However, in the former case, it will be unacceptable to employers. Consequently, the needed make-up pay would have to come from government and may thus generate objections from taxpayers.

If regular taxes cannot supply the needed funds, special taxes must be levied on the economic sectors particularly responsible for the decline in jobs: capital-intensive industries, employers that computerize jobs, and those that send American jobs overseas.

A second problem: The policy can be viewed as assuming that economic growth has ended. Because this view is pessimistic, WTR's opponents have sometimes called it a "sharing of poverty."

WTR also flies in the face of an old and deeply believed faith that economies can prosper only through economic growth and that such growth can never be allowed to stop. Businesses in competitive industries believe that they must compete in order to survive and that such competition requires growth. This is one reason that they have generally opposed national attempts at reducing work time.

Whether and how capitalist enterprises survive without economic growth and what form capitalism would then take are much debated questions. However, WTR is causally independent of economic growth. A diversified economy is diversified also in its employment levels, and industries, occupations, and even individual workplaces with high unemployment and underemployment could, with government help, resort to WTR while the rest of the economy retains longer work hours.

Third, WTR flies in the face of contemporary capitalism, which has been steadily minimizing the role of labor in creating goods and services. Employers therefore have an additional reason for opposing WTR and trying to avoid participation in it.

Among their objections are the extra bureaucratic, training, and other costs that employers incur when they recruit and hire additional workers. If allowed, they prefer to pay overtime to their existing workers, to increase computerization, or simply to resort to old-fashioned speedup methods.

For this and other reasons, the supporters of WTR have not yet been able to provide persuasive evidence that it can create new jobs. Although the logic of the policy implies that a 10 percent decrease in work time would lead to a 10 percent increase in the number of jobs, Bosch and Lehndorff (2001) estimate that the actual number is somewhere between 3 and 6 percent and that it varies among workplaces and across an economy and its labor politics. It is probably easier to implement in large bureaucratized and routinized workplaces and perhaps impossible to make practicable in small workplaces with highly specialized and thus indispensable or irreplaceable workers.

In addition, WTR's advocates have not spoken up about its contribution to worker and familial wellness. Although there are studies about harmful work and its effects on health (e.g., Marmot et al. 1991), research on the relationship between work time and health are still rare.

Despite these problems, WTR is worth trying, in firms, public agencies, and nonprofit organizations. Even if the job gain is less than expected, working fewer hours may increase productivity. Worker health may increase as well, with appropriate savings in medical and related expenditures.

The likelihood that WTR could add jobs would be increased if competing industries overseas instituted the same policy at the same time. A firm with a thirty- or thirty-two-hour week might be unable to compete with one that can keep the same workers for forty or forty-eight hours, even if pay rates and other working conditions are the same.

If policies that shorten the workweek become feasible, WTR could also be designed for workplaces in which workers were eager—or could be incentivized to be eager—to take parental, child-rearing, and other types of leave. Even longer vacations open up opportunities for job creation, for example in areas where workers are interested in taking time off for hunting season.

In these cases, the replacements would most likely have to be temps—either people who want to work for a limited period or permanent temps but in a reorganized and government-regulated temp industry in which temps would obtain the same pay and benefits as other workers. Workplace routines would have to be adapted to the absence of the regular workers, and the latter would need guarantees that they would get their jobs back after their return.

Whether WTR could obtain the necessary political traction is hard to tell. Its fate during the Great Depression suggests another negative business reaction, which might be even greater now, considering the heightened shareholder and executive pressure for rising profits and stock prices. However, under other political conditions, and with more attention to externalities, WTR might be more feasible. After all, work time has been declining for centuries now, and economies seem to have become more productive nonetheless. Perhaps WTR should be introduced when an economy is healthy and unemployment is low.

Reducing work time for health and health-related reasons might become a topic of public discussion if family and women's organizations sought to obtain more parenting time and if such extra time could be quickly proven beneficial for children. Unfortunately, American workers have always wanted or needed more money rather than less work time, and the policy would require government income makeup or would have to wait for a period of rising worker pay.

Thus, it could be undertaken almost immediately in professional or technical workplaces that do not encounter internal or external competitive pressure to maximize their products or services and are staffed by highly paid employees. If workers voted for longer weekends, such workplaces could adopt thirty-two-hour workweeks; if they wanted more daily quality time at home, they could shift to six-hour workdays.

If global warming proceeds as predicted—and energy costs rise—workplaces in some regions may find it economical to close for several weeks during the height of summer.

In an ideal world, liberating WTR would begin in workplaces in which work is especially dangerous, dirty, exhausting, or otherwise inimical to longevity and good health. Unfortunately, such jobs are usually held by immigrant or other low-status workers who, lacking political and economic power, can be underpaid and overworked. They also need their wages so badly that they might oppose WTR.

Political Requirements

Several contextual requirements and conditions are needed to make WTR politically viable. One is a U.S. economy in which a larger and growing proportion of the population is underemployed or jobless and both are generating pressure for government job creation. The second is public understanding of the destructive political, social, and emotional effects of high levels of unemployment and underemployment.

The third requirement is the realization by the business community that reducing unemployment and underemployment delivers funds mainly to households that spend most of their earnings. If the business community can accept the fact that these households help keep the consumer economy vibrant, the overall economy healthy, and business profits high, it could learn to give up its obsession with lower taxes and deregulation. However, the consumer economy might have to decline severely before the business community is ready to give it up.

The fourth requirement for making WTR feasible: that government be, and be accepted as, the incentivizer as well as the employer and income-support provider of last resort.

Equally important, government must be enabled to create a tax program that will pay for the wages and salaries lost by reduced work time and ensure every worker at least a living wage.

None of these requirements will become applicable until the political and social climate is right. For one thing, the current trend of rising involuntary part-time work and other forms of underemployment, as well as declining salaries, wages, and benefits even for full-time work, must grow larger and probably spread upward into the now better-off sectors of the population.

Until that happens, the activists, movements, and voters with an economic, ideological, and cultural interest in maintaining the economic status quo will seek to veto all change. Moreover, those who perceive themselves as the "makers" of economic wealth and the rest of the population as "takers" of various kinds of public benefits will be particularly hostile toward policies in which people are rewarded for working less. Thus, willingness to support WTR cannot take place until enough of the self-defined makers lose their jobs and some of their economic resources. And then they must first realize that they can no longer afford an ideology that mainly benefits the economic elites.

Change might also take place if the jobless, underemployed, and under-paid portion of the below-median-income population mobilizes its demographic strength and can turn it into political strength on behalf of this and other job-creation policies.

Conversely, WTR might not become a politically feasible option until the economy is so healthy and incomes are rising so regularly that enough employees—and employers—are ready to seek liberation from excessive work time.

They could then decide if they want shorter workweeks, more leaves, vacations, or sabbaticals, or a shorter work life, with later entry into or earlier departure from the labor force. However, whether they can make such a choice will depend on whether employers are able and willing to let them choose—and whether an economy with a variety of work times is able to function.

Social Requirements

Keynes was neither the first nor the last member of the cultural elite to worry about what workers would do with and in their leisure time if their workweek were reduced. Some of these worriers predicted that the workers would not choose to improve themselves intellectually and culturally, thus holding back humanity's ennoblement. Others may have feared living with or being attacked by drunken, stoned, and media-sodden masses.

Undoubtedly, some people, including members of the cultural elite, will have trouble keeping themselves busy. However, if the workweek were reduced to thirty hours, many people would spend their new free hours in familial quality time. A modest family allowance might encourage finding and enriching such time.

Others would, if legally able, moonlight in second jobs, frequently in the informal economy. Eventually, some might turn to growing vegetables in their backyards, selling homemade foods and arts and crafts, and exchanging goods and services in a local barter economy. Some people might go back to school or volunteer, but unless WTR permits longer and subsidized vacations, most people will probably devote only a little more time to leisure activities.

Nonetheless, a wise government would, with the aid of nonprofit agencies, increase the opportunities for volunteering, for example, for workaholics and those needing help to fill up their new free time with useful activities. The opportunities must provide satisfaction and usefulness to avoid being labeled as "make-work," and they must be carefully regulated to prevent an unpaid volunteer from replacing a paid worker.

However, such a government would also subsidize travel costs to make vacationing easier or lean on domestic and foreign tourist industries to do so.

Fears of overconsumption seem equally overdone. The Great Recession showed again that when people had to, most were able to forgo what they defined as luxuries and prioritize the necessities. Those for whom consumption is an addiction, whether of drugs or luxuries, and those who use conspicuousness for status-seeking may have a harder time if austerity is required and if they cannot substitute window shopping for shopping.

Actually, WTR might require some austerity in a slowly growing or stable economy, especially if pay must shrink along with work time. Reductions in the standard of living will not be politically popular, although they might be compensated for in part by transforming health, education, and perhaps even commuting into public goods that are free for everyone.

Government and other institutions should also monitor possible WTR effects on education. Presumably the demand for good jobs will always outpace the supply, thereby maintaining the intense competition for places in "selective" and other academically high-quality schools at all levels.

However, a reduced workweek could also reduce the educational involvement of students with average levels of academic talent, and fewer might want to attend college. Then the quality of a U.S. high school education might finally have to equal that of Europe's, and other ways of postponing young people's entry into the labor force might have to be found.

Alternatively, education, including higher education, might shift some of its curricular and other programming toward developing student interest in avocations. Even now, many people find avocations that compensate for boring or otherwise unpleasant work, and avocational schooling might help others find avocations of their choice.

Perhaps WTR's most serious effect would be some downgrading of work's social functions. Work is a major source of social life, the best supplier of social usefulness, and thus a major creator of social and self-respect. Work also remains the most widely used way of determining and indicating social status.

These functions would survive a thirty- or even twenty-four-hour workweek, but they might be imperiled by a Keynesian fifteen-hour workweek. Eventually, the country would develop substitutes for the social functions of work, but meanwhile, a sufficient number of volunteer work opportunities must remain available when enough paid jobs are not available.

Work-Time Reduction in the Very Long Run

If technological and other innovations enable employers to continue to do away with jobs, future generations may yet have to adjust to Keynes's fifteen-hour workweek. However, if the country can concurrently bring about economic democracy, income and wealth may be sufficiently equalized to make the brief workweek economically feasible.

Conversely, and if the climate scientists are right, eventually global warming may overwhelm the coastlines and overheat the southern portion of the country so that its populations will have to move inland and northward. They would perhaps generate enough physical building and other infrastructural jobs to bring back fuller employment and a longer workweek.

Note

Reprinted from *Challenge*, vol. 56, no. 5, 2013, by permission of Taylor & Francis Group.

Further Reading

Baker, D. 2011. "Work Sharing: The Quick Route Back to Full Employment." Washington, DC: Center for Economic and Policy Research, June.

Bosch, G., and S. Lehndorff. 2001. "Working-Time Reduction and Employment: Experiences in Europe and Economic Policy Recommendations." *Cambridge Journal of Economics* 25: 209−43.

Coote, A., A. Simms, and J. Franklin. 2010. "21 Hours: Why a Shorter Working Week Can Help Us All to Flourish in the Twenty-first Century." London: New Economics Foundation.

Gans, H. 1990. "Planning for Worksharing: Toward Egalitarian Work Time Reduction." In *The Nature of Work,* ed. K. Erikson and S. Vallas, 258−76. New Haven, CT: Yale University Press.

Hunnicut, B. 1988. *Work Without End: Abandoning Shorter Hours for the Right to Work.* Philadephia, PA: Temple University Press.

_____ . 2013. *Free Time: The Forgotten American Dream.* Philadelphia, PA: Temple University Press.

Huntington, J. 2012. *Work's New Age: The End of Full Employment and What It Means to You.* Eldred, NY: Royal Flush Press.

Keynes, J. 1968. "Economic Possibilities for Our Grandchildren." In *Essays in Persuasion,* 358−74. New York: Norton.

Marmot, M., et al. 1991. "Health Inequalities Among British Civil Servants: The Whitehall II Study." *Lancet* 337, no. 8754 (June 8): 1387−93.

More, T. 1516/1965. *Utopia,* trans. with an introduction by Paul Turner. Harmondsworth, UK: Penguin.

Pecci, L., and G. Piga, ed. 2008. *Revisiting Keynes Economic Possibilities for Our Children.* Cambridge, MA: MIT Press.

Sharpe, M. 2013, "Keynes's Hundred Year Forecast." *Challenge* 56, no. 3 (May-June): 101−9.

Skidelsky, R., and E. Skidelsky. 2012. *How Much Is Enough? The Love of Money and the Case for the Good Life.* New York: Other Press.

CHAPTER 10

Basic Income

A Remedy for a Sick Labor Market?

No one can tell now what will happen if what might be called the current Labor Market Recession turns into a permanent one, and how many jobs of what kind will be available when future waves of computerization and robotization arrive.

However, a number of observers of the economic scene, especially in Western Europe but also in other countries, are already thinking about a future economy in which there will no longer be jobs for all and unknown numbers will have to depend on income from other sources.

Among the policies under discussion, one is an adaptation of an old Utopian idea: the basic income, sometimes also called the citizen's income, which is "unconditionally granted to all on an individual basis without means test or work requirement."[1]

In its Utopian form, the basic income is universal and untargeted, intended as a guaranteed government subsistence payment to all adults as their shares of the wealth of their society. Once upon a time, that wealth came out of the land; today is it more often earned by machines, including those that have replaced workers.

In theory, the basic income makes it possible to live without having to work, albeit modestly, although in practice, its recipients are assumed to work for the rest of their livelihood as in any other economy.

More recently, the advocates of this Utopian idea have also proposed a partial basic income, generally in lieu of welfare and unemployment benefits targeted to specific population groups. As I suggest further below, it holds promise as one income-support program for the United States if and when the labor market's health declines further.

The Utopian Basic Income

In its Utopian version, the basic income program is justified in two slightly different ways. The first is as an entitlement due every adult citizen simply as a member of society—therefore, the term *citizen's income;* the second is as that individual's share of the total public resources of his or her society.[2]

Whether the rationale is political or economic, basic income also promises to lessen people's economic dependence on governments and bureaucracies. Thus, most basic income proposals are accompanied by provisions to eliminate other income supports, preserving only those needed for emergencies. In some respects, the basic income ideal is radically libertarian.

Such an asocial ideal may seem somewhat strange today, but basic income's history goes back many centuries. Consequently, it already made some sense in a past when only a minority of the society could count on secure incomes. It offered another kind of security when the arbitrary or capricious exercise of authority might have meant unexpected poverty for people on the wrong political side.

Thomas Paine, one of the Revolutionary era's prime radical activists, was an early advocate of the basic income ideal and can be viewed as its American originator. In his 1795 pamphlet, "Agrarian Justice," he argued that in the precapitalist past, before land became private property, it belonged to everyone, and that this common ownership should still be honored.

Paine proposed that in lieu of people taking title to their share of the land, they would receive 15 pounds at the age of twenty-one and 10 pounds a year after reaching the age of fifty—this at a time when laborers earned about 23 pounds a year (Paine 1795).

While most advocates of the basic income guarantee situate themselves somewhere on the political left, some libertarians, here and overseas, are also thinking about it (e.g., Zwolinski 2012). Theoretical disagreements about the nature of liberty lead them to differing conclusions, but the conservative or market-oriented libertarians favor it as a way to abolish the major "entitlements" and as much else of the welfare state as possible. In the long run, they will probably be the most vocal and, financially as well as politically, the best-supported libertarian advocates of a basic income.

A good recent example is Charles Murray, who has suggested the provision of an annual basic income of $10,000 for each adult citizen, of which about $3,000 would be preempted for health insurance and another $2,000 might be taken for a retirement plan (Murray 2006). In effect, Murray's basic income can be viewed as a reimbursement, albeit a miserly one, for turning the United States into an almost government-free libertarian society.

Basic Income and Its Problems

Basic income is a provocative idea, put forth by an international sociopolitical movement with some well-known scholarly advocates (e.g., Offe 2008; Van Parijs 1995). Despite the fact that the movement has not done a great deal to obtain popular support, and that the idea itself seems both economically and politically unrealistic, attempts to implement it take place regularly all over the world (Caputo 2012).

True, none of these attempts has gotten very far, not very surprising in a world that still believes that people should obtain their incomes by working for them. Even so, attempts to implement basic income schemes continue, and the Swiss government may soon vote on a citizen petition drive calling for a universal basic income of $2,800 a month (Lowrie 2013).

Another political shortcoming: the movement's thinkers have not yet figured out how much a basic income scheme would cost, how it would be paid for, whether and how the richest citizens could be required to pay their share of its cost, and whether society could even afford it.

One exception is Allan Sheahen, an American advocate who has worked out some general cost estimates for an annual basic income of $10,000 per adult (Sheahen 2012). Using mostly 2010 figures, he estimated that it would cost an impractical $2 trillion a year, but he also showed that a large portion of this amount could be retrieved by eliminating other governmental monetary payouts.

These include welfare and other benefits now going mostly to poor and moderate-income people, and a variety of tax loopholes, most now benefiting the very rich and Big Business. Sheahen also proposed levying some new taxes on the latter two and cutting the defense budget back to its 2000 level.

However, Sheahen's analysis also demonstrates that retrieving these monies would require the elimination of a significant number of existing government programs and agencies. Each of these has its own political leaders, employees, beneficiaries, supporters, and other vested interests—all of which have more political power than the basic income movement.

The Partial Basic Income

Although the basic income movement has complemented its universal basic income idea with a partial one, others not affiliated with or even aware of basic income have created similar programs for a long time. Most were antipoverty warriors looking for new ways of providing incomes to the poor, or forecasters of technological and other economic changes that would create large numbers of newly jobless people.

Of the partial income schemes that have been considered in the United States in the post-World War II era, the following deserve discussion.

The first of these is the negative income tax, which is literally an income grant paid to people filing an income tax return but earning so little that they are eligible for the grant instead of having to pay taxes. The grant thus sets a minimum income floor for the country. One of its drawbacks: It requires filing a tax return, which would likely exclude the neediest of the poor from ever obtaining the income.

In the United States, the negative income tax was proposed by Milton Friedman in 1962. It would have paid poor people $1,500 a year in lieu of welfare benefits and represented an early conservative attempt to roll back the New Deal's welfare state. The amount of the tax was also lower than most existing welfare payments, which helped condemn it to political oblivion.

The second scheme was Daniel P. Moynihan's Family Assistance Plan (FAP) of 1970, the most important of a series of family allowance schemes Moynihan had advocated during the prior decade (Steensland 2007). Like the negative income tax, FAP was an income grant to replace welfare benefits, but unlike Friedman's proposal, not out to replace other parts of the welfare state.

FAP would have raised the incomes of welfare recipients in eight Southern states, thereby increasing the incomes of poor blacks, which distressed Southern white politicians. At the same time, the plan would have lowered recipients' incomes in more than forty other states, which generated vocal opposition by liberals and the Left.

For this and other reasons, President Richard Nixon eventually withdrew his support of FAP, but its demise led indirectly to the earned income tax credit. It is in many respects simply a negative income tax payment but available only to the working poor.

For that reason, and perhaps because its title suggested that it was a bonus for earning an income through work, it is still in existence forty years later, and with several increases in payments during that time. That it is, in effect, a wage supplement that subsidizes employers not paying a living wage may also explain its survival.

Subsequently, FAP helped to bring about a series of federally funded income tax experiments that sought to discover whether negative income tax-like supports would reduce incentives among poor families to work.

One result of the experiments was a decline in working hours for a number of mothers, presumably to spend more time with their children. Another was an increased divorce rate among recipients, who used the extra money to escape unhappy marriages. However, both results were interpreted as solely negative effects and so helped put an end to the government's interest in partial basic income programs.

Meanwhile, George McGovern, the 1972 Democratic presidential candidate, had proposed what he called a Demogrant, which would have paid $1,000 a year to every family. Unfortunately, he failed to offer a persuasive rationale for his proposal and was forced to withdraw it shortly after presenting it.

Since then, no government official with the power to do so has sought to set up a basic income program or anything resembling it. Just the reverse, for in 1996, President Bill Clinton terminated Aid to Families with Dependent Children (AFDC), the existing welfare program, and its replacement, Temporary Assistance for Needy Families (TANF), serves only a small proportion of needy people and even less adequately than its predecessor.

A number of indirect income-support programs remain, in the form of either material goods or services, of which food stamps and Medicaid reach the largest number of people. Other income support programs are targeted to specific poor clients, among them the old, the jobless, children, and people living in the colder parts of the country who need help to pay their heating bills.

In recent years, a number of these programs have been reduced or threatened with elimination by Tea Party and other conservatives unwilling to aid poor people they consider undeserving—a category that increasingly includes all poor and even moderate-income people.

In addition, the Great Recession has helped to create a set of conservative voters who seem to see the country's economy turning into a zero-sum game. As a result, they perceive any monies or services now going to low-income populations as depriving themselves of benefits to which they are already entitled or to which they might be entitled in the future should the economy begin to hurt *them*.

Toward Implementing a Basic Income

The universal and untargeted basic income idea is still so little known in the United States that it is rarely discussed, even by scholars. Nonetheless, basic income deserves to become better known, if only as an intriguing economic policy idea that differs significantly from those normally considered. Once a little more widely known, it might even inspire some innovative thinking about future income support programs.

The partial and targeted basic income idea deserves even earlier discussion. In fact, a case could be made now for its early reintroduction, and by whatever name that would increase its chance of becoming politically acceptable.

For example, in today's politics, it might be associated with the earned income tax credit, since that has survived politically even in the Tea Party era. Conversely, calling it a negative income tax might gain it enough Republican support to make it feasible, if only because Milton Friedman introduced it to the United States.

Still, the more fundamental question is whether taxpayers, now or in the future, will support a basic income grant to people who are not working, especially able-bodied ones.

Perhaps the question would receive a positive answer if this income grant, whatever it is called, could be paid first to help poor people who are thought of as especially deserving, such as jobless veterans, who are prime victims of the country's recent wars. Maybe impoverished victims of natural disasters could also be allowed to become eligible.

After the income grant helps casualties of these disasters, it could be extended to aid the casualties of economic disasters. Treating poor people as economic disaster victims will, however, require a drastic change in the country's perception of poverty.

That change might come if liberal ideas and liberals regain political power, or if the number of poor unemployed people rises so significantly that even conservative constituencies will demand economic help.

Until this happens, however, conservative politicians can assert that giving money to the jobless will reduce or kill their incentive to work. Consequently, the first economic disaster casualties to become eligible for the basic income grant have to be long-term unemployed people who are too old ever to be rehired. They should receive the tax until they are eligible for Social Security.

A number of older long-term jobless have already dropped out of the labor force permanently and are now classified as discouraged workers. Their chances of reemployment being equally small, they ought to be equally eligible for this grant.

Even less visible economic casualties are the so-called NEETs, young people "not in employment, education, or training." Many of them have never yet held a decent full-time job and deserve to be eligible for the income grant until they have found such a job or, better still, until they have obtained a foothold in the labor market.

Whatever the basic income grant is called, it should be designed to incorporate some qualities of a tax. For example, it should not be paid out by a welfare or antipoverty agency but by the IRS, Social Security, or another government agency that serves the broad middle class. Then it cannot easily be withheld from people whom others consider undeserving. Nor can it be held back until eligible recipients have been administered drug and other tests that actually seek to exclude them from receiving income support. Admittedly, the amount of the income grant could be reduced by political opponents, but that danger always faces government programs aimed at the lower-income population.

Getting the taxpayers used to what is in effect a basic income may take a while, but meanwhile, other, already known programs are available to supplement what is left of the welfare program.

One is the expansion of the material benefits program, now limited mainly to food stamps—and even that now rests on a wobbly political foundation. In the 1960s, the national welfare rights movement was able to require welfare agencies to issue winter coats to welfare recipients. However, other goods and services could be provided in lieu of funds, including furniture and appliances and even used cars if poor people lacked access to other transportation. Services, especially free care for poor people of all ages, are even more badly needed.

In fact, the more goods and services made eligible, the harder it may become to target a single one for reduction or elimination.

Suppliers of these goods would benefit as well, just like the farmers and the food industry that now benefit from the food stamp program. Some might even throw some political weight behind such a program.

Another way of helping the poor is via universal programs for the entire population that are subsequently taxed away from affluent recipients. In the early 1960s, Daniel P. Moynihan and others lobbied unsuccessfully for a universal family allowance, but today's middle-class families who did not need it then may need it now. So many families have two breadwinners with static or declining wages and could use allowance funds to help with extra expenses, such as school costs, day care, and parental leave time.

Many European countries have long provided family allowance programs. Although the programs of other countries are not easily copied, there should be some that might inspire American policy makers and the politicians whose approval is needed.

Yet another idea is Hillary Clinton's 2007 proposal of a $5,000 grant to every baby born in the United States, which can be spent at age eighteen for college or at age twenty-one for directly job-related expenditures.

The Clinton proposal is actually a variant on the Ackerman and Alstott (1999) stakeholder program, which advocated awarding an $80,000 grant to every eighteen- or twenty-one-year-old, to be used for college or career investment.

Another related proposal is Sherraden's Individual Development Account, a public IRA that would enable grantees to save for the future (Sherraden 1991).

Conclusion

Needless to say, proposing a basic income grant, whatever its name, is still a Utopian idea in the current U.S. polity. It can probably only be thought of as a realistic idea when the country's economy can no longer function without far greater government intervention.

Although it is too early to think apocalyptically about the future of jobs in the United States, it is not too early to think about possible negative futures and ways of dealing with them. Even if the unemployment rate declines to near a past normal, the labor participation rate must rise, too, as well as the proportion of decent and secure jobs that pay a living wage or more.

If these changes do not come about, the basic income concept may be one such way to confront negative futures. Alternatively, a kind of allowance scheme could be developed—and at a level that maintains as much of the country's standard of living as possible even as it grows the level of consumer demand needed for the economy.

What if someday the global economy, increasing robotization, and other new labor-saving schemes take enough jobs from enough citizens with the political ability to demand change? Then these citizens might demand a universal basic income program and force those profiting from their jobless-ness or low wages to pay for it.

Notes

Reprinted from *Challenge*, vol. 57, no. 2, 2014, by permission of Taylor & Francis Group.

1. Basic Income Earth Network (BIEN, www.basicincome.org/bien/) has the best website for a detailed description of the basic income idea. It also includes a newsletter, which reports news about basic income-related activities all over the world, and a journal, *Basic Income Studies.*

2. Indeed, Alaska's Permanent Fund currently pays all Alaskans about $1,000 a year as their share of the state's oil royalties. However, it is, strictly speaking, only a temporary profit-sharing plan that will end when the oil runs out, but meanwhile, it establishes a temporary basic income principle that could be used by other energy- and mineral-rich states, as well as those with natural tourist destinations.

Further Reading

Ackerman, Bruce A., and Anne Alstott. 1999. *The Stakeholder Society.* New Haven, CT: Yale University Press.

Caputo, Richard K., ed. 2012. *Basic Income Guarantee and Politics: International Experiences and Perspectives on the Viability of Income Guarantee.* New York: Palgrave Macmillan.

Lowrie, Annie. 2013. "Switzerland's Proposal to Pay People for Being Alive." *New York Times*, November 12.

Murray, Charles. 2006. *In Our Hands: A Plan to Replace the Welfare State*. Washington, DC: American Enterprise Institute Press.

Offe, Claus. 2008. "Basic Income and the Labor Contract." *Basic Income Studies* 3, no. 1 (April). www.bepress.com/bis/vo13/iss1/art4/.

Paine, Thomas. 1795. "Agrarian Justice." www.constitution.org/tp/agjustice/htm.

Sheahen, Allan. 2012. *Basic Income Guarantee: Your Right to Economic Security*. New York: Palgrave Macmillan.

Sherraden, Michael. 1991. *Assets and the Poor: A New American Welfare Policy*. Armonk, NY: M.E. Sharpe.

Steensland, Brian. 2007. *The Failed Welfare Revolution: America's Struggle Over Guaranteed Income Policy*. Princeton, NJ: Princeton University Press.

Van Parijs, Philippe. 1995. *Real Freedom for All: What (If Anything) Can Justify Capitalism*. Oxford, UK: Clarendon Press.

Zwolinski, Matt. 2012. "Classical Liberalism and the Basic Income." *Basic Income Studies* 6, no. 2 (January): 1–14.

CHAPTER 11

Seeking a Political Solution to the Economy's Problems

M ore and more economists and other observers now see the country in the throes of an economic decline that began in the 1970s and that shows no sign of ending soon. Some now call it the Long Recession, and a few writers have even described it as a permanent one.

A number of economists have also proposed corrective economic policies, but like many social scientists, they stop there. They forget that policy and politics begin with the same three letters and that policies are not implemented unless they are politically feasible.

To be sure, sometimes economic problems correct themselves, but increasingly, I would argue, they have to be corrected politically. This article is based on that premise and resorts to a thought exercise describing a political process that could produce feasible economic policies.

A Long Recession

The Long Recession that seems to have succeeded the Great Recession is marked by the continuing rise in economic inequality. It is accompanied by slow economic growth and a dismal labor market that creates too many poorly paid and unstable jobs and drives down consumer demand that further slows economic growth.

Economic inequality in turn breeds political inequality. Corporations and the very rich have always had an outsize influence on American politics, but now they can spend as much as they want to finance election campaigns, lobbies, and other means to persuade legislators to put their interests over those of much of the citizenry.

Furthermore, the intertwining of economic and political inequality enlarges the economic gaps between the several income strata. The very richest people are moving further and further away from their fellow Americans—so far away that many do not seem to even understand why their immense wealth is resented.

The professional-technical upper-middle class may be comfortable rather than rich, but even it possesses less economic security than in the past and worries about the possibility of downward mobility, especially by its children. However, the middle- and moderate-income populations are experiencing much greater economic insecurity, with the latter also worrying about becoming poor. And the poor live with the constant fear of extreme poverty.

As a result, many believe that America is becoming a zero-sum society, in which each economic stratum fears that others will deprive it of its monies and other resources. The resulting paranoia is felt even by the very rich, but it is most visible in the upper-middle and middle-class Tea Partiers and their ideological peers who see themselves as the sole makers of their fortune and those below them economically as "takers" of their fortune by government.

One already apparent effect is heightened political and ideological polarization, a politics of distrust and conflict. Thanks mainly to the Far Right, the polarization has resulted in a federal government that is currently not permitted to make needed decisions.

The Future of the Long Recession

Extrapolating current trends is risky. Undoubtedly, dramatic technological and other innovations will continue to take place, but like most recent ones, they are likely to be capital-intensive. Capitalism has been on a labor-saving if not labor-destroying trend for centuries, and will continue to be so as long as new machines are more profitable than workers.

Caregiving, retailing, and other work that serves and services people and cannot be outsourced or fully computerized is expected to increase. Even when it pays a living wage, which is not often, it will supply many part-time and insecure jobs.

A reversal of political inequality is equally unlikely. The top strata are not going to be more altruistic, and the rest of the population is divided in its interests. Many aim to maintain their economic and social superiority to those below them in the pecking order.

Moreover, except at presidential election time, large numbers of Americans ignore or reject politics. Nationwide protest movements that successfully press for even minimal redistributive economic change have never yet appeared in this continent-sized country.

Surprises are always possible, and the amount and kind of protest needed to produce political change will vary with economic and political conditions. However, despite the public veneration of the American Dream, many people down on their luck seem to have been able to lower or postpone expectations, endure temporary downward mobility, and resign themselves to just getting by economically. The situation is most critical for the poor, as always, and while the more fortunate Americans may be unhappy, they might live with a recessionary economy and a paralyzed polity longer than can now be imagined.

Still, shrinking labor participation, economic insecurity and deprivation, as well as overall economic stasis could become sufficiently pervasive so that eventually government has to intervene drastically in the economy even without much prior significant protest from the public.

The government might act particularly if job- and income-related troubles spread to a significant proportion of the higher levels of the middle and the upper-middle class. It might also intervene if national joblessness climbs to Great Depression levels. These were estimated to be close to 50 percent even though the official rate reached only 25 percent.

If government has to act, its economic policy should emphasize labor-intensive economic growth, making sure that no further jobs are lost and that as many new ones as possible are created. If greater full-time employment and job security cannot be achieved, income-support programs that do not stigmatize their recipients must be made available.

The jobs and incomes programs should help to grow the consumer economy and the larger economy with it. However, since a large number of these programs will have to be funded by government, some redistribution of wealth and income will be necessary. Economic reform involving redistributional policies will be extremely difficult, if not impossible, in anything like today's polity because the economic power holders can summon the resources to fight it.

In the past, America moved toward full employment and somewhat more economic equality because two world wars and the Great Depression reduced those resources. The arrival of politically militant labor unions and heightened action on the Left also helped—as did the labor shortages caused by so many workers going off to war. Many West European countries accomplished a more pervasive economic change because of the prior existence of worker parties able to take advantage of postwar economic conditions.

None of these preconditions exist in today's America. In addition, American democracy is far from representative, and the people who need economic change the most are also the least well represented. Thus, government and politics will have to become more democratic before the needed economic changes can take place.

How that might be initiated will be discussed in the remainder of this article.

A Political Thought Exercise

Considering what could happen in the future and what should happen are the bases of long-range planning, but plans made without a political base and the political clout to affect the future are better called thought exercises.

Thought exercises about how change might actually be accomplished politically are badly needed, but future political feasibility is impossible even to guess. This article describes the politically most feasible one I can now imagine, although even its likelihood of being achieved is not very high.

While the easiest solution is to imagine a large and militant movement of angry, radicalized, and economically suffering people demanding economic change, a thought exercise that builds on conventional politics is more realistic.

That exercise would begin with an election victory that enables a political party dedicated to moving toward a fuller-employment economy to take firm control of all three branches of government.

This outcome itself might take just one landslide election, or more likely several elections, even in a less polarized America. It might happen if and when enough people realize that they need and can get government help to make a living and will then be motivated to vote.

Perhaps the imagined election victory or sets of victories would be more likely if the winning party were a coalition of centrist and liberal Democrats as well as independents. Whatever its membership, the majority of this coalition's program would have to be devoted to economic reform, avoiding as much as possible other issues that could lose it supporters.

If properly organized, this coalition could even be moderately bipartisan, attracting Republicans whose constituents need economic help badly enough to demand action from their representatives. The coalition should also attempt to obtain corporate support from firms, industries, and even oligarchs whose profits depend on a revival of consumer demand.

As already noted, the moment the coalition has acquired sufficient control over the government, it would have to move quickly, as did FDR in 1933, toward whatever jobs and income support-related reforms are politically feasible at that moment. If at all possible, the reforms must quickly demonstrate enough successes so as to prevent the governing party from losing control at the next midterm election.

At the same time that it initiates its economic programs, the reform coalition must take two necessary political steps.

The first: to bring about a rapid expansion of the electorate, in primaries and November elections, so that current sporadic voters and nonvoters, many of whom need and support economic reform, can be encouraged and then convinced to become regular voters.

The fastest way to enlarge the electorate is to institute at-home voting, but where this is not feasible, quick and easy voting in a nearby voting booth should be available. In addition, elections should become festive, with work holidays, celebratory events, and parties. Previous nonvoters, or all voters, might be rewarded with modest gifts after they have voted.

Electoral enlargement could be encouraged by special federal funding but first, using legislative and judicial efforts, will have to overcome opposition from voter restriction forces. Governmental reaffirmation of the one-person-one-vote principle would help; court cases to enable the Supreme Court to restate and reinforce its past precedent setting for that principle might eventually end voter-restriction efforts. Court action is also needed for the eventual reform of the Senate and the House, which, as discussed further below, violate that principle in their very structures.

Someday, if and when a politically sufficient number of states follow much the same election procedures, federal elections can perhaps be nationalized. If voter turnout is not high enough, compulsory voting might have to be tried when the political time is ripe, which may occur only in some distant future.

The second necessary political step is to institute public financing of election campaigns. A liberal Supreme Court should be able to overturn past decisions that treat money as speech, and in that case only public financing satisfies the one person-one vote principle.

Sufficient political support for public financing may not appear instantly and may actually have to wait until enough people feel that they can trust elected officials to act on their behalf.

The likelihood of the entire change process from initial election victories to expansion of the electorate and the democratization of the electoral process would be increased if, at all stages, social movements would be active in supporting and pressuring roles to make sure that the political and economic objectives of the process continue to be pursued.

During this entire period, government must continue to do whatever it can in support of job maintenance and creation, as well as of necessary income supports for those who cannot find work or work that pays a living wage. The greater its success, the higher its level of public support, which, all other things being equal, will enable it to be more successful yet in the future.

If government demonstrates that it can often be as, or more, effective economically as private enterprise, and if the latter is facing increasing challenge in a recessionary economy, the historic adversary relationship between the two might be reduced.

Perhaps some cooperative arrangements could be worked out, but if insufficient jobs are being created, government may eventually have to establish labor-intensive public firms that compete with private firms.

Meanwhile, government will need all the successes and other forms of obtaining public support it can accumulate, for it will have to resort to tax reform and other means of redistributing some of the country's income and wealth to pay for its jobs and income-support programs.

By the time political conditions for redistributive tax reform are in place, the Western European welfare states and others are likely to have already instituted such reforms. This will help to discourage capital flight and other ways by which the very rich evade paying taxes.

If the shift of income and wealth from the very rich is insufficient to fund the needed programs, the much more numerous upper-middle class may have to be taxed more heavily as well. However, because they are numerous and politically more active than others, they may be able to oppose redistributive legislation more effectively than the richest Americans.

Once the coalition or a liberal Democratic Party has achieved enough of a representative electorate as well as some economic successes to maintain control of the government over a number of elections, it can and must move on to the next step: to further democratize the country's major political institutions so that these will more often respond to the economic needs of the majority of the population.

Reforming Government

Since many of the founding fathers envisaged the country as a republic with a limited electorate, they could not foresee that it would eventually turn into more of a representative democracy. However, thanks in part to the rigidity of the Constitution, some of the country's major political institutions have not yet been adapted to the requirements of a representative democracy and thus violate the one person–one vote principle.

All political institutions probably need democratizing reform, but the list that follows limits itself to the three branches of government.

1. *The Senate.* This branch of government represents the most formidable obstacle to the one person–one vote principle and to representative democracy. With every state having two senators regardless of size, those from the four smallest states, with less than 1 percent of the total population, cast the same number of votes as their colleagues from the four largest states, with one third of the country's population.

In fact, the small states, many of which elect conservative politicians, have frequently been able to block the liberal economic reforms sought by the country's biggest states. Were the Senate to reflect the American population accurately, it would likely have passed much economic legislation that benefits a majority of the electorate and lessened the economic decline of the median- and below median-income populations that began in the 1970s.

The Constitution now makes it virtually impossible to reorganize the government's branches. Otherwise, the Senate could revise its rules to award senators from larger states as many votes as their proportion of the country's total population or electorate.

2. *House of Representatives.* In the House, equality of representation can be increased by a professionally designed redistricting scheme to eliminate or minimize gerrymandering but that would also align each state's distribution of congressional districts with its election results.

A better solution would be to allow states to elect at-large representatives or establish enlarged districts that can elect several members, but such solutions would probably first require nationalizing of all elections and eliminating primaries in which tiny numbers of highly committed voters nominate the candidates.

The public funding of election campaigns will relieve incumbents and challengers from fund-raising and increase the time they spend representing and serving their constituents. If congressional offices can be supplied with more staff, the members of Congress should increase their representation activities and be in touch with more than their wealthy constituents and those who attend their town meetings.

For example, since members of Congress most likely know all or many of the major employers in their districts, they should also be able to learn where and when jobs will be available in the future and thus help their job-seeking constituents. In addition, their staffs can keep an eye on agencies providing job and income supports and related government services to make sure that as many eligible people as possible are receiving them.

3. *The Presidency.* Considerable agreement exists already that the Electoral College violates the idea of a representative democracy and that the president should be elected by a national majority vote.

However, even then, presidents need more authority over domestic decision making, giving them the same power in economic and other domestic emergencies that they already have in dealing with disasters that are deemed natural. That power will need to include access to sufficient emergency funds, although it could be checked and balanced by a committee of the top decision makers in the other branches of government.

4. *The Supreme Court.* Right now, the Supreme Court is unaccountable to anyone, and five unelected members appointed by long-ago administrations can impose drastic changes on the country's government, politics, and economy. A number of the Court's critics have suggested its members, and all federal judges, ought to serve staggered terms for fourteen or eighteen years.

The practice of some state courts that divide seats up equally between Democrats, Republicans, and independents would at least balance ideologically weighted judicial decision-making. If the judicial branch were subject to checks and balances similar to those applying to other government branches, all major Supreme Court decisions would be reviewed and subject to revision or even veto—maybe by a committee consisting of the president and the leaders of the Senate and the House.

Changes like those suggested here are unlikely to be undertaken as a result of public demand or political calculations. However, they could come about in economic and other emergencies in which present procedures prevent necessary and agreed-on solutions. For example, if the economy was in free fall and senators from the small states could block a workable solution agreed upon by large-state senators, the Senate might be forced to decide that, as suggested above, senatorial votes be determined by the size of the state's population.

Likewise, if the Supreme Court continually rejected legislation absolutely essential to a foundering economy, something in its structure or membership—or in its interpretation of the Constitution—would eventually have to give.

Economic Democracy

Long before reforming the three branches of government is possible, Congress and the president can attempt to take some fledgling steps to bring a modicum of democracy to the economy. These steps could be first required from large employers that obtain federal contracts, subsidies, and tax benefits. They ought to be obligated or incentivized to help establish employee or worker councils and not to interfere with unionization. Corporate governance regulations for firms with federal funding should require the placing of workers and customers on corporate boards and their important committees and create profit-sharing schemes for workers.

Conclusion

The thought exercise outlined above assumes that political means can be found to force the country's economic power holders to give up enough of their political power to drive both polity and economy in a more democratic direction. The exercise must also try to figure out whether expanding the electorate and campaign finance reform might be feasible and whether they could put processes in play both to further democratize the country and to bring about government intervention in the economy on behalf of those needing job and income supports.

If the exercise suggests that these initiatives cannot achieve the desired ends, other exercises can be designed to determine whether different politically feasible initiatives can produce government economic intervention on behalf of those needing it most.

Perhaps several diverse thought exercises need to be developed and discussed so that the most feasible solutions to current problems become topics of the public conversation.

Thought exercises alone cannot produce plans and policies that are guaranteed to work in the actual economy and polity, but troubled times make it necessary to think actively about desired futures before an undesirable one becomes the present.

Note

Reprinted from *Challenge*, vol. 57, no. 5, 2014, by permission of Taylor & Francis Group.

CHAPTER 12

High School Economics Texts
and the American Economy

The November 2014 election appears to have been just another midterm event in which the president's party lost control of Congress. However, it was at a time when many voters (and nonvoters) were still encountering economic difficulty and might have voted differently had they received an economic education, or a better one than they have so far been given.

Although a majority of poll respondents told the pollsters that the state of the economy was their major problem, a landslide majority of the voters elected the very political party that had sabotaged attempts to heal the economy. Worse yet, it was the same party that had sickened the economy while its man was president. Worst of all, many of the citizens who were the prime victims of the Republican assaults on the economy did not vote.

Actually, one would think that with rising educational levels, more people would know enough to blame the politicians mainly responsible for the ills of the economy. Moreover, in hard economic times, one could expect more people to vote, and to vote their economic interests ahead of all but the most deeply felt noneconomic values.

If Thomas Piketty and his colleagues are correct to predict yet greater economic inequality and further declines in incomes and job security, the victims will have to obtain an economic education oriented to increasing their understanding of the economy.

Since many future political battles are likely to be fought over whether and how government should intervene on behalf of those hurt by economic inequality, their economic education will also have to include a potent dose of politics and political economy.

Admittedly, improving economic education now will not bear fruit until today's young people become voters. Even then, such an education alone will not persuade the victims of inequality to vote their economic interests. Still, it could add support to political and other efforts to reduce the country's inequality.

High School Economics

In theory, a democracy should be expected to make a special effort to educate its people to be effective citizens. However, many of the Founding Fathers sought to minimize mass political participation, and perhaps they learned from their slave-owning colleagues that withholding an education might help to minimize that participation.

The invention of mass public education included little or nothing in the way of an economic or political education, but eventually, courses in civics and social studies were added to the high school curriculum. Today's social studies courses often include some economics, although much of it is devoted to personal finance. It teaches students about handling checking accounts, buying cars, financing a college education, and the like, but not about the rest of the economy.

Now, several of the social sciences are being added, including economics. In fact, in 2014, twenty-four states required the offering of a high school course in economics, although only thirteen demanded that students be tested on the subject (Council for Economic Education 2014b). Still, in 2009, nearly 60 percent of high school graduates had taken an economics course (Walstad and Rebeck 2012).

Up to now, few economics researchers or educators seem to have gone into the classrooms to learn how and what economics is taught and what students are learning. Currently, the most accessible evidence is the textbooks being used in high schools, although not all teachers actually use a text. Even so, a study of the texts would shed some light on what the country's high school students are being taught about the economy.

Doing such a study is no easy task, since most texts run to 600 pages or more. They are also divided into semester and year-long texts as well as regular and advanced ones, the latter for advanced placement courses giving students college credit for an economics course.

However, the study is made easier by the fact that the texts are remarkably similar. Although individual authors may devote a few more pages to subjects that particularly interest them, the texts all follow a significantly common structure.

They do so because, like most high school texts, they must satisfy a set of standards established by disciplinary or other associations before local or state textbook buyers will purchase them for their school districts. In effect, the texts are standardized.

High school economics texts are primarily guided by a set of twenty standards suggested by the Council for Economic Education, a nonprofit organization describing itself as devoted to the advancement of economic literacy (Council for Economic Education 2010).

The twenty standards are written by a team of well-known university economics professors. They not only suggest general subjects to be covered, but they also shape much of the organization, content, and even tone of the texts.

Although the Council seeks to make students economically literate, the substantive requirements of that literacy are not spelled out, other than by the standards. Judging by them, and the texts, literacy means a conceptual, substantive, and implicit political understanding, not of the actual economy but of a model of an ideal American market economy.

One possible explanation for this conception of economic literacy can be obtained from the membership of the Council's twenty-six-person board of directors. It includes fifteen executives and other officers of a variety of financial, corporate, and other private firms; five academics; three foundation representatives, two of them supporting economic literacy; and three others (Council for Economic Education 2014a).

The first standard is titled scarcity, and the next three—on decision-making, allocation, and incentives—describe what goes into the case of people having to choose among scarce resources.

However, the remaining standards deal mainly with the components of the competitive market economy. The next six standards lay out the basics of that economy, the prices, and other activities that elaborate on the workings of supply and demand.

The three following standards basically concern money: its role in infla-tion, then in interest rates, and finally as income. A further two standards are about what the Council seems to consider crucial to a market economy: entrepreneurship and economic growth, with the former being described as an important source of the latter.

Three more standards concern government-market relationships. One is titled "Government and Market Failure," although the standard itself says nothing about that failure and instead emphasizes government's protection of property rights and attempts to make markets competitive. The second is about government failure, including government's social goals that inter-fere with economic efficiency. The third covers fiscal and monetary policy, although mainly its effects on the market economy.

The final two are nominally about economic fluctuation as well as unemployment and inflation, but also about the role these factors play in recessions—perhaps because this edition of the standards was published just after the Great Recession. However, nothing is said about the role that other economic institutions and practices play in recessions.

The Textbooks

Guided by reviews of the major and most widely used texts (Leet and Lopus 2003; Marri et al. 2012), I examined seven of these texts: Arnold 2001, Clayton 2001, Krueger and Anderson 2014, Krugman and Wells 2009, Mankiw 2007, McConnell and Brue 2008, and O'Sullivan and Sheffrin 2007.

Since current editions are not held by university libraries, and each costs around $300, I ended up purchasing cheaper and therefore older editions, but a look at yet older editions suggested that new editions rarely change the basic structure and content of the texts.

Before I opened these texts, I thought they would teach students about the economy in which they must someday function as adults. Since these students will shortly become eligible to vote, I assumed that the texts would also teach them enough about the government's economic role so that the newly eligible voters could vote and otherwise participate intelligently in the politics relevant to that role.

In fact, however, the texts I examined are not about the economy but about economics. They teach students how the discipline describes, concep-tualizes, and analyzes a variety of economic processes, actions, and institutions.

Above all else, the texts teach the apparently timeless principles of a discipline that studies an economy in constant flux and frequent turmoil.

Although the texts illustrate their analyses with examples from the American economy, they emphasize concepts. Glossaries of such concepts at the ends of the texts number mostly in the 400s and 500s, ranging from just under 300 in one case to over 1,000 in another. But concepts are tools for studying economies and can do little to teach students about the economy in which they will live.

A systematic content analysis of the texts is a research team task, and what follows is a superficial read-through and an impressionistic analysis—and one, I must note, conducted by a sociologist. In addition, I analyzed the attention given to a variety of subjects by counting the total number of pages associated with each subject as reported in the index, being careful to choose only those playing important roles in the economy prior to the texts' publication dates.

This measure is imperfect, for the seven texts were not chosen systematically. Also, the number of pages shown in the index cannot report the actual number of words and paragraphs devoted to each subject. Further, authors emphasize some subjects over others, and indexers may classify similar ideas differently.

Nonetheless, all of the texts are built on a theoretical and conceptual foundation of mainstream neoclassical economics, sometimes updated to apply to a few of today's economic institutions. However, their authors do not pay much attention to the global and other large corporations and related organizations that now dominate the economy. Consequently, the texts often seem to describe an eighteenth- or nineteenth-century economy of individual producers and small businesses.

Every text begins with meeting the first Council for Economic Education standard, describing the main task of economics as instructing students that resources are almost always scarce. They go on to teach that everyone must make choices among these resources, not only individuals who include sneaker-buying high school students, but also firms and governments that must allocate the scarce resources available to them.

None of the texts notice that some individuals, firms, and institutions have more than enough in the way of resources to avoid worries about scarcity when they make allocation decisions.

More important, no authors suggest other priorities for economics or definitions of the discipline—for example, a more general one that covers the financing, production, distribution, and consumption of resources, goods, and services.

Subsequently, the texts describe an economic world dominated by an abstract entity called the market. It is, in turn, ruled by the law of supply and demand, which determines prices, wages, and much else. The texts are full of supply-and-demand charts and curves to back up this lesson. They portray people, institutions, and the larger economy as striving for perfect competition and equilibrium, although monopolies, cartels, and other obstacles stand in the way.

This emphasis is supported by the count of page mentions in text indexes. Market and market-related concepts appeared on 449 pages of the seven texts, equilibrium on 169 pages, and various applications of marginality on 222 pages. Perfect competition was mentioned on 94 pages.

Conversely, components of the actually existing economy appeared frequently only if they were included in the standards, but those considered problematic, especially recent ones, were hard to find. Multinational corporations received 15 page mentions, outsourcing, 7 pages, but hedge funds and insider trading none.

Likewise, subjects that do not fit the neoclassical conception of economics and problems that some students might eventually confront received few mentions. Thus, the minimum wage was discussed on 34 pages, and part-time employment on 4. However, involuntary part-time employment did not appear in the index, nor did downsizing. Poverty was discussed on 44 pages.

Government participation in the economy was underplayed as well. The welfare state appeared on 27 pages of one text and once in another. Public investment obtained 3 mentions, and while public resources, goods, and spending were mentioned on 136 pages, 101 of them were concentrated in three texts. Regulation and deregulation were discussed on 34 and 9 pages, respectively, and redistribution on 11.

Economic growth is a more favored topic, however, being cited on 178 text pages. So are entrepreneurs, who are seen as playing a vital role in economic growth. Although they were mentioned only 50 times, some texts also describe and praise a number of American entrepreneurs by name, particularly the texts that advertise a relationship with a business magazine or newspaper.

However, entrepreneurs are most prominently emphasized in a list of what are called factors of production, presented at the beginning of all the texts. Sometimes also called resources, the four are land, labor, capital (financial and human), and entrepreneurs. Although they are mentioned last, they are the only actual humans in the quartet, employees and employers being conceptualized only as labor and human capital. Incidentally, employees appear on only 16 pages of the seven texts.

In some respects, the four factors also seem to have been left over from another era, since land, other than real estate, and raw material extraction no longer seem as important in the American economy as they once were. For example, in today's economy, technology, information, and cyberspace deserve being added to the list of factors. So should government, especially since even in a textbook economy centered on markets, it often supplies the capital and subsidies that help entrepreneurs get started or keep going.

The current list of factors also suggests the scarcity of what social scientists call agency. The overall picture of the economy is, with some notable exceptions, one of impersonal processes that seemingly operate without or with only occasional human intervention.

This pattern is established from the very beginning of the texts, for in the discussion of scarcity and resource allocation, the allocating is done by society. Whatever its metaphorical or conceptual usefulness, society is an imagined social body that lacks the body parts that actually allocate. However, claiming that society can allocate preempts potentially political—and perhaps classroom—controversy about which individuals, populations, institutions, and other human agents actually participate in allocation processes.

The reference to society may not be accidental, since the texts avoid references to politics as much as possible. The words politics or political appear on 37 pages in the indexes of the seven texts, and political economy on 5 pages, all in one text. By the same token, the two government texts I looked at (McClenaghan 2007; Teachers Curriculum Institute 2009) pay equally little attention to the economy. The duo referred to economics or the economy on only 21 pages, and political economy on none.

Moreover, the economics texts are remarkably free of explicit position taking and ideology. Instead they try to be balanced, much like the mainstream news media that must also deal with diverse constituencies and with pressure and interest groups that watch for ideological deviance.

For example, when the texts discuss the minimum wage, they also mention the dispute about its effect on employment, and when they discuss the national debt, they consider its effects on the economy. The writers almost always report both sides, although some will use empirical data or judgmental language to suggest which side they support.

Even so, the textbook authored by Paul Krugman and Robin Wells and that written by Gregory Mankiw are not very different in structure or in ideology. They both adhere to the Council for Economic Education standards, and while both give more attention at times to their favorite subjects, neither text reads like the columns the authors write for the *New York Times*.

The texts are so devoid of explicit politics as well as ideology and the values these represent that unless teachers bring them in via lectures or class discussions, students are given an economic world that omits a good deal of human social input (Marglin 2012). As one study of the texts puts it: "what is missing is a careful examination of how everyday citizens can gain knowledge, acknowledge values and work toward a reasoned and reality-based view" (Marri et al. 2012, 294).

Grading the Courses

As noted earlier, more than half of all high school graduates have now taken an economics course, but we do not know what they have been taught or what they have learned. A 2005 Harris poll that quizzed a sample of students on their knowledge of some textbook subjects reflecting the standards of the Council for Economic Education (then called the National Council on Economic Education) reported that six in ten students received a failing grade (National Council on Economic Education 2005).

We know only a little more about the teachers. In some places, they need undergraduate degrees with majors in economics, although how many actually meet that requirement or are social studies teachers drafted to teach economics is not known.

A survey of a national sample of economics teachers showed that they are somewhat more market-oriented and otherwise conservative about economic issues than other social studies teachers (Schug, Dieterle, and Clark 2009). While they think economics should be used to turn students into "critically minded, reflective citizens," they do not believe it should develop "activists to . . . solve current societal problems" (ibid., table 1). In addition, they place "injustice in the economic system" low on a list of important curriculum topics (ibid., table 2).

The survey sample was small, but if the study reflects a national pattern, it would seem that either the teachers reflect the general tenor of the texts or the texts are designed to fit the teachers.

In any case, there is no indication that either texts or teachers aim to train students to learn to deal with the economy they will enter sooner or later. Admittedly, training even seniors in this way could be difficult. Except for those who need to work while in high school, they will have had little contact with that economy, other than the adolescent consumption markets that are covered in personal finance sections of the texts, or in entire courses devoted to personal finance.

Furthermore, the textbooks, or at least current ones, are embedded in, and thus governed by, the same free-enterprise economy their authors are describing. Like many other consumer goods, the texts are manufactured and distributed by profit-seeking oligopolies. About half a dozen large corporations dominate the overall high school text market.

The texts are also expensive and massively labor-intensive enterprises, for each is produced by up to twenty editorial and production staff members. In addition, the texts are looked over by fact checkers and reviewed by several dozen high school and college instructors; one text thanked over a hundred of them.

In some respects, the textbook industry resembles the automobile industry, manufacturing a standard product but with a raft of stylistic and other variations. Some economics texts come in year-long and semester versions; others divide their subject matter into micro- and macroeconomics.

There are also student and teacher editions, the latter often outlining a sample course for the novice teacher, complete with homework assignments. Student editions all have accessory features, such as highlights, illustrative case studies, lists of important points to remember, and a variety of quizzes.

Because the texts are produced for purchase by school boards and other governmental bodies, their content is shaped by a variety of political requirements. Like the abovementioned standards, these are influenced by a handful of private and nonprofit interest groups, most promoting and protecting the hegemony of free enterprise.

Moreover, the texts must be acceptable to school boards, many of which include local businessmen and women, as well as to potential parent and other citizen protesters, many of them advocating conservative social and economic values.

A handful of politically and socially conservative states are particularly influential, Texas being so powerful that special Texas editions are produced by some textbook publishers (Collins 2012). Indeed, an economics text that emphasizes the social and other costs of private enterprise is probably unpublishable.

Unless teachers depart from their texts, the critical thinking from students that they consider important may have to wait until students enter college or the university of hard knocks. Despite the belief that education can change society, public education is in most places firmly cemented to the status quo.

What Might be Done

If the country becomes yet more unequal and its labor markets are even less able to produce decent paying and secure jobs, the affected citizenry must be taught how to understand the political economy that creates these conditions.

Today's adults must fend for themselves, but at least the children can still be taught, and on paper, there is a simple solution: required courses on the economy, not on economics.

The textbook publishing industry should be able to produce texts that describe and analyze the American economy, including chapters on the country's political economy and the politics that most directly affect the economy.

The textbooks and their eventual digital successors can be so designed that instructors will be able to supplement and update the texts with current economic news. Discussing the week's economic news relevant to the course may sometimes benefit student learning as much as textbook readings. Publishers or their successors can certainly create websites that prepare the economic news for both students and teachers.

Textbooks on the American economy must deal with current issues and controversies and may therefore run into opposition from the guardians of conservative economic ideology. For that reason alone, parallel organizations advocating textbook standards and defending textbooks that support a liberal market economy supported by welfare-state institutions must be established. In fact, such organizations should already have been established long ago.

Wherever the political climate is favorable and students are receptive, teachers should be free to go beyond the texts and the news to help their students learn to cope with the economic conditions they are likely to face.

Needless to say, private and charter schools need courses about the American economy as well, although elite schools that are teaching likely future economic and political decision makers may need somewhat different courses.

Undoubtedly, some high school economics teachers are already teaching courses about the American economy, and specialists in economics education should be identifying and describing them. Even so, professional economists and university economics professors should become involved as well and take an active interest how their discipline is and ought to be taught in high school Perhaps some can even begin to write the needed texts.

Note

Reprinted from *Challenge*, vol. 58, no. 3, 2015, by permission of Taylor & Francis Group. I am grateful to Amand Marri for helping me enter the world of high school economics texts.

Further Reading

Arnold, Roger A. 2001. *Economics in Our Times*, 2d ed. Chicago, IL: National Textbook Company.

Clayton, Gary E. 2001. *Economics: Principles and Practices.* Columbus, OH: Glencoe/McGraw Hill.

Collins, Gail. 2012. "How Texas Inflicts Bad Textbooks on Us." *New York Review of Books* 59, no. 11: June 21.

Council for Economic Education. 2010. "Voluntary National Content Standards in Economics," 2d ed. New York: The Council.

———. 2014a. "About CEE." New York: The Council.

———. 2014b. "Survey of the States: Economic and Personal Finance Education in Our National Schools 2014." New York: The Council.

Krueger, Alan B., and David Anderson. 2014. *Explorations in Economics.* New York: Worth.

Krugman, Paul, and Robin Wells. 2009. *Economics.* New York: Worth.

Leet, Don R., and Jane S. Lopus. 2003. "A Review of High School Economics Textbooks." Social Science Research Network, February 13.

Mankiw, N. Gregory. 2007. *Principles of Economics*, 4th ed. Mason, OH: Thomson.

Marglin, Stephen A. 2012. "Saving the Children: A Rant." *Journal of Economic Education* 43, no. 3: 283–92.

Marri, Anand R., et al. 2012. "Analyzing Content About the Federal Budget, National Debt, and Budget Deficit in High School and College-Level Economics Textbooks." *Journal of Social Studies Research* 36, no. 3: 283–97.

McClenaghan, William A. 2007. *Magruder's American Government*. Boston, MA: Pearson Prentice Hall.

McConnell, Campbell R., and Stanley L. Brue. 2008. *Economics: Principles, Problems, and Policies*, 17th ed. New York: McGraw-Hill Irwin.

National Council on Economic Education. 2005. "What American Teens & Adults Know About Economics." New York: The National Council.

O'Sullivan, Arthur, and Steven M. Sheffrin. 2007. *Economics: Principles in Action*. Boston, MA: Pearson Prentice Hall.

Schug, Mark C., David A. Dieterle, and J. R. Clark. 2009. "Are High School Economics Teachers the Same as Other Social Studies Teachers?" *Social Education* 72, no. 2: 71–75.

Teachers Curriculum Institute. 2009. *Government Alive! Power, Politics and You*. Palo Alto, CA: Teachers Curriculum Institute.

Walstad, William B., and Ken Rebeck. 2012. "Economics Course Enrollments in U.S. High Schools." *Journal of Economic Education* 43, no. 3: 339–47.

PART FOUR

RACE AND CLASS

R ace is not only a weapon people use to discriminate and harass others but also an an indicator of class.

Thus, skin color or other visible physical characteristics correlate sufficiently with class position to serve as rough guides for identifying the higher and lower classes. Oversimplifying only a little, the darker the skin, the lower the class.

Class-related characteristics are therefore also useful for excluding people from equal access to valued resources and social positions; for example, the better jobs, good housing, and the higher levels of prestige and political power.

Chapter 13 spells out this argument in greater detail. However, this part of the book focuses particularly on what I consider two of today's major research and policy-relevant questions: why are so many African Americans still mired at the bottom of the class hierarchy 150 years after the end of slavery; and why are many of the better-off ones prevented from moving up too fast and too much in that hierarchy compared to some other nonwhite populations?

Chapters 14 and 15 explore this analysis in some other ways. Chapter 14 points out that, because race is a social construct, the meanings of racial characteristics can be altered. Even perceptions of nonwhite skin colors can be changed, particularly if enough whites are ready to do so.

So far, one of the major alterations has been "whitening," the process by which whites who once saw skins as nonwhite now see them as white. The best example: the predominantly poor Eastern and Southern European immigrants who were transformed from "swarthy" races to white ethnic groups when they moved into the middle class in large numbers after World War II.

The same process is now starting to repeat itself with the new waves of immigrants that came after 1965, notably Asian Americans and the lighter-skinned Latinos—and again, once they were solidly middle class. However, their whitening process is being hastened by rapidly rising rates of intermarriage with whites by the second and later generations.

The process may have been speeded up further by the increasing worry on the part of whites that they would become a racial minority before midcentury. Since I wrote chapter 14, that worry has turned to hysteria among some whites, helping to create an intense enough anti-immigration and even white nationalist faction in the Republican party to enable Donald Trump to win the 2016 presidential election.

Since the newly whitened populations are likely to participate to keep poor blacks at America's bottom, the country's racial hierarchy may begin to turn into a tripartite structure, with whites at the top, blacks at the bottom, and everyone else, including those awaiting possible whitening, in the middle.

For many centuries now, the better-off classes have divided the poor into the deserving and undeserving poor. The former were praised for working and the latter were blamed for being unwilling to work, but also for a long list of alleged behavioral, moral, law-breaking, and other shortcomings.

Chapter 16 provides a recent example of this blaming practice. It reports my 2012 reexamination of the Moynihan Report, which, when written in 1965, demonized the black single-parent family as pathological. That family structure was also blamed for preventing poor blacks from escaping poverty.

I wrote chapter 16 with an additional agenda: to reanalyze some of Moynihan's data and analysis in order to question the continued celebration of the Report as a sterling example of high-quality social science research.

The Moynihan Report included some positive and even influential ideas, and its author played a significant role in the country's effort to reduce poverty. Even so, his legacy will long be affected by his unjustified attack on the black single-parent family.

CHAPTER 13

Race as Class

Humans of all colors and shapes can make babies with each other. Consequently most biologists, who define races as subspecies that cannot interbreed, argue that scientifically there can be no human races. Nonetheless, lay people still see and distinguish between races. Thus, it is worth asking again why the lay notion of race continues to exist and to exert so much influence in human affairs.

Lay persons are not biologists, nor are they sociologists, who argue these days that race is a social construction arbitrary enough to be eliminated if "society" chose to do so. The laity operates with a very different definition of race. They see that humans vary, notably in skin color, the shape of the head, nose, and lips, and quality of hair, and they choose to define the variations as individual races.

More important, the lay public uses this definition of race to decide whether strangers (the so-called "other") are to be treated as superior, inferior, or equal. Race is even more useful for deciding quickly whether strangers might be threatening and thus should be excluded. Whites often consider dark-skinned strangers threatening until they prove otherwise, and none more than African Americans.

Scholars believe the color differences in human skins can be traced to climatic adaptation. They argue that the high levels of melanin in dark skin originally protected people living outside in hot, sunny climates, notably in Africa and South Asia, from skin cancer. Conversely, in cold climates, the low amount of melanin in light skins enabled the early humans to soak up vitamin D from a sun often hidden behind clouds. These color differences were reinforced by millennia of inbreeding when humans lived in small groups that were geographically and socially isolated. This inbreeding also produced variations in head and nose shapes and other facial features so that Northern Europeans look different from people from the Mediterranean area, such as Italians and, long ago, Jews. Likewise, East African faces differ from West African ones, and Chinese faces from Japanese ones. (Presumably the inbreeding and isolation also produced the DNA patterns that geneticists refer to in the latest scientific revival and redefinition of race.)

Geographic and social isolation ended long ago, however, and human population movements, intermarriage, and other occasions for mixing are eroding physical differences in bodily features. Skin color stopped being adaptive too after people found ways to protect themselves from the sun and could get their vitamin D from the grocery or vitamin store. Even so, enough color variety persists to justify America's perception of white, yellow, red, brown, and black races.

Never mind for the moment that the skin of "whites," as well as many East Asians and Latinos is actually pink; that Native Americans are not red; that most African Americans come in various shades of brown; and that really black skin is rare. Never mind either that color differences within each of these populations are as great as the differences between them, and that, as DNA testing makes quite clear, most people are of racially mixed origins even if they do not know it. But remember that this color palette was invented by whites. Nonwhite people would probably divide the range of skin colors quite differently.

Advocates of racial equality use these contradictions to fight against racism. However, the general public also has other priorities. As long as people can roughly agree about who looks "white," "yellow," or "black" and find that their notion of race works for their purposes, they ignore its inaccuracies, inconsistencies, and other deficiencies.

Note, however, that only some facial and bodily features are selected for the lay definition of race. Some, like the color of women's nipples or the shape of toes (and male navels) cannot serve because they are kept covered. Most other visible ones, like height, weight, hairlines, ear lobes, finger or hand sizes—and even skin texture—vary too randomly and frequently to be useful for categorizing and ranking people or judging strangers. After all, your own child is apt to have the same stubby fingers as a child of another skin color or, what is equally important, a child from a very different income level.

Race, Class, and Status

In fact, the skin colors and facial features commonly used to define race are selected precisely because, when arranged hierarchically, they resemble the country's class-and-status hierarchy. Thus, whites are on top of the socioeconomic pecking order as they are on top of the racial one, while variously shaded nonwhites are below them in socioeconomic position (class) and prestige (status).

The darkest people are for the most part at the bottom of the class-status hierarchy. This is no accident, and Americans have therefore always used race as a marker or indicator of both class and status. Sometimes they also use it to enforce class position, to keep some people "in their place." Indeed, these uses are a major reason for its persistence.

Of course, race functions as more than a class marker, and the correlation between race and the socioeconomic pecking order is far from statistically perfect: All races can be found at every level of that order. Still, the race-class correlation is strong enough to utilize race for the general ranking of others. It also becomes more useful for ranking dark-skinned people as white poverty declines so much that whiteness becomes equivalent to being middle or upper class.

The relation between race and class is unmistakable. For example, the 1998–2000 median household income of non-Hispanic whites was $45,500; of Hispanics (currently seen by many as a race) as well as Native Americans, $32,000; and of African Americans, $29,000. The poverty rates for these same groups were 7.8 percent among whites, 23.1 among Hispanics, 23.9 among blacks, and 25.9 among Native Americans. (Asians' median income was $52,600—which does much to explain why we see them as a model minority.)

True, race is not the only indicator used as a clue to socioeconomic status. Others exist and are useful because they can also be applied to ranking co-racials. They include language (itself a rough indicator of education), dress, and various kinds of taste, from given names to cultural preferences, among others.

American English has no widely known working-class dialect like the English Cockney, although "Brooklynese" is a rough equivalent, as is "black vernacular." Most blue-collar people dress differently at work from white-collar, professional, and managerial workers. Although contemporary American leisure-time dress no longer signifies the wearer's class, middle-income Americans do not usually wear Armani suits or French haute couture, and the people who do can spot the knockoffs bought by the less affluent.

Actually, the cultural differences in language, dress, and so forth that were socially most noticeable are declining. Consequently, race could become yet more useful as a status marker, since it is so easily noticed and so hard to hide or change. And in a society that likes to see itself as classless, race comes in very handy as a substitute.

The Historical Background

Race became a marker of class and status almost with the first settling of the United States. The country's initial holders of cultural and political power were mostly WASPs (with a smattering of Dutch and Spanish in some parts of what later became the United States). They thus automatically assumed that their kind of whiteness marked the top of the class hierarchy. The bottom was assigned to the most powerless, who at first were Native Americans and slaves. However, even before the former had been virtually eradicated or pushed to the country's edges, the skin color and related facial features of the majority of colonial America's slaves had become the markers for the lowest class in the colonies.

Although dislike and fear of the dark are as old as the hills and found all over the world, the distinction between black and white skin became important in America only with slavery and was actually established only some decades after the first importation of black slaves. Originally, slave owners justified their enslavement of black Africans by their being heathens, not by their skin color.

In fact, early Southern plantation owners could have relied on white indentured servants to pick tobacco and cotton or purchased the white slaves that were available then, including the Slavs, from whom the term *slave* is derived. They also had access to enslaved Native Americans. Blacks, however, were cheaper, more plentiful, more easily controlled, and physically more able to survive the intense heat and brutal working conditions of Southern plantations.

After slavery ended, blacks became farm laborers and sharecroppers, de facto indentured servants, really, and thus they remained at the bottom of the class hierarchy. When the pace of industrialization quickened, the country needed new sources of cheap labor. Northern industrialists, unable and unwilling to recruit southern African Americans, brought in very poor European immigrants, mostly peasants. Because these people were near the bottom of the class hierarchy, they were considered nonwhite and classified into races. Irish and Italian newcomers were sometimes even described as black (Italians as "guineas"), and the eastern and southern European immigrants were deemed "swarthy."

However, because skin color is socially constructed, it can also be reconstructed. Thus, when the descendants of the European immigrants began to move up economically and socially, their skins apparently began to look lighter to the whites who had come to America before them. When enough of these descendants became visibly middle class, their skin was seen as fully white. The biological skin color of the second and third generations had not changed, but it was socially blanched or whitened. The process probably began in earnest just before the Great Depression and resumed after World War II. As the cultural and other differences of the original European immigrants disappeared, their descendants became known as white ethnics.

This pattern is now repeating itself among the peoples of the post-1965 immigration. Many of the new immigrants came with money and higher education, and descriptions of their skin color have been shaped by their class position. Unlike the poor Chinese who were imported in the nineteenth century to build the West and who were hated and feared by whites as a "yellow horde," today's affluent Asian newcomers do not seem to look yellow. In fact, they are already sometimes thought of as honorary whites, and later in the twenty-first century they may well turn into a new set of white ethnics. Poor East and Southeast Asians may not be so privileged, however, although they are too few to be called a "yellow horde."

Hispanics are today's equivalent of a "swarthy" race. However, the children and grandchildren of immigrants among them will probably undergo "whitening" as they become middle class. Poor Mexicans, particularly in the Southwest, are less likely to be whitened, however. (Recently a WASP Harvard professor came close to describing these Mexican immigrants as a brown horde.)

Meanwhile, black Hispanics from Puerto Rico, the Dominican Republic, and other Caribbean countries may continue to be perceived, treated, and mistreated as if they were African American. One result of that mistreatment is their low median household income of $35,000, which was just $1,000 more than that of non-Hispanic blacks but $4,000 below that of so-called white Hispanics.

Perhaps South Asians provide the best example of how race correlates with class and how it is affected by class position. Although the highly educated Indians and Sri Lankans who started coming to America after 1965 were often darker than African Americans, whites only noticed their economic success. They have rarely been seen as nonwhites, and are also often praised as a model minority.

Of course, even favorable color perceptions have not ended racial discrimination against newcomers, including model minorities and other affluent ones. When they become competitors for valued resources such as highly paid jobs, top schools, housing, and the like, they also become a threat to whites. California's Japanese-Americans still suffer from discrimination and prejudice four generations after their ancestors arrived here.

African-American Exceptionalism

The only population whose racial features are not automatically perceived differently with upward mobility are African Americans: Those who are affluent and well educated remain as visibly black to whites as before. Although a significant number of African Americans have become middle class since the civil rights legislation of the 1960s, they still suffer from far harsher and more pervasive discrimination and segregation than non-white immigrants of equivalent class position. This not only keeps whites and blacks apart but prevents blacks from moving toward equality with whites. In their case, race is used both as a marker of class and, by keeping blacks "in their place," an enforcer of class position and a brake on upward mobility.

In the white South of the past, African Americans were lynched for being "uppity." Today the enforcement of class position is less deadly but, for example, the glass ceiling for professional and managerial African Americans is set lower than for Asian Americans, and on-the-job harassment remains routine.

Why African-American upward economic mobility is either blocked or, if allowed, not followed by public blanching of skin color remains a mystery. Many explanations have been proposed for the white exceptionalism with which African Americans are treated. The most common is "racism," an almost innate prejudice against people of different skin color that takes both personal and institutional forms. But this does not tell us why such prejudice toward African Americans remains stronger than that toward other nonwhites.

A second explanation is the previously mentioned white antipathy to blackness, with an allegedly primeval fear of darkness extrapolated into a primordial fear of dark-skinned people. But according to this explanation, dark-skinned immigrants such as South Asians should be treated much like African Americans.

A better explanation might focus on "Negroid" features. African as well as Caribbean immigrants with such features—for example, West Indians and Haitians—seem to be treated somewhat better than African Americans. But this remains true only for new immigrants; their children are generally treated like African Americans.

Two additional explanations are class-related. For generations, a majority or plurality of all African Americans were poor, and about a quarter still remain so. In addition, African Americans continue to commit a proportionally greater share of the street crime, especially street drug sales—often because legitimate job opportunities are scarce. African Americans are apparently also more often arrested without cause. As one result, poor African Americans are more often considered undeserving than are other poor people, although in some parts of America, poor Hispanics, especially those who are black, are similarly stigmatized.

The second class-based explanation proposes that white exceptionalist treatment of African Americans is a continuing effect of slavery: They are still perceived as ex-slaves. Many hateful stereotypes with which today's African Americans are demonized have changed little from those used to dehumanize the slaves. (Black Hispanics seem to be equally demonized, but then they were also slaves, if not on the North American continent.) Although slavery ended officially in 1864, ever since the end of Reconstruction subtle efforts to discourage African-American upward mobility have not abated, although these efforts are today much less pervasive or effective than earlier.

Some African Americans are now millionaires, but the gap in wealth between average African Americans and whites is much greater than the gap between incomes. The African-American middle class continues to grow, but many of its members barely have a toehold in it, and some are only a few paychecks away from a return to poverty. And the African-American poor still face the most formidable obstacles to upward mobility. Close to a majority of working-age African-American men are jobless or out of the labor force. Many women, including single mothers, now work in the low-wage economy, but they must do without most of the support systems that help middle-class working mothers. Both federal and state governments have been punitive, even in recent Democratic administrations, and the Republicans have cut back nearly every antipoverty program they cannot abolish.

Daily life in a white-dominated society reminds many African Americans that they are perceived as inferiors, and these reminders are louder and more relentless for the poor, especially young men. Regularly suspected of being criminals, they must constantly prove that they are worthy of equal access to the American Dream. For generations, African Americans have watched immigrants pass them in the class hierarchy, and those who are poor must continue to compete with current immigrants for the lowest-paying jobs. If unskilled African Americans reject such jobs or fail to act as deferentially as immigrants, they justify the white belief that they are less deserving than immigrants. Blacks' resentment of such treatment gives whites additional evidence of their unworthiness, thereby justifying another cycle of efforts to keep them from moving up in class and status.

Such practices raise the suspicion that the white political economy and white Americans may, with the help of nonwhites who are not black, use African Americans to anchor the American class structure with a permanently lower-class population. In effect, America, or those making decisions in its name, could be seeking, not necessarily consciously, to establish an undercaste that cannot move out and up. Such undercastes exist in other societies: the gypsies of Eastern Europe, India's untouchables, "indigenous people" and "aborigines" in yet other places. But these are far poorer countries than the United States.

Some Implications

The conventional wisdom and its accompanying morality treat racial prejudice, discrimination, and segregation as irrational social and individual evils that public policy can reduce but only changes in white behavior and values can eliminate. In fact, over the years, white prejudice as measured by attitude surveys has dramatically declined, far more dramatically than behavioral and institutional discrimination.

But what if discrimination and segregation are more than just a social evil? If they are used to keep African Americans down, then they also serve to eliminate or restrain competitors for valued or scarce resources, material and symbolic. Keeping African Americans from decent jobs and incomes as well as quality schools and housing makes more of these available to all the rest of the population. In that case, discrimination and segregation may decline significantly only if the rules of the competition change or if scarce resources, such as decent jobs, become plentiful enough to relax the competition, so that the African-American population can become as predominantly middle class as the white population. Then the stigmas, the stereotypes inherited from slavery, and the social and other arrangements that maintain segregation and discrimination could begin to lose their credibility. Perhaps "black" skin would eventually become as invisible as "yellow" skin is becoming.

The Multiracial Future

One trend that encourages upward mobility is the rapid increase in interracial marriage that began about a quarter century ago. As the children born to parents of different races also intermarry, more and more Americans will be multiracial, so that at some point far in the future the current quintet of skin colors will be irrelevant. About 40 percent of young Hispanics and two thirds of young Asians now "marry out," but only about 10 percent of blacks now marry nonblacks—yet another instance of the exceptionalism that differentiates blacks.

Moreover, if race remains a class marker, new variations in skin color and in other visible bodily features will be taken to indicate class position. Thus, multiracials with "Negroid" characteristics could still find themselves disproportionately at the bottom of the class hierarchy. But what if at some point in the future everyone's skin color varied by only a few shades of brown? At that point, the dominant American classes might have to invent some new class markers.

If in some Utopian future the class hierarchy disappears, people will probably stop judging differences in skin color and other features. Then lay

Americans would probably agree with biologists that race does not exist. They might even insist that race does not need to exist.

Note

Reprinted from *Contexts*, vol. 4, no. 4, 2005, by permission of Sage Publications DOI 1525/ctx.2005.4.4.17

Further Reading

David Brion Davis. *Challenging the Boundaries of Slavery* (Harvard University Press, 2001). A historical account of the relation between race and slavery.

Joe R. Feagin and Melvin P. Sikes. *Living with Racism: The Black Middle-Class Experience* (Beacon, 1994). Documents continuing discrimination against middle- and upper-middle-class African Americans.

Barbara Jeanne Fields. "Slavery, Race and Ideology in the United States of America." *New Left Review* 181 (May/June 1990): 95–118. A provocative analysis of the relations between class and race.

Marvin Harris. "How Our Skins Got Their Color." In *Who We Are, Where We Came From, and Where We Are Going* (HarperCollins, 1989). An anthropologist explains the origins of different skin colors.

Jennifer Lee and Frank D. Bean. "Beyond Black and White: Remaking Race in America." *Contexts* (Summer 2003): 26–33. A concise analysis of changing perceptions and realities of race in America.

CHAPTER 14

"Whitening" and the Changing American Racial Hierarchy

Introduction

In recent decades, pundits, journalists, demographers, and even some social scientists have been warning the country that by the middle of the twenty-first century Latinos, Asians, and others, defined by most whites as nonwhite races, would turn whites into a demographic minority. Most of the prophets were merely predicting a more diverse future, but some were intentionally scaring whites, to get backing for one or another measure against immigration or to get rid of immigrants, undocumented and otherwise. Whatever the reason, the prediction is sociologically not credible. The continuing rise in racial intermarriages and more informal couplings are creating with every generation ever larger numbers of people now labeled as biracials and multiracials.[1]

Moreover, even if the Bureau of the Census persists in using old racial categories and names (Prewitt, forthcoming), popular conceptions of Asian, Latino, and other descendants of immigrants should change and might eventually become irrelevant for categorizing and ranking people (Warren and Twine, 1997). Furthermore, unless current trends are somehow halted, by 2050, two generations hence, many of these hybrids will have been whitened. However, a rising number of monoracials currently still considered nonwhite will likewise be whitened. In fact, East Asians and light-skinned Latinos, particularly middle-class ones, are already heading in that direction. If the processes repeat themselves that turned the 1880–1924 waves of Italian, Jewish, and other Southern and Eastern European immigrants, then called races, into white ethnics after the end of World War II, many Latinos and Asians will be perceived and counted as whites by whites before midcentury. Consequently, whites are likely to remain a demographic majority.

True, such a prediction is risky; we do not know how many immigrants with what phenotypical features and socioeconomic status will arrive here in the coming decades. Predictions can only project some current trends for a decade or so; projecting any trends for forty years hence has to be guesswork. Thus, if the country's economy remains in bad shape and its politics continues to be polarized, white racial and ethnic hysteria could generate new judgments about who is white and who is not and even lead to some unwhitening (McDermott and Samson, 2005; Richeson and Craig, 2011).

Under other conditions, white racial and class discrimination against blacks might decline, for example, if anti-immigrant feelings intensify, or if the labor market finds poor blacks attractive for other reasons. Alternatively, panicked whites might deliberately hasten the whitening process to make sure that they remain a majority. This is more easily said than done, because how people judge the skin color of others is not easily controlled by politics or policy. Still, the government has some weapons, beginning with the U.S. Census, which could be persuaded to tweak the racial categories—something it has done in any case from time to time.

Though 2050 is nearly forty years away, racial intermarriage, biracials, multiracials, and the whitening process are here to stay. Many researchers are already looking at how these factors are beginning to change today's America, but research programs should be established now to track these changes systematically, and most importantly, to reassess frequently what they could mean for the country's future racial hierarchy.[2]

Even more attention must be paid to the position of poor and moderate-income African Americans and black Latinos who are currently at the bottom of this hierarchy. No one can say if they will be so placed in 2050, but this topic requires the most careful following of trends for both empirical and policy purposes. Although black intermarriage rates are also rising, and the intermarrieds will be adding further to the biracial and multiracial population, for the foreseeable future whites are likely to consider a limited proportion of this group as acceptable candidates for whitening.

Where blacks are placed in the racial hierarchy will depend in part on how whites and the already whitened will construct the biracial and multiracial descendants of racially intermarried blacks, particularly those in the more affluent classes. Hypodescent and the one-drop rule will probably become less significant even in the South, except among those who still believe in the existence of racially differentiated blood. Researchers therefore have a special responsibility to follow where whites will position black and hybrid populations in coming decades. Monitoring whom whites will treat more equally is particularly important, because public policy could encourage this process in the right political climate.

Although much of the needed research and tracking will have to deal with whether and how whites whiten or otherwise allow current non-whites to move up in the racial hierarchy, researchers must also look for— and at—changes in the class hierarchy of the future. In fact, the racial hierarchy combines race and class; whether race trumps class in placing people or vice versa may become a question more relevant than it is today. Researchers must ask questions about where societal processes relevant to race and class are headed and make projections. Policy-minded researchers can be drawn in to suggest policies for today that could bring about greater racial and class equality in the future.

A voluminous research literature has already developed on many of the subjects to be discussed below. These are covered in a special issue of *Daedalus* (Bobo 2011a), particularly in articles by Bobo (2011b), Cohen (2011), Hochschild et al. (2011), and Richeson and Craig (2011). Consequently, this article will discuss and speculate on what could begin to happen between now and 2050.

Whitening

The contemporary study of whitening began in the 1990s (Brodkin 1998; Ignatiev 1995; Roediger 1991; Twine 1996), in part to demonstrate to whites that they were as much a race as any other. In fact, the early writers mainly used the concept in the fight against racial discrimination. Whitening is more often used now to describe the social process by which the descendants of the European immigration were accepted by non-immigrant America. As many critics of the term have rightly pointed out, the mostly Southeastern and Eastern Europeans were already white, even though some were considered swarthy.

Whitening is a white activity, although others can act in support or in opposition. As a social process, whitening works at various speeds, depending on many factors, including among others the size of the nonwhite population being considered for whitening. When such populations are large and mainly of low status—such as Latinos in today's California and the Southwest—whitening is likely to proceed slowly. The speed of whitening is also determined by how much the candidates for whitening resemble middle-class whites socially and culturally. Nonwhites who are able to move into lily-white communities and live like whites, at least publicly, have similar cultural and other tastes and vote for white politicians to thereby help whiten themselves. Their ability to achieve the American Dream counts, too. All other things being equal, successful nonwhites whiten more easily than others.

Nonetheless, the people who are whitened do not have to accept a white identity. Most whites probably do not care or even notice what identity these former nonwhites choose for themselves, unless it interferes with their relationship with the whiteners. So far at least, those already whitened gravitate toward behavior and attitudes associated with whiteness, particularly to increase the gap between them and darker-skinned people, notably African Americans (O'Brien 2008). Some whitened people exercise their racial option instrumentally, biracials choosing to be white when that is helpful, or nonwhite when that is advantageous: biracial college students at scholarship time, for example.

That some biracials and monoracial East Asian, other Asian, and Latino peoples are on the way to being whitened does not preclude white discrimination against similar others, for racial or class reasons (Kim 2007). Quotas, glass ceilings, and other obstacles to upward mobility do not necessarily disappear with whitening; white favoring of East Asians and light-skinned Latinos does not prevent whites from discriminating against Southeast Asians and dark-skinned Latinos.

Whitening presumably does not exclude subsequent unwhitening, if and when whites decide to exclude or otherwise discriminate against those they have whitened. If populations which had been whitened become a threat numerically, economically, or politically, white behavior and attitude can change dramatically. Numbers are particularly important; if the whitened become a numerical majority, whites, who are rarely comfortable being a minority, could find ways to unwhiten them.

It was thus probably no coincidence that white ethnics were fully whitened when large numbers of African Americans and dark-skinned Puerto Ricans came to the cities dominated by white ethnics. Perhaps today the speed with which Asians are being whitened is connected to the concurrent large immigration of Mexicans—especially undocumented ones—but then, whites have whitened Asians before in order to protect themselves from a dark-skinned majority (Loewen 1971).

Whether the whitening of light-skinned Latinos will be affected by the size of the Mexican immigration needs to be monitored. If the whitening is slower or faster in cities with a larger Mexican population than in other cities, we need to determine whether and how population size either raises white fears about Mexican immigrants or provides more opportunity for Mexican-white intermarriages, or both.

Impressionistic evidence suggests that the children of East Asians married to whites are probably the first to be whitened. However, the same can be said about East Asian monoracials, particularly those who are middle or upper-middle class, or living in almost entirely white suburbs. Conversely, South and Southeast Asians, notably Indians, Filipinos, Malayans, and Indonesians, who are often darker in skin color and not upper-middle class probably are currently not whitened as quickly or as often, but how far whitening occurs along the light-to-dark skin color array and down the social-class hierarchy is a major future research question.

The Latino whitening process is most important, not only because Latinos are by far the largest immigrant group in the country, but also because class, skin color, and other phenotypical characteristics may vary more greatly with this group than among Asians (Alba et al., 2011). As among East Asians, the children of Latino and white parentage as well as some light-skinned Latinos are already being whitened. However, dark-skinned Latinos and Caribbeans often suffer racial and class discrimination and exclusion, in some cases not very different from those inflicted on African Americans.[3] Even so, immigrants differ not only racially but ethnically, which raises the question of whether adherence to immigrant ethnic culture makes a difference. People who remain inside the enclave and are endogamous are probably not candidates for whitening, since they may not have much social contact with whites.

Deracialization

In retrospect, whitening was an unfortunate choice of words. Literally, the people in question were being socially bleached, but a more accurate term for the process would be *deracialization*. In fact, when white Anglo-Saxon Protestants (WASPs) and other whites turned the Eastern European immigrants into white ethnics, they in effect deracialized them.[4] As I use the term, deracialization is the opposite of racialization (Barot and Bird, 2001). It describes a process which begins when one group ceases to stigmatize the phenotypical distinctiveness of another, continues when that group no longer views the other as a race, progresses as the group, which does not think of itself as a race, ceases to pay attention to the other's phenotypical differences, and culminates when the first group eventually stops noticing these differences altogether.[5] At some point, the fact that people once distinguished themselves from others by selected phenotypical differences could become a historical curiosity.

Because deracialization is not a common term, the rest of this paper will instead employ the term "whitening," particularly since empirical and other studies of whitening are now available (Twine and Gallagher, 2008).

Intermarriages and Biracials

All other things being equal, the whitening process is likely to become publicly visible as more Americans intermarry racially and their children are described and identify themselves as biracial and multiracial. Black and white intermarriage has been studied for decades, but the study of other interracial marriages is now also well under way (Lee and Bean, 2010; Sanjek 1994). So far, the number of racial intermarriages of nonwhites and whites remains small, though the intermarriage rates continue to rise. According to a recent Pew Research Center study (Wang 2012), almost 10 percent of all marriages, but 15 percent of new marriages in 2010 were interracial; 70 percent of these involved marriages to whites.

Asian and Latino intermarriages with whites are most numerous, while Black and white intermarriages lag behind, although even they are now increasing.[6] While racial intermarriages still take place largely among middle-class people, researchers also need to study interracial common law and other cohabiting relationships, especially as marriage rates continue to decline.[7] The sociological study of biracials themselves has been limited almost entirely to how biracials identify themselves, and to the possibilities and problems of living with a biracial or multiracial identity (Khanna 2011). The more significant topic—how whites identify biracials—has not yet received much attention.[8] However, as long as whites are in charge of the country's racial definitions, their identification decisions are the ones that count.[9]

The Changing Racial Hierarchy

The differential treatment by whites of the various participants in the post-1965 immigration is also creating changes in the arrangement of the races in the American social, economic, and political hierarchy. No single nationwide racial hierarchy exists that fits all regions of the country; positions in the hierarchy differ somewhat between regions, particularly those with many immigrants of diverse racial, national, and class origins. The hierarchy may, however, be more similar in regions that have experienced little immigration in the last few decades.

The hierarchy was probably also more similar across the country during most of the last half of the twentieth century. Then, the hierarchy constructed by whites as the dominant race put themselves at the top, followed by Asians, Latinos, Afro-Caribbean, and black Latinos, with Native Americans and African Americans at the bottom.

Because racial discrimination toward all nonwhites (and in the first half of the twentieth century, white ethnics) was still rampant, it was once possible to construct a simpler hierarchy: white and nonwhite. Then, in the 1990s, some of us, realizing that many of the new immigrants were being incorporated and assimilated at a faster rate than the Europeans who had arrived between 1880 and 1924, suggested that the hierarchy was being rearranged.

If the class differences between whites and light-skinned nonwhites were going to be reduced—skin color differences to be de-emphasized—and if whites were to begin whitening the latter, the American racial hierarchy might move toward becoming nonblack and black someday (Gans 1999; Lee and Bean, 2004; Yancey 2003).[10] Whites were of course still free to distinguish themselves from other nonblacks, but before the intense demonization of undocumented Mexican immigrants began, African Americans—and some others whose skin color whites constructed as black—were clearly the lowest stratum.

The fact that African Americans were losing jobs to Latino newcomers made it even clearer. Even though whites treated middle- and upper-middle-class African Americans with more respect, they nonetheless continued to discriminate against and harass them in a variety of ways (Feagin and Sikes, 1994).

While the nonblack–black duality was being proposed, other observers added a third category—brown—in the middle (O'Brien 2008). However, Bonilla-Silva (2002), feeling that the whitening process had not yet sufficiently advanced, saw the middle category in his tripartite hierarchy as honorary whites and the bottom one as "collective blacks" (p. 4), which included very dark-skinned Asian and Latino immigrants as well as African Americans (Bonilla-Silva 2002).

When I wrote about a nonblack–black hierarchy (Gans 1999), I qualified it as "an exercise in speculative analysis," (p. 371) which I justified by the need to think about where the country might be headed in the future. The experiences of the last decade suggest that the analysis has to be reconsidered, especially because of the acceleration of intermarriage, the rising number of white-appearing biracials, and the whitening of nonblack newcomers. In retrospect, the notion of a nonblack–black hierarchy may also have been naive. Although it is phenotypically accurate enough to serve as an analytic concept, we should have realized that most whites would strenuously reject being described as nonblacks. For this reason, and because of the likelihood of continued white domination of the hierarchy, its description should have placed whites at the top.

Some researchers are still reporting a nonblack and black hierarchy; since they are doing empirical work in particular regions of the country, they have good reason to do so (Marrow 2011). Still, I believe the currently evolving hierarchy is better described, at least for now and for the country as a whole, as a tripartite one, with whites as well as whitened Asians, Latinos, and some others at the top and African Americans at the bottom, together with others perceived by whites as black, including Latinos and Caribbeans.

Between these two strata, I would hypothesize a heterogenous stratum of dark but not black Americans, some of whom, such as Southeast Asians, are closer to the immigrants once perceived as yellow and others more like Latino browns.[11] This stratum could also be constructed as a broader nonwhite but nonblack stratum.[12] This stratum could also become an interstitial one, perhaps in continuing flux, in which white America will locate all those, including new nonwhite immigrants, it is not yet able or willing to assign a place in the hierarchy. The stratum could be further subdivided by a variety of other phenotypical and class criteria as white America tries to figure out how to identify the increasing variety of biracials and multiracials.

Much of the flux will stem from widespread white confusion about how and where to place the growing number of biracials and multiracials. How whites will classify the rising phenotypical varieties is impossible to predict, although they will probably use class and other criteria to reduce their confusion. There is some empirical indication that the confusion is already beginning (Harman 2010; Harris 2002), and it should be a major research topic someday. If white confusion becomes too disturbing, phenotypical classification might be de-emphasized, with whites and other Americans exploring alternate ways of ranking each other. Researchers studying the racial hierarchy must look carefully to see if an interstitial stratum develops as well as who is placed in it and by what criteria.

Needless to say, all possible scenarios can evolve quickly with new immigrations or with other macro changes in America—for example, the possible replacement of aging whites by Latinos and other now nonwhites in the professional and managerial upper-middle class (Alba 2009). If enough now poor African Americans and other blacks were allowed to enter the middle class, blacks might no longer be consigned to the bottom of the hierarchy. Conversely, if whites are sufficiently fear-driven, if future conservatives continue to think as do today's, and if they obtain enough power, the government could turn overtly racist, or race blind.

Race and Class

The racial hierarchy is actually part of a larger race-class hierarchy, for the two categories are generally treated as conjoined, as in the race-class nexus (Franklin 1991). Which one is more important is itself an empirical issue that has become more visible because of the class diversity of the post-1965 immigration. In fact, what may once have been a race-class hierarchy could be turning into a class-race one, for the early moves to whiten East Asian newcomers were in large part an effect of their higher-than-average class status, as immigrants but even more so as second-generation Asian Americans.[13]

To put it another way, class appears to be trumping race in the ranking process, but only up to a point, for as already noted, blacks, and particularly African Americans, including black-white biracials, are now almost never whitened. If or when class trumps race, then successful dark-skinned people may become honorary whites, or perhaps the hierarchy will consist of high-status lights at the top and low-status darks at the bottom. If race trumps class, very dark-skinned people will continue to be ranked lower and possibly discriminated against more severely regardless of their class status.[14] High-status African Americans whom white taxi drivers will not pick up have been experiencing this brand of race-class inconsistency for a long time.[15]

Whatever the future shape of the race-class nexus, the likelihood of America soon becoming postracial seems small, at least for African Americans. Despite the enthusiasm for postracialism evoked by the 2008 Obama campaign, the Obama presidency quickly discovered that the president could not appear to favor African Americans in any way. In fact, if today's austere economy continues, race and class conflicts may harden, and young people in the future may not be as racially tolerant and postracial as are some of today's youth. In the near future, researchers can begin to determine whether and how today's tolerant and postracial young feel and act in later adulthood (Bobo 2011b; Cohen 2011; Hochschild et al., 2011).

The race-class (or class-race) hierarchy is a metaphorical concept, but how people rank and are ranked is an existential reality that affects their lives in innumerable ways. A higher rank means having and exercising more economic, social, and political power. As a result, voting and other political activities may affect the racial hierarchy. Until now, most people at the higher levels of this and other hierarchies, with some exceptions, are likely to vote Republican.

However, Asian, Latino, and other immigrants and their children have so far voted Democratic more often than Republican. Upward mobility is likely to persuade some to switch parties, but what they will do if they are whitened remains to be seen. The political choices of whitened Latinos will be most significant; their numbers alone could swing elections in several states if not the country some day. Even so, how whitened populations will vote in the future also depends on whether and how global and other economic and political forces remake the political parties and national political demographics. No one can guess now whether the two major parties will survive to midcentury.

Policy Implications

Keeping track of trends in intermarriage, biracialism, and multiracialism, changes in the race-class hierarchy, and in the realities and politics of migration are not just topics for research, but issues relevant to public policy. The following four points are of paramount importance.

Reducing White Fears and Deconstructing Race

White fears about becoming a racial minority must be stilled, if only to prevent additional fear-driven politics by government or social movements. Perhaps ways can be found to persuade the fearful that race is a social construction—and that they are therefore likely to remain a majority. Indeed, learning that they would remain demographically dominant might get whites to understand the constructionist nature of race and therefore perhaps reduce racism.

Preventing Downward Mobility

Downward mobility has many destructive effects on the downwardly mobile. One of these effects would probably be racial, driving darker races further down the racial and class hierarchies. Economic policies which minimize downward mobility are therefore essential on racial grounds as well.

Encouraging Upward Mobility at the Bottom

The people assigned to the bottom of any hierarchy are always the most vulnerable; consequently any policies that enable them to move up economically will also have other positive effects. If class and intermarriage remain correlated, economic upward mobility will raise black-white intermarriage rates, which will subsequently add to the number of biracials and multiracials.

The people at the bottom are also politically the weakest; politicians are rarely eager to support policies that help them move up. Full employment has traditionally been the most effective policy, but it is probably unachievable, even by maximal bribing of private enterprise. Political conditions in which government is forced to become the employer of last resort for job seekers at the bottom, especially those now considered unemployable, must therefore be exploited (Gans 2012). Meanwhile, economic and other public policies are needed to reduce the size of the economic and social gap between those at the bottom and in the rest of the hierarchy. Someone must always be at the bottom, but the people assigned to it are better off with an income 10 percent below the country's median income than one that is 50 percent below it. People at all levels in the hierarchy generally oppose reducing all gaps, especially the one between them and the people just below them; what policy and which politics can alter the gaps still needs to be understood.

Preventing Undercaste Growth

Although rarely noticed by its higher strata, American society includes an undercaste, a racially distinctive population at the bottom of the class structure.[16] Today it consists largely of the poorest segments of the African American, dark-skinned Latino, and Native American populations. Once institutionalized by slavery and its aftermath, today's undercaste is much less visible. Nonetheless it is currently growing, partly because it has been the major victim of the Great Recession.

Other societies include undercastes: gypsies in Europe, untouchables in India and elsewhere, "indios" in Latin America. Whether the dominant racial groups "need" an undercaste to construct as inferior, dangerous, or undeserving in order to justify their own positions and powers should be investigated.

Research Implications

Although this paper already suggests needed research, if only indirectly, four of the most urgent projects deserve individual mention.

Whitening Demographics

Basic information on which whites whiten (and deracialize) which perceived nonwhites is needed, whether these are East and other Asians, light-skinned Latinos, or their biracial or multiracial descendants. Research about whom whites refuse to whiten is also needed: who is not whitened helps us understand who is. Since whitening takes place both privately and publicly, each process need to be studied separately.

The Whitening Process

Whitening (and deracialization) are social processes; who starts them and makes them persist is important to know. For example, what roles do public officials, politicians, the courts, celebrities, other prominent figures, and the media play? The possibility that the process occurs in stages, from the reduction of discrimination and limited inclusion in white society to honorary whiteness to whiteness—and equivalent stages of deracialization—should be studied over time. Unwhitening and re-racialization should also be on the research agenda.

Phenotype and Class

We need to know what phenotypical characteristics and qualities, real and imagined, whites invoke in approving or rejecting whitening for the now phenotypically nonwhite. If color continues to be significant, what colors and shades do different people see and evaluate, and what other phenotypical characteristics play significant roles?

In each case, boundary judgments are needed as well. What makes whites construct others as white or nonwhite? When does light brown become white, when is dark brown treated as black, and when are "Asian" eyes no longer distinguished from others? Phenotype has no meaning until people add social associations; the associations whites make with whiteness and other phenotypical characteristics are at least as relevant as phenotype itself.

How do people see phenotype in conjunction with class, and what class-related attributes become relevant in whitening? Higher status is correlated with whiteness, but when do class judgments lead to racial ones, and vice versa? The phenotypical and class cues that lead whites to reject whitening are as important to know as those which help.

Blackness

Given the possibly permanent lower status of blackness, the questions about phenotype and class must be explored in greater detail concerning blacks of all class levels. The particular phenotypical characteristics that whites use to distinguish African Americans from other blacks, especially African immigrants, and from dark brown peoples require determination. Social and other associations are particularly important, including whether, when, and why whites still describe African Americans with stereotypes and blaming terms used against their enslaved ancestors.

Research attention needs to be given to successful blacks, especially those living in white communities (Lacy 2007), working in white-dominated workplaces, and married to whites. Instances of the whitening of African Americans and other blacks deserve particular attention. Ideally, the policy analyses and research projects described above should be pursued under special institutional auspices, not only to underline their importance, but also to make sure that they are framed as long-term projects and can be continued over time.

Researchers need to study whites' identification of major monoracial, biracial, and multiracial nonwhites, especially in a variety of actual social situations, but also in interviews using photographic cues (Harman 2010; Harris 2002; Roth 2012). These populations can be asked whether and why they believe they have been whitened, are being whitened, or might be whitened in the future.

Conclusion

If Du Bois were writing today, he might identify the existence and future of what I have called an undercaste as a principal racial problem of the current century. He would also recognize that African Americans could be pushed further and further below the next higher social and economic strata. Consequently, he would likely call for special attention to the class components of the American race and class hierarchy that makes an under-caste possible.

Notes

Reprinted from *Du Bois Review*, vol. 9, no. 2, 2012, by permission of Cambridge University Press.

1. Perhaps even concepts such as biracial and multiracial will eventually disappear, since they are based on an essentialist conception of race—as well as on a quantifiable notion of racial "blood." In that case, race may be described phenotypically, mainly or solely in terms of appearance or simply skin color.

2. Although it is often called a racial order, this term fails to convey the characteristics and attributes of its hierarchical structure.

3. Whether and how whites distinguish between "indios" and "mestizos" is not yet clear, but the former look more unlike whites and are poorer than the latter. Researchers interested in phenotypical subtleties need to study how whites deal with the children of Latino-Asian intermarriages and other less numerous mixtures.

4. Actually, many of the Jewish immigrants who came earlier in the nineteenth century seem to have been WASPed, if I may coin that term. A significant number later converted to high-status Protestant denominations. The arrival of the poor Eastern European Jews put an end to WASPing and led to the racialization of even the richest and most assimilated German Jews, as well as to a drastic increase in antisemitism.

5. So far, deracialization has been used mainly by political scientists to describe race-blind election campaigning for local offices.

6. In 2010, about a quarter of Asian and Latino marriages, and 17 percent of black ones were racial intermarriages. Asian intermarriages are currently declining somewhat, probably because of the rapid increase in second-generation Asian Americans of marriageable age (Wang 2012).

7. According to Batson et al. (2006), interracial cohabitation takes place at a higher rate among blacks than interracial marriage.

8. Recall that the Chicago School began its study of the immigrant second generation by focusing on its identity and its problems, notably marginality (Park 1928). Researchers find it easier to study how a small number of biracials identify themselves than to analyze how a huge and diverse aggregate such as whites categorizes the variety of biracials.

9. Needless to say, the targets of such identification may reject or be troubled by it, particularly because of its effects on how they identify themselves (Davila 2008).

10. Sanjek (1994) has a prominent place on this list as well. He constructed several scenarios, one of which divided the racial hierarchy into light and dark, thereby anticipating the nonblack–black binary by several years.

11. Perhaps there will be two middle strata, but a stratum is a sociological construction with fluid and fuzzy boundaries. In fact, strata should perhaps be placed in quotes for this reason.

12. The populations Bonilla-Silva (2002) describes as collective blacks may ultimately describe themselves as browns, since such immigrants and their descendants will probably want to place themselves above African Americans in the pecking order.

13. Working-class Asians and Asian Americans are very different from their middle- and upper- middle-class coracials. They fit the model minority stereotype even less, but despite their large numbers in some parts of the country, they are also less visible to whites (Lee 2005).

14. One can also argue that race is itself a proxy for class, and that blacks are at the bottom of the American hierarchy because they were enslaved and not because they were black (Fields 1990; Gans 2005). Had the Chinese slaves who first worked the plantations not been replaced by Africans, today's poor Asian Americans might be at the bottom of the racial hierarchy.

15. In this connection, it would be important to study how whites perceive and treat high-status Africans and very dark South Asians who are black but not African American. If the whites see whites, class trumps race; if not, race trumps class.

16. My notion of the undercaste derives from Myrdal's (1963) underclass concept. Myrdal viewed the underclass as an economic stratum occupying "the basement of the stately American mansion" (p. 49), but said nothing about its racial characteristics.

References

Alba, Richard. 2009. *Blurring the Color Line: The New Chance for a More Integrated America*. Cambridge, MA: Harvard University Press.

Alba, Richard, Tomas R. Jimenez, and Helen B. Marrow. 2011. *Mexican-Americans as a Paradigm for Contemporary Intragroup Heterogeneity*. Unpublished working paper.

Barot, Rohit and John Bird (2001). Racialization: The Genealogy and Critique of a Concept. *Ethnic and Racial Studies*, 24(4): 601–618.

Batson, Christie D., Zhenchao Quian, and Daniel T. Lichter (2006). Interracial and Intraracial Patterns of Mate Selection Among America's Diverse Black Populations. *Journal of Marriage and Family*, 68(3): 658–672.

Bobo, Lawrence D. (Ed.) (2011a). Race, Inequality and Culture, vol. 2. *Daedalus*, 140(2): 11–36.

———. (2011b). Somewhere Between Jim Crow and Post-Racialism: Reflections on the Racial Divide in America Today. *Daedalus*, 140(2): 11–36.

Bonilla-Silva, Eduardo (2002). We Are All Americans: The Latin Americanization of Racial Stratification in the USA. *Race and Society*, 5: 3–16.

Brodkin, Karen (1998). *How Jews Became White Folks and What That Says About Race in America*. New Brunswick, NJ: Rutgers University Press.

Cohen, Cathy J. (2011). Millenials and the Myth of the Post-Racial Society: Black Youth, Intra-generational Divisions, and the Continuing Racial Divide in American Politics. *Daedalus* 140(2): 197–205.

Davila, Arlene M. (2008). *Latino Spin: Public Image and the Whitewashing of Race*. New York: New York University Press.

Feagin, Joe R. and Melvin P Sikes (1994). *Living with Racism: The Black Middle-Class Experience*. Boston, MA: Beacon Press.

Fields, Barbara J. (1990). Slavery, Race and Ideology in the United States of America. *New Left Review*, 181:95–118.

Franklin, Raymond S. (1991). *Shadows of Race and Class*. Minneapolis, MN: University of Minnesota Press.

Gans, Herbert J. (1999). The Possibility of a New Racial Hierarchy in the Twenty-First Century United States. In Michele Lamont (Ed.), *The Cultural Territories of Race: Black and White Boundaries*, pp. 371–390. Chicago, IL and New York: University of Chicago Press and Russell Sage Foundation.

Gans, Herbert J. (2005). Race as Class. *Contexts*, 4(4): 17–21.

Gans, Herbert J. (2012). Superfluous Workers: The Labor Market's Invisible Discards. *Challenge*, 55(4): 94–103.

Harman, Melissa R. (2010). Do You See What I Am: How Observers' Backgrounds Affect their Perceptions of Multiracial Faces. *Social Psychology Quarterly*, 73(1): 58–78.

Harris, David R. (2002). In the Eyes of the Beholder: Observed Race and Observer Characteristics. *PSC Research Report No. 02-522*. Ann Arbor, MI: Population Studies Center, University of Michigan.

Hochschild, Jennifer L., Vesla M. Weaver, and Traci Burch (2011). Destabilizing the Racial Order, *Daedalus*, 140(2): 151–165.

Ignatiev, Noel (1995). *How the Irish Became White*. New York: Routledge.

Khanna, Nikki (2011). *Biracial in America: Forming and Performing Racial Identity*. Lanham, MD: Lexington Books.

Kim, Nadia (2007). Critical Thoughts on Asian American Assimilation in the Whitening Literature. *Social Forces*, 86(2): 53–66.

Lacy, Karyn R. (2007). *Blue Chip Black: Race, Class and Status in the New Black Middle Class*. Berkeley, CA: University of California Press.

Lee, Jennifer and Frank D. Bean (2004). America's Changing Color Line: Immigration, Race/Ethnicity, and Multiracial Identification. *Annual Review of Sociology*, 30: 221–242.

Lee, Jennifer and Frank D. Bean (2010). *The Diversity Paradox: Immigration and the Color Line in Twenty-First Century America.* New York: Russell Sage.

Lee, Sara S. (2005). Class Matters: Racial and Ethnic Identities of Working- and Middle-Class Second-Generation Korean-Americans in New York City. In Philip Kasinitz, John H. Mollenkopf, and Mary C. Waters (Eds.), *Becoming New Yorkers: Ethnographies of the New Second Generation,* pp. 313–338. New York: Russell Sage

Loewen, James W. (1971). *The Mississippi Chinese: Between Black and White.* Cambridge, MA: Harvard University Press.

Marrow, Helen B. (2011). *New Destination Dreaming: Immigration, Race, and Legal Status in the Rural American South.* Stanford, CA: Stanford University Press.

McDermott, Monica and Frank L. Samson (2005). White Racial and Ethnic Identity in the United States. *Annual Review of Sociology,* 31: 245–261.

Myrdal, Gunnar (1963). *Challenge to Affluence.* New York: Pantheon Books.

O'Brien, Eileen (2008). *The Racial Middle: Latinos and Asian Americans Living Beyond the Racial Divide.* New York: New York University Press.

Park, Robert (1928). Human Migration and the Marginal Man. *American Journal of Sociology,* 33(6): 881–893.

Prewitt, Kenneth (Forthcoming). *What's Your Race: The Census and the Flawed Effort to Classify Americans.* Princeton, NJ: Princeton University Press.

Richeson, Jennifer A. and Maureen A. Craig (2011). Intra-minority Intergroup Relations in the Twenty-First Century. *Daedalus,* 140(2): 166–175.

Roediger, David (1991). *The Wages of Whiteness: Race and the Making of the American Working Class.* New York: Verso.

Roth, Wendy D. (2012). *Race Migrations: Latinos and the Cultural Transformation of Race.* Stanford, CA: Stanford University Press.

Sanjek, Roger (1994). Intermarriage and the Future of the Races. In Steven Gregory and Roger Sanjek (Eds.), *Race,* pp. 103–130. New Brunswick, NJ: Rutgers University Press.

Twine, France Windance (1996). Brown-Skinned White Girls: Class, Culture, and the Construction of White Identities in Suburban Communities. *Gender, Place, and Culture,* 3(2): 205–224.

Twine, France Windance and Charles Gallagher (2008). The Future of Whiteness: A Map of the Third Wave. *Ethnic and Racial Studies,* 31(1): 4–24.

Wang, Wendy (2012). *The Rise of Intermarriage: Rates Vary by Race and Gender.* Washington DC: Pew Research Center. http://www.pewsocialtrends.org/2012/02/16/the-rise-of-intermarriage/ (accessed September 13, 2012).

Warren, Jonathan W. and France Windance Twine (1997). White Americans: The New Minority? Non-Blacks and the Ever-Expanding Boundaries of Whiteness. *Journal of Black Studies,* 28(2): 200–218.

Yancey, George (2003). *Who Is White? Latinos, Asians, and the New Black/Nonblack Divide.* Boulder, CO: Lynne Rienner.

CHAPTER 15

The Moynihan Report and Its Aftermaths

A Critical Analysis[1]

Introduction

In four years, the so-called Moynihan Report of 1965, "The Negro Family: The Case for Federal Action" (Moynihan 1967),[2] will be fifty years old, but there are already signs that it could become immortal. In this century alone, it has been memorialized and celebrated in Hodgson's (2000) sympathetic biography of Moynihan, by the creation of a Moynihan Prize, at two conferences (Massey and Sampson, 2009a; Moynihan et al., 2004), and most recently by an entire book (Patterson 2010).

The memorializing has pursued three agendas. First, it celebrates the Report's social science, remembering its author as "prescient" and "prophetic." Although Moynihan did not try to be either, his Report is now read as having predicted a continuing increase in black family instability and *ghetto* pathology.

Second, the celebrations have continued and sometimes escalated Moynihan's long-ago attack on unnamed "liberals" and social scientists who failed to do further research and writing on the failings of the black family.

Third, some celebrants have reframed Moynihan's findings as partially cultural, thus enrolling the Report in the current drive to emphasize "culture," sometimes at the expense of "structure," in the study of poverty.

However, rereading the Report today raises questions about whether it ever deserved so much praise, for even at the time of its writing, it displayed serious shortcomings as both social science and social policy.

Moreover, I believe these problems could have been avoided when Moynihan wrote the Report, for sufficient research findings and other necessary information were available to him.

I do not want to engage in a blaming exercise; Moynihan was a creative and constructive thinker about antipoverty and other public policy, who tried to persuade the federal government and the country to attack the economic and other inequalities of the poor black population. The Report was in some respects an unusual federal research venture, written under less than optimum conditions. Nor could its author have predicted the conditions under which the Report would be released and the reception it would meet. Had he been able to do so, some of the Report's shortcomings might have been corrected before it saw the light of day.[3] Still, the shortcomings remain; the praise that continues to be showered on the Report and its enduring influence justify another analysis of these shortcomings.

The Report

"The Negro Family" argued that the basic problem of the black (then called Negro) population was male unemployment and low wages paid to poor black workers. As its title suggests, the Report devoted most of its attention to the instability of black family life, particularly the proliferation of the single-parent or female-headed family and its illegitimate offspring. These Moynihan considered major causes of what he called a "tangle of pathology" that helped to mire many blacks in poverty. In addition, he warned about the associated occurrence of poor school performance, street crime, delinquency, and drug use. However, the Report attracted most attention for its claim that the single-parent family is accompanied by a self-perpetuating mechanism that causes it to produce another generation of such families with all the accompanying pathologies.

Moynihan warned that unless the black single-parent family was replaced by the two-parent nuclear family, *ghetto* pathology was likely to worsen further. Although the Report made no concrete policy recommendations, it suggested that a jobs policy was needed to deal with unemployment, hinted at the need for what was later called affirmative action, and proposed that the country's pursuit of equality of opportunity be replaced by one for an equality of results. Nonetheless, Moynihan also urged action by the black community itself, in effect demanding that it pull itself up by its familial bootstraps.

The Report initially found favor with President Lyndon B. Johnson, who made it one theme in a presidential address. The White House plans for a subsequent conference to begin implementing the Report were scuttled, however, once the Report became public knowledge and generated considerable public criticism. That criticism came from both the Left and the Right: from commentators, social scientists, the Civil Rights Movement, and black leaders. That the violence in Watts, the black *ghetto* of Los Angeles, took place shortly after the Report first became known did not help matters.

The criticism by liberals and social scientists led Moynihan to develop a lifelong antagonism to them, blaming the social scientists, among other things, for being too cowardly to do research on the problems he had identified in the Report. At the same time, Moynihan continued to press for economic help to the black community, beginning in his initial position on the Harvard faculty later in the 1960s.

As an adviser to the Nixon administration in the early 1970s, Moynihan worked hard if unsuccessfully to obtain Congressional approval for his welfare-reforming Family Assistance Plan. He continued to support antipoverty policies during his four terms as U.S. Senator from New York, and opposed Bill Clinton's ending of welfare "as we know it." In short, on poverty-related issues he remained a liberal himself, even though at the same time he sided with the neoconservatives, many of them personal friends, on other domestic and foreign policy issues.[4]

The Report's Shortcomings

I believe I can reanalyze the Report without indulging in undue hindsight because, unlike most of today's celebrants of the Report, I participated in public and other discussions, including one with a senior White House adviser, following the Report's arrival in the public arena.[5] I had gotten to know Moynihan before the Report was released, but I probably first read the entire Report in August 1965. After seeing the early critical newspaper stories about the Report, I was concerned about how it might be received. Specifically, I worried that because of the lack of policy proposals to solve the economic problems that Moynihan laid out, the Report's reception would emphasize the prevalence of the single-parent family and the tangle of pathology rather than Moynihan's references to black male unemployment.

Consequently, when I was asked to review the Report for *Commonweal* magazine (Gans 1965) I suggested that the single-parent family was now, as in other societies with high male joblessness, adaptive rather than pathological. In addition, I made some specific economic-program proposals to reinforce the Report's understated thesis about the connection between family structure in the *ghetto* and its poverty and racial inequality.

When, forty-six years later—in a very different political context—I reread the Report in order to participate in a Columbia University faculty seminar discussing James Patterson's (2010) book on the subject, I was struck by its many shortcomings. *However, my discussion is restricted to those shortcomings that I believe were avoidable when the Report was drafted, even under the conditions in which Moynihan and his assistants prepared it.*

The Report as Social Science[6]

Thinking of the Report as social science is both inaccurate and unfair, for it is somewhere between a polemic and a position paper, with U.S. Census and other federal data as supporting evidence.[7] It is unfair also because Moynihan was then not, strictly speaking, a social scientist. His PhD was in International Relations, then a professional rather a research-training program. Thus, his chapter on the New York Irish in *Beyond the Melting Pot* (Glazer and Moynihan, 1963) was not a social science analysis but primarily a discussion of the group's political history.

Unlike today's celebrants of the Report, Moynihan may not even have thought of the Report as social science analysis or a data-gathering enterprise. While he reported on the findings of some sociological and other social science authors, he was writing for an audience of policy makers and other public officials, not for social scientists.

Moynihan's initial knowledge of research about the black community appears to have come from the work of Nathan Glazer (1963), who had begun his own discussion of the Negro family in *Beyond the Melting Pot* with observations on the female-headed family, illegitimacy, child abandonment, and related problems.[8] For his observations on the harshness of American slavery, Moynihan drew from Glazer's (1963) recently written introduction to Stanley Elkins' *Slavery*. Beyond that, the Report included only brief quotations from the work of Franklin Frazier, Kenneth Clark, Thomas Pettigrew, Margaret Mead, and a few other social scientists.

In later years, some of Moynihan's writing appeared in academic books and journals, and he came to know and work with many important social scientists. Still, in 2000 his biographer and friend, Godfrey Hodgson, wrote: "He thinks anecdotally. He thinks in narrative. . . . He is an intellectual . . . but not an academic" (p. 23). As quoted in Weisman (2010), Moynihan himself once wrote in the same vein, "I do not have the stamina for a professor. I can't study like that . . ." (p. 12).

In any case, the Report was flawed in a number of ways. First, Moynihan could even then have been criticized for failing to look at studies of the poor black family and community other than those by Frazier (1939) and Clark (1965). For example, he might have quoted from Drake and Cayton's (1945) *Black Metropolis* which, in a few pages, offers a more comprehensive and balanced analysis of the situation of poor black families.

Further, as an Assistant Secretary of Labor, Moynihan should have been able to obtain more recent analyses from the black sociologists, most of them directly or indirectly connected with Howard University in Washington DC, who were then studying and writing about the black community.

Second, and more seriously, Moynihan apparently looked at the poor black population with a belief system which viewed any family form that did not include a two-parent nuclear unit as unstable and pathological. Moynihan must have known or could have found out that stability and family structure were not perfectly correlated, and that a two-parent family could be unstable and a single-parent one, stable.

Moynihan was aware that jobless black men were not good candidates for marriage, but he was seemingly blind to the effects of socioeconomic class on family structure. As a result, he failed to see that poor people lacked many of the material and nonmaterial resources that make a two-parent family possible, and that for poor blacks, the single-parent family was sometimes the only solution. He also did not consider the ways in which it was adaptive and in fact provided a modicum of stability for a population living under conditions of high economic instability.

Although little research had been done on the single-parent family when Moynihan wrote the Report, black family researchers would also have been able to tell him that single-parent families were not necessarily single-parent households, and might have included a female grandparent or other relative. In addition, unmarried mothers often had some help from the fathers of their children and were surrounded by a familial support network.[9]

Moynihan could also have learned that the single-parent family was found in most societies in which large numbers of males were unemployed or under employed.[10] He must have known from his writings on the Irish that during economic crises husbands leave or are often pushed out of two-parent families. By describing a family structure that could be found in many economies suffering from male joblessness as pathological, Moynihan was in fact defining deviance up.[11]

Moreover, Moynihan did not seem to know that the children of single mothers were considered statistically normal and socially acceptable in the poor black community. Instead, Moynihan viewed their legal status through the lens of white mainstream respectability, and saw it as an indicator of both family instability and pathology.

To be fair to Moynihan, he was not alone in making these observations and charges. In 1964, the year before Moynihan wrote his Report, the Harvard social psychologist Thomas Pettigrew published *A Profile of the Negro American*, the first two chapters of which reported many observations also found in the Report. Pettigrew's initial chapter also included a section on "family disorganization" (pp. 15–24) that covered much the same territory as Moynihan's report. Pettigrew's (1964) book was supported by hundreds of citations of other studies; some forty citations supported the nine pages on family disorganization alone.[12]

Even so, Pettigrew's analysis diverged significantly from Moynihan's. He used the term pathology only sparingly and framed his findings as reactions to what he called oppression, a term that covered everything from slavery to contemporary forms of racial and class subjugation and exploitation. The oppressor was white America, and although many of the studies to which Pettigrew referred identified or implied black moral failings, Pettigrew—who is himself white—pointed the moral finger directly at the white oppressor.

Third, Moynihan misused the concept of pathology, treating it not as a synonym for individual or community illnesses and dysfunctions, but as a term to describe phenomena he considered socially or morally undesirable.[13] Had he used the conventional definition of pathology, he could have described a number of social and individual pathologies found among the *ghetto's* poor, including chronic health and mental health problems, child abuse, alcoholism and other addictions, and interpersonal violence. Even in the 1960s, sociologists could have told him that these were far more likely to be caused by poverty and racial inequality than by the single-parent family, illegitimacy, and matriarchy, the latter another one of Moynihan's proxies for instability and pathology.

Moynihan misused the term further by describing the poor black community as being enmeshed in "a tangle of pathology." Since he did not describe what was tangled or explain the impact of the tangling on the poor black family or the *ghetto*, the "tangle of pathology" became a synonym for social chaos; it was a sensational phrase that automatically attracted media attention.[14]

For Moynihan, the single-parent family seemed to be at the center of the black community's tangle of pathology. He came back to it and to the subject of illegitimate offspring repeatedly; almost half of the Report's more than sixty tables and graphs were devoted to these two topics, while only six dealt with unemployment.[15] Indeed, the Report's second chapter makes this point in its first sentences: "At the heart of the deterioration of . . . Negro society is the deterioration of the Negro family. It is the fundamental source of the weakness of the Negro community at the present time" (1967, p. 51).

Fourth, the Report's causal analysis had a fundamental flaw: the absence of data on the effects of the poor single-parent family. No one had then done an empirical study that followed a sample of such families over a generation or more in order to measure pathological effects if any, and to determine whether these effects could be traced to the structure of the family rather than to its poverty or to what is now called racism. Consequently, Moynihan could not properly argue that the single-parent family played a causal role in the *ghetto's* "tangle of pathology." He did so nevertheless, for he claimed to have found a self-perpetuating familial mechanism, what Clark (1965) called a "self-perpetuating pathology" (p. 81) that would reproduce itself in the future.

As Moynihan (1967) pointed out in the last chapter of his report, "The situation may indeed have begun to feed on itself. . . . The present tangle of pathology is capable of perpetuating itself without assistance from the white world" (p. 93). Despite the fact that he is now considered to have been prophetic, Moynihan never predicted that rates of black single-parent-family formation would rise for the rest of the twentieth century and into the next.

In his report, Moynihan (1967) based the existence of a self-perpetuating pathology on his so-called "scissors" analysis, which showed in his Table 22 that from 1948 to 1962, unemployment and the number of newly opened Aid to Families with Dependent Children (AFDC) cases had risen and fallen in tandem, but that in 1960, 1963, and 1964, unemployment declined while the number of new AFDC cases increased (p. 124).[16]

The analysis, however, was unconvincing. Moynihan (1967) not only assigned great weight to a mere three years of deviant data, but here as elsewhere in the Report, he or his assistants treated a statistical correlation as a cause. Also, Moynihan should have known that the basic unemployment rate was too simple a measure to support a causal analysis. Earlier in the Report, he had mentioned low wages as one of the *ghetto's* employment problems, but the scissors analysis failed to indicate that even if poor black men found jobs, most were neither well paying nor stable enough to enable the men holding them to marry.

Actually, Moynihan lacked the data even to hypothesize a self-perpetuating mechanism. When poor black single parents produce another generation of such parents, the most likely explanation is that poverty and racism have continued and people continue to practice the coping patterns that have enabled them to survive. A self-perpetuating mechanism can only be posited if conditions change and people do not adapt: for example, if the many forms of racial and class inequality declined but the rate of single parent family formation in subsequent generations did not.

Moynihan's resort to a self-perpetuating pathological process became particularly noteworthy because in the late 1950s the anthropologist Oscar Lewis (1959), who had done fieldwork in Mexico, had come up with the notion of a "culture of poverty," which included the same mechanism.[17] In 1965, Lewis's work had not yet obtained widespread public attention, but social scientists familiar both with Lewis's concept and the Report put the two together, and critics of both studies accused their authors of what William Ryan (1971) later called "blaming the victim."[18]

Admittedly, Moynihan could not anticipate that his ideas would be associated with Lewis's work, but as an experienced public official who had been active in New York politics, he should have expected some of the other criticisms with which the Report was met. Consequently, one would have thought he would have had a draft of the Report read by representatives of the various constituencies in and out of the government who would be affected by it. They could have corrected factual mistakes and rewritten politically risky statements. As quoted in Weisman (2010), Moynihan himself wrote to a federal official in 1966: "The United States government is the most powerful research organization in the world. It can find out anything it wants to find out" (p. 130).

Perhaps Moynihan did not worry about potential criticism of the Report, since he wrote it solely for consumption inside the U.S. Department of Labor.[19] Still, he sent it immediately to the Secretary of Labor, and must therefore have had plans or hopes that the Report or at least its ideas would receive wider distribution. Ultimately, in fact, some students of the period have reported that he himself released it to the press (Lemann 1991).

The Report as Social Policy

Since most of the contemporary celebrants of the Report are social scientists, they might be inclined to pay less attention to the Report's implications for social action or social policy. However, Moynihan (1967) used the final chapter of the Report to make "the case for national action" (pp. 93–94) although he did not propose specific programs to implement it.[20]

Outlining elements of a "national effort . . . to bring the Negro American to a full and equal sharing of the responsibilities and rewards of citizenship," Moynihan (1967) suggested that federal programs should have "the effect . . . of enhancing the stability and resources of the Negro American family" (p. 94). Unfortunately, he did not spell out what he meant by a full and equal sharing of the rewards he had in mind. A literal such sharing would have implied the equality of results he urged earlier in the Report. If he had been more specific, he might have initiated an innovative public discussion which addressed, among other subjects, what resources had to be redistributed from and to whom.

In the mid-1960s, when the War on Poverty had not yet deteriorated into a skirmish, enhancing the resources of the family might have been politically feasible; in several places elsewhere in the Report, Moynihan indicated that greater male employment and better jobs could bring about the enhancement. Had he given more attention and space to these subjects, and written about them with the same rhetorical intensity he devoted to the single-parent family, the Report's conclusions about black family pathology might have received less attention. Perhaps the Report would then have met with less criticism from the black and liberal communities—and more importantly, with greater political support from the White House. Some employment programs might even have been initiated.

However, even Moynihan's (1967) hints about the desirability of such programs were partly neutralized by his cyclical argument, at the start of the

Report's final chapter, that the ability to obtain jobs "reflects educational achievement, which depends in large part on family stability, which reflects employment" (p. 93).

Moynihan went on to indicate that where to break into this cycle was "one of the most difficult domestic questions" (p. 93), but framing the problem as a cycle without proposing a break-in point crippled the Report's potential contribution to national action.

Had Moynihan replaced the cycle with a more open-ended process model, he might have been able to suggest that the process could begin with job creation. He would have reinforced that suggestion if he could have shown that secure employment led to, or at least correlated with a higher rate of two-parent family formation.

Part of the Report's policy shortcomings must be attributed to Moynihan's emphasis on family stability, a condition neither he nor anyone else knew how to bring about. Even if he had in mind only the establishment of two-parent families, policy to encourage and help people to marry did not exist, although Moynihan exerted effort to make married, two-parent families eligible for welfare.[21]

Criticism of the Report's social policy discussion may be unfair to Moynihan, since at the time Moynihan wrote the Report, he was not a social policy analyst and might not have had access to one at the U.S. Department of Labor. Still, as an intellectual and a politician, he might have realized that federal officials should not advocate an end state like family stability unless they could also propose policies and programs that would achieve it.

Aftermaths

The Report was officially forgotten soon after the White House refused to act on it. However, the debate over the Report continued for years afterwards, especially in the social science community, until it too shifted its attention elsewhere.

Moynihan himself supplied the first installment of the Report's aftermath. As indicated above, he was principally unhappy with social scientists for not undertaking research that would support his findings on the harmful effects of the single-parent family and the *ghetto's* tangle of pathology—what he called, quoted in Patterson (2010), "the great silence" (p. 105).

Moynihan's criticisms were unreasonable. He wanted researchers not only to become social critics of the black community but to generalize about nonexistent data. Do children of poor black single mothers grow up with problems that are caused purely by the absence of a male parent? To this day there is no persuasive evidence that they do. Also, not having yet been a grant-seeking academic, Moynihan may not have known that researchers or the agencies that fund them are normally not eager to explore a subject that the White House has determined to be a political hot potato.

Once Moynihan had joined the Harvard faculty, and especially after he had been named the director of the MIT-Harvard Joint Center for Urban Studies, he could have proposed studies to test the assertions he made in the Report. He could also have done so during his tenure at Harvard, later during his time in the Nixon White House, and in the quarter century he served as a U.S. Senator from New York.

Celebrations

I leave it to historians and citation analysts to determine the exact origins of the current celebration of the Report, but the phenomenon became visible in 1987, when William Julius Wilson praised Moynihan's work early in the first chapter of his now classic *The Truly Disadvantaged* (p. 4). Wilson then viewed poor blacks as members of an underclass, and, like Moynihan, saw them as suffering from a self-perpetuating pathology.

More importantly, Wilson emphasized the connection between high male unemployment among poor blacks and the prevalence of single mothers. Perhaps as a consequence, Wilson (1987) praised the Moynihan Report as "the only non-impressionistic study of the changing black family structure" and criticized "liberal scholars (who) shied away from researching behavior construed as unflattering or stigmatizing to particular racial groups" (p. 4).

The Truly Disadvantaged became, and remains, one of the most influential studies, if not *the* most influential study, of the poor black community in America, particularly among researchers, policy analysts, and the political elite. Consequently, Wilson's praise of the Report may have returned it to public attention.

In 2002, just before Moynihan's death, Syracuse University, where he had finished writing his PhD dissertation, held a conference that presented a number of studies relevant to the Report (Moynihan et al., 2004).

In 2007, the American Academy of Political and Social Science and Harvard University held a similar conference. The resulting issue of the *Annals of the American Academy of Political and Social Science* opened with Massey and Sampson (2009) describing the report as "the most famous piece of social scientific analysis never published" (p. 6) and suggesting that the purpose of the report was "to make an impassioned moral case for a massive federal intervention to break the cycle of black poverty . . ." (p. 6). The introduction to the *Annals* issue also reinvigorated Moynihan's attack on liberals and escalated the one on social scientists, claiming that "the calumny heaped on . . . [Moynihan and Oscar Lewis] . . . had a chilling effect on social science over the next two decades. Sociologists avoided studying controversial issues relating to race, culture and intelligence . . ." (Massey and Sampson 2009, p. 12). Subsequently, the Nobel prize-winning economist James Heckman even described the critics of the Report as "venomous" (Heckman 2011, p. 72).

William Julius Wilson's (2009a) article in the 2009 *Annals* volume once more praised the Report as a "prophetic document" (p. 34), but also added a new theme, reinterpreting the Report as an early contribution to the cultural analysis of poverty. Wilson has long been concerned with the extent to which the problems of the poor black community can be explained by "structural" causes (i.e., mainly economic and political forces and institutions), and how much by "cultural" causes which determine the ways people feel, think, and act. Even so, ultimately Wilson (2009b) has always concluded that structural factors have priority over cultural ones.

However, in discussing the Report, Wilson (2009a) suggested that Moynihan had already pointed to the role of cultural factors in black poverty, describing Moynihan's analysis as being in part an "implicit cultural argument on the impact of black family fragmentation" (p. 40). Wilson reinforced his point by quoting Orlando Patterson's (2006) argument that the "deep-seated dogma against cultural analysis of the fragmentation of the black family . . . was caused in no small part by reaction to the Moynihan Report" (Wilson 2009a, p. 40). Wilson also supported Patterson's view that cultural factors play a significant role in understanding black poverty as a whole, agreeing with his criticism that structural theorists show a "relentless preference for relying on structural factors like low income, joblessness, poor schools and bad housing" (Wilson 2009a, p. 40).

Orlando Patterson's criticism reflects the so-called "cultural turn." This late twentieth-century intellectual movement which, in its sociological incarnation, has turned into cultural sociology, likes to claim that cultural analysis is better suited than structural analysis to comprehending modern society. I find it difficult to understand why the effects of slavery, long-term male unemployment, low wages, poverty, and racial discrimination should be defined as cultural, especially since cultural sociologists cannot agree on a definition of culture (Small et al., 2010). When behaviorally defined, culture can be used to help explain the choices people make when they have options among alternative actions. The conditions under which poor blacks have lived during and after slavery, and indeed for much of the twentieth century, did not give them much choice in familial and other survival methods.

When employed in poverty and antipoverty policy research, cultural analyses that downplay the relevance of economic, political, and related "structural" factors can be used to undermine the need for economic and other policies to fight poverty and discrimination. As Cohen (2010) points out, discussions of cultural analysis can even lead to revivals of culture of poverty concepts, although most cultural sociologists are careful to avoid reviving Oscar Lewis's much criticized concept (Small et al., 2010). Still, connecting culture and poverty enables conservative thinkers and apolitical researchers to avoid research and policy issues relevant to the struggle against poverty.

The most recent celebration of the Report, by James Patterson (2010), a well-known historian of poverty, is mainly a detailed analytic history of the Report. The book also describes its more public aftermaths, notably Moynihan-like appeals for the nuclear family from comedian Bill Cosby and President Barack Obama.

James Patterson shares Moynihan's concerns with and characterizations of black family and community pathologies, and devotes many pages to updating Moynihan's statistics to the present day; for example, the drastic rise in the number of single-parent families and of jobless black men. While James Patterson (2010) also feels that Moynihan has been unfairly criticized, his book discusses both the positive and negative aspects of the Report.

Conclusion

Given the Report's continued stream of admirers and their work, someone will most likely soon be planning a special celebration on its fiftieth anniversary. However, another replay of Moynihan's list of black familial and communal pathologies is inappropriate. Instead, Moynihan could be honored by a comprehensive study of single-parent families from the gamut of classes and races to determine exactly whether, when, and how they are problematic and to what extent, if any, they pass problems on to the next generation. He might be honored even more by focusing attention on a previously ignored part of the Report: an exploration and elaboration of the equality of results—the idea that blacks and whites ought to be equal in income, rate of employment, education, civil rights, and other entitlements of being Americans—and of public policies that could move the black community and the country in that direction.

If Moynihan's name and work retain sufficient political clout, perhaps they could be used to generate support for the job and income programs he advocated all his life. I am sure that if Pat Moynihan were still alive, he would work energetically for these policies.

Notes

Reprinted from *Du Bois Review*, vol. 8, no. 2, 2011, by permission of Cambridge University Press.

1. The author is grateful to Merlin Chowkwanyun and Alice O'Connor for very helpful comments on an earlier draft of this paper and to Nathan Glazer, Nicholas Lemann, and James Patterson for answers to his several questions about the Report's history.

2. Although issued as a federal report by the U.S. Department of Labor in 1965, the Report was not actually published until it appeared in the first major study of the Report by Rainwater and Yancey (1967). Rainwater and Yancey published a true copy of the original Report that included its own paging, but my references are to the paging of the Rainwater and Yancey volume.

3. For the most detailed study of the creation and initial reception of the Moynihan Report, see Rainwater and Yancey (1967). The book also presents the authors' incisive analysis of the Report's rise and fall, the Report itself, as well as a collection of the official and unofficial documents and writings about the Report. Later histories and critical analyses of the Report can be found in several places, notably Steinfels (1979), Lemann (1991), and O'Connor (2001), still the most thoughtful critique of the Report. For a complete history of the Report up to the present, see J. Patterson (2010).

4. Although it ends in the late 1970s, the most incisive analysis of Moynihan's ideological positions and political stances remains that of Peter Steinfels (1979, pp. 108–160).

5. Strictly speaking, I am of course writing with hindsight but I believe that my memory of the relevant social science findings and ideas at the time is reasonably accurate. What hindsight adds, mostly, is the years of subsequent reflection as well as the knowledge of what has happened since the Report was written. My participation in the events following the release of the Report is described in Rainwater and Yancey (1967, pp. 195, 210, and passim) and in J. Patterson (2010, pp. 78–79).

6. For their analysis of the Report as social science and particularly of its implications for social science in the mid-1960s, see Rainwater and Yancey (1967, pp. 292–313).

7. Rainwater and Yancey (1967) had already described the Report as a polemic at the time, writing, "It is a polemic which makes use of social science techniques and findings to convince others" (p. 297). They argue further that Moynihan relied almost exclusively on government statistics because he wrote the Report for government officials, not for social scientists. Even so, a more academic companion piece to the Report, published about the same time in *Daedalus* and written in a less polemical style, was also filled with government statistics (Moynihan 1965).

8. However, in Glazer and Moynihan (1963), Glazer noted that "broken homes and illegitimacy do not necessarily mean poor upbringing and emotional problems" (p. 50), although he then discussed problems associated with such homes.

9. Moynihan probably could have learned a great deal more about the actual functioning of the poor black family from researchers and experts at various government agencies, including the Women's Bureau inside his own Department of Labor. However, whether by his own choice or lack of choice, Moynihan undertook to write a one-person report, not a departmental or an interagency one.

10. Moynihan himself grew up in a single-parent family during part of his childhood, although his father deserted the family for reasons other than unemployment and family finances. However, the family was solidly middle class, and his mother remarried later. Even as a single-parent family, it was poor only a short time. Many observers have noted this personal familial fact about Moynihan, but as far as I know, no one ever asked him whether and how this affected his writing, in the Report and elsewhere, about poor single-parent families.

11. Moynihan was here judging a normal adaptation as deviant, but later he coined and often resorted to the phrase "defining deviance down," to criticize those who treated what he thought was deviant as normal or acceptable.

12. Interestingly enough, Moynihan cited only a paragraph of Pettigrew's nine pages in the Report.

13. I suspect Moynihan used pathology as a replacement for social disorganization, the term initially employed by the Chicago School of sociology to describe conditions deviating from WASP middle-class norms among Chicago's poor immigrants. Frazier was a member of that school and thus resorted to the phrase to describe the black family in the Frazier quotation that Moynihan (1967) included at

the end of the Report (p. 94). Moynihan may not have known that the phrase fell into disrepute long before he wrote the Report, when community researchers and others (Whyte 1943) showed that poor communities were organized differently than middle-class ones. This is not to say that poor communities were not also disorganized. However, the Chicago sociologists used social disorganization vaguely and promiscuously. If they or anyone else thought about specific and concrete proxies for community disorganization—such as miscommunication, incompetence, corruption, dysfunctional divisions of responsibility and labor, for example—poor communities likely would have been more disorganized than better-off ones.

14. Moynihan took the tangle of pathology metaphor from Kenneth Clark's (1965) *Dark Ghetto*, although Clark used it only a couple of times to describe the interaction between individual and community pathology. More often he wrote about individual and social pathologies, as well as multiple ones, and he found pathology even in the "gilded suburban *ghetto*" (p. 108). Although *Dark Ghetto* reads like a scholarly study, Clark (1965) pointed out at its beginning that the book was not a "report . . . but rather the anguished cry of its author" (p. xx).

15. A further six dealt with unemployment and single-parent family relationships, three with black fertility, and six with school performance-related data. The remainder were mostly background demographic information.

16. The analysis was so named because the decline of joblessness and the rise of AFDC applications were diverging like an open scissors. For the definitive critique of the scissors analysis, see O'Connor (2001, pp. 205–206).

17. Lewis's self-perpetuating mechanism was a set of values he noticed among young children, but Lewis had no data about whether the adults' behavior reflected the childhood values that Lewis saw, especially in communities which offered these adults the opportunity to escape poverty.

18. Moynihan later invited Lewis to join his year-long seminar on poverty, held under the auspices of the American Academy of Arts and Sciences. Lewis prepared a concise statement of the culture of poverty for the seminar volume (Lewis 1968), but Moynihan's discussion of the Lewis chapter in his introduction to the volume (Moynihan 1968) was carefully neutral.

19. Since Moynihan had already planned to resign his post to stand for a New York City Council election, he might not then have developed as much emotional investment in the Report—its tone notwithstanding—as he did later when it and he were criticized so strongly.

20. Why the Report did not include such proposals remains unclear. However, even before Moynihan had finished the Report, President Johnson had already indicated that little money would be available for the War on Poverty, and perhaps Moynihan's superiors at the Labor Department did not want to antagonize the White House by proposing costly programs. Nonetheless, Moynihan's (1965) *Daedalus* article was mainly about the unemployment and related economic problems

of the poor black population, and devoted only a couple of pages to what he now called "The Ordeal of the Negro Family." However, he managed to include most of his Report argument about black family instability and illegitimacy, including his description of the self-perpetuating pathology and the "scissors" analyses. Since the *Daedalus* article and the Report were written about the same time, it is worth speculating whether Moynihan should have used the former—with its emphasis on joblessness as the Department of Labor report; and the latter, with its emphasis on the poor black single-parent family, as the *Daedalus* article. Since that journal is written for and mainly read by an academic audience, such a switch might have reduced the public criticism leveled at Moynihan for his observations about black family pathology.

21. In 2009, Moynihan's close friend James Q. Wilson, remembering his many years of discussion with him, wrote: "You might wonder what Pat Moynihan thought should be done about the family problem. He didn't know . . ." (J. Wilson 2009, p. 32).

References

Clark, Kenneth B. 1965. *The Dark Ghetto: Dilemmas of Social Power.* New York: Harper and Row.

Cohen, Patricia. 2010. 'Culture of Poverty' Makes a Comeback. *New York Times,* October 18, A1.

Drake, St. Clair and Horace R. Cayton. 1945. *Black Metropolis: A Study of Negro Life in a Northern City.* New York: Harper and Row.

Frazier, E. Franklin. 1939. *The Negro Family in the United States.* Chicago, IL: University of Chicago Press.

Gans, Herbert J. 1965. The Negro Family: Reflections on the 'Moynihan Report.' *Commonweal,* 83: 47–51.

Glazer, Nathan. 1963. Introduction. In Stanley Elkins, *Slavery: A Problem in American Institutional and Intellectual Life,* pp. ix–xvi. New York: Grosset & Dunlap.

Glazer, Nathan and Daniel P. Moynihan. 1963. *Beyond the Melting Pot.* Cambridge, MA: MIT Press.

Heckman, James J. 2011. A Post-Racial Strategy for Improving Skills to Promote Equality. *Daedalus,* 140(2): 70–89.

Hodgson, Godfrey. 2000. *The Gentleman from New York: Daniel Patrick Moynihan—A Biography.* Boston, MA: Houghton Mifflin.

Lemann, Nicholas. 1991. *The Promised Land: The Great Black Migration and How It Changed America.* New York: Random House.

Lewis, Oscar. 1959. *Five Families: Mexican Case Studies in the Culture of Poverty.* New York: Basic Books.

Lewis, Oscar. 1968. The Culture of Poverty. In Daniel P. Moynihan (Ed.), *On Understanding Poverty: Perspectives from the Social Sciences*, pp. 187–200. New York: Basic Books.

Massey, Douglas S. and Robert J Sampson. 2009. Moynihan Redux: Legacies and Lessons. In The Moynihan Report Revisited: Lessons and Reflections after Four Decades. *Annals of the American Academy of Political and Social Science*, 621: 6–27.

Moynihan, Daniel P. 1965. Employment, Income and the Ordeal of the Negro Family. *Daedalus*, 94(4): 134–159.

Moynihan, Daniel P. 1967. The Moynihan Report: The Negro Family: The Case for National Action. In Lee Rainwater and William L. Yancey, *The Moynihan Report and the Politics of Controversy*, pp. 39–124. Cambridge, MA: MIT Press.

Moynihan, Daniel P. (Ed.) 1968. *On Understanding Poverty: Perspectives from the Social Sciences*. New York: Basic Books.

Moynihan, Daniel P., Timothy M. Smeeding, and Lee Rainwater (Eds.) 2004. *The Future of the Family*. New York: Russell Sage Foundation.

O'Connor, Alice. 2001. *Poverty Knowledge: Social Science, Social Policy, and the Poor in Twentieth-Century U.S. History*. Princeton, NJ: Princeton University Press.

Patterson, James T. 2010. *Freedom Is Not Enough: The Moynihan Report and America's Struggle over Black Family Life—from LBJ to Obama*. New York: Basic Books.

Patterson, Orlando. 2006. A Poverty of the Mind. *New York Times*, March 26.

Pettigrew, Thomas F. 1964. *A Profile of the Negro-American*. Princeton, NJ: Van Nostrand.

Rainwater, Lee and William L. Yancey. 1967. *The Moynihan Report and the Politics of Controversy*. Cambridge, MA: MIT Press.

Ryan, William. 1971. *Blaming the Victim*. New York: Random House.

Small, Mario, David J. Harding, and Michele Lamont. 2010. Introduction: Reconsidering Culture and Poverty. *Annals of the American Academy of Political and Social Science*, 629: 6–27.

Steinfels, Peter. 1979. *The Neoconservatives: The Men Who Are Changing America's Politics*. New York: Simon and Schuster.

Weisman, Steven K. 2010. *Daniel Patrick Moynihan: A Portrait in Letters of an American Visionary*. New York: Public Affairs.

Whyte, William F. Jr. 1943. *Street Corner Society*. Chicago, IL: University of Chicago Press.

Wilson, James Q. 2009. Pat Moynihan Thinks About Families. *The Annals of the American Academy of Political and Social Science*, 621: 28–33.

Wilson, William J. 1987. *The Truly Disadvantaged: The Inner City, the Underclass, and Public Policy*. Chicago, IL: University of Chicago Press.

Wilson, William J. 2009a. The Moynihan Report and Research on the Black Community. *The Annals of the American Academy of Political and Social Science*, 621: 34–46.

Wilson, William J. 2009b. *More Than Just Race: Being Black and Poor in the Inner City*. New York: Norton.

PART FIVE

ETHNICITY

Although some sociologists believe that there are no differences between race and ethnicity, I think the concepts describe very different social realities. People can change or shed their ethnicity but not their race.

In the two chapters of part 5, the descendants of the European immigrants I first wrote about in chapter 14 have, like the descendants of most other newcomers, been almost completely acculturated, i.e., Americanized.

They have also been assimilated, i.e., accepted by nonethnic groups, organizations, and institutions. Although some ethnic groups achieve that status faster than others, it is usually close to complete by the third generation, after which most ethnicity researchers usually stop studying them.

However, I have long been curious about what happens to them subsequently, and chapters 16 and 17 report on subsequent generations whom I describe as late-generation ethnics.

Chapter 16 describes what I see as the last stages of their ethnicity, while chapter 17 speculates on when and how that ethnicity will disappear completely. The immigrants who have been coming here since 1965 will probably follow the same path to Americanization, but many of those with darker skin may not be accepted by non–ethnic America.

Both articles briefly mention the religious institutions the European immigrants brought with them. They have been similarly Americanized but, as chapter 17 points out, some late-generation ethnics are giving up religion as well. In this respect, too, they are like other Americans, about a fifth of whom—and a third of young ones—now say they belong to no religion.

Perhaps the sociologies of ethnicity and religion will soon have to come closer to each other.

The Coming Darkness of Late-Generation European-American Ethnicity

Introduction

In 1985, Richard Alba published a book about Italian Americans subtitled *Into the Twilight of Ethnicity*. He was writing about the third and fourth generations of the Italian immigrants who arrived in America between about 1870 and 1924, but the same book could have been written about the other European populations who came across the Atlantic during the same period.

Now, twenty-eight years after the appearance of Alba's volume, their descendants are of the fifth and maybe even sixth generation. They are sometimes called later-generation ethnics (LGEs hereafter) and their ethnicity, which has so far been little studied, deserves further research.

A review of the major and some minor ethnic journals and a 'Quick Search' of the many databases at Columbia University's library using the phrase 'fourth-generation ethnicity' found very few citations. Since I wanted to focus solely on ethnicity, I purposely omitted citations about ethnoreligious populations, for example, Jews and Greeks for whom religious membership helps keep late-generation ethnicity alive.

My search suggested two basic hypotheses: first, late-generation European ethnicity has virtually disappeared or at least is no longer visible; and second, researchers have more or less stopped studying the descendants of the European immigration, and paid only minimal attention to the newest European immigrants who arrived here in the last half century. Perhaps both hypotheses are relevant; but more important for my purpose, they suggest many other interesting and important questions for future study, some of which are described below.

That the old European ethnicity may be becoming invisible is almost true by definition. By now the descendants of that immigration are far enough removed from their immigrant ancestors in time, place, and social space that most probably do not even know their names.

More important, by now three or more generations of interethnic intermarriage have taken place, and today's young LGEs may have grandparents with half a dozen or more ethnic or multi-ethnic origins.[1] As a result, they have so many ethnic options (Waters 1990) that choosing one or two is impossible and choosing none may be the easiest solution.

Whatever is left of their ethnicity, whether as practice or identity, is likely to be dominated by some material or non-material symbols from the past that stand for the real and imagined ethnicity of their ancestors. Indeed, if ethnicity of any kind is of interest to the LGEs, it would either be a family tradition or an ethnic symbol, probably in an Americanized version.

Thus, if symbolic ethnicity survives (Gans 1979), it is likely to be heavily nostalgic. At the same time, however, ethnicity has turned into an increasingly widespread source of diversion for ever more Americans—or at least those people who enjoy exercising a large variety of ethnic restaurant options. Whether and how they feel ethnic might make for an interesting study.

Late-Generation Ethnicity

In order to look for and at ethnicity among the LGEs, one can distinguish between (1) ethnic structure: the formal and informal organizations and institutions that conduct literal and figurative ethnic business; (2) private ethnic practice: the familial and other primary group rituals, routines, and other activities; and (3) ethnic identity: whether, when, where, and how people perceive themselves as ethnics and how they feel and express this identity.

Ethnic Organizations

Formal ethnic organizations and institutions are the most visible evidence of ethnicity's persistence, and even simple Googling reveals lists of national, regional, and local organizations for every European population that arrived in the United States between 1870 and 1924—and even before then. Informal organizations, from social and card-playing clubs to family circles, if any such still exist among LGEs, are surely more numerous, but they will be visible only to empirical researchers, particularly ethnographers, studying the communities where their members live.

Even the formal organizations call for close empirical study, since some lack offices and are merely phone numbers, while others are kept alive by a handful of people. These may be LGEs, so-called ethnic converts (Kelly 1996), including white Anglo Saxon Protestants (WASPs) who have married LGEs, and other LGEs who have made professional careers or avocations devoted to keeping ethnic organizations alive. Most likely they will also include recent European newcomers, some of whom may have altered these organizations to fit their own ethnic and acculturative requirements.

My Googling suggests that these organizations fall into four types—promotional, commercial, performing, and preserving—although some may combine two or more of these functions. Promotional organizations publicize and keep visible the ethnic population, its ethnicity, and the label by which the population is known. They may also include social clubs that promote the ethnicity simply by being so labeled. Other promotional organizations may defend that population against stereotyping, stigmatization, and discrimination.

Commercial organizations are businesses that sell a variety of ethnic products and symbols such as foods, holiday paraphernalia, and arts and crafts, some of them especially to tourists. Ethnic food manufacturers and distributors remain numerous, although some produce foods for several ethnic tastes. Others, particularly large corporate firms, produce and sell ethnic foods such as bagels and pizza that have become part of mainstream nonethnic fare.

Performing organizations primarily hold festivals, many of them annual, with programmes of folk dances, ethnic music, theatre pieces, and the like. Most are labeled traditional, although some offer reconstructed and newly constructed tradition. For example, the stores of Lindsborg, Kansas, which calls itself 'Little Sweden USA,' offer visitors an 'Adventure in Swedish Tradition' (Schnell 2003).

Many of the performing organizations seek to attract tourists, whether LGEs and other ethnics curious about their ethnic pasts, or visitors looking for something new and different to entertain the kids. Who offers what versions of an ethnic past or present to what kinds of audiences is a worthwhile topic of study, including for sociologists of tourism (Wood 1998).

Although all of the organizations aim to preserve one or another component of their ethnicity, the preserving organizations are mainly concerned with saving the arts, literature, scholarship, and other forms of the ethnic culture—higher rather than popular, and past more than present. Often the culture to be preserved is in a version of its initial immigration form; second-, third- and later-generation American representations of that culture may not offer the desired nostalgic ethnicity.

Preserving organizations take many forms: language classes, ethnic studies enterprises, community centres, as well as university teaching and research centres and museums. The educational preservation organizations often seek to encourage future ethnic literacy and sometimes simply to preserve the language among whoever wants to learn it. A number receive support and subsidies from the European countries whose Americanized structures and cultures they are preserving.

Other surviving institutions with ethnic features include industries that have long been dominated by one or maybe two ethnic groups and that have been profitable enough for LGEs to remain in them—even though they do not necessarily produce ethnic goods or services. Some are low-status occupations and industries that immigrants moved into as laborers perhaps because no one else would do such work, such as garbage removal. LGEs may still dominate them, but now as owners and managers.

Some are prestigious enterprises with creative or well-paid jobs, the most visible being the entertainment industry. This industry remains heavily Eastern European Jewish, although many of its contemporary workers only identify as Jews.

Private Ethnic Practices

LGE organizations with ethnic identifiers are at least visible on Google, and so are storefronts selling ethnic goods and services. However, private LGE practices, which would normally be found in families, other primary groups, and networks, are nearly invisible. Empirical researchers need to find them and their participants; not an easy task since almost all are scattered in physical and social space, as well as cyberspace.

By practices I mean at-home and micro-social activities and actions, many of them occasional, including rituals but also some routines. Practices require tools, and therefore also the toolkits in Swidler's (1986) metaphorical definition of culture—as well as the material and symbolic objects associated with both practices and tools. These become ethnic practices if the people practicing them think of them as ethnic, or connect them to the ways of earlier ancestors, or if they can be identified as such by researchers.

Research projects on ethnic practices may end up with many negative findings, for LGEs may retain few, if any, practices that fit my definition of ethnic ones. These are apt to be family habits associated with foods and cooking or other shared activities, the recital of family and children's stories, as well as favorite words and phrases left over from the language that the immigrants brought with them. These words could even be ethnic first or pet names.

Some practices require literal tools of immigrant or derivative immigrant origin, including ethnic objects. Among these are history and cookbooks, family heirlooms, ancestral photographs, letters, and other keepsakes from earlier generations.

Most practices will be occasional activities, some perhaps associated with religious and secular holidays or with familial anniversaries. Moreover, these practices will frequently be Americanized versions of the immigrant original, perhaps derived from those created by the second or third generations.

Since most LGEs are by now multi-ethnic, researchers might find an array of practices that were handed down by ancestors of different ethnic origin. An LGE family of Irish-Italian-German-Polish ancestry might have preserved an interesting mix of such practices and may not even remember their ethnic origin.[2]

Organizational ethnic practices should also be studied. Most relevant to study would be which of the four types of ethnic organizations use what practices, tools, objects, and symbols, and from what generations. However, researchers might also discover organizations that do without ethnic practices, seeking only to attract people who identify with, or are curious about, the organization's ethnicity. Social or card-playing clubs are most likely to fall into this category, unless the card (or other) games are of ethnic origin. In any case, there is much to study.

Ethnic Identity

Symbolic ethnicity came into being in part to express an ethnic identity and to feel ethnic, but occasions for feeling ethnic, whether voluntary or involuntary, are fewer than before. Involuntary ones are especially rare, because LGEs are not often identified as such and are therefore rarely asked about their ancestry.

Nonetheless, at that time, many of the descendants of European immigrants, including LGEs, still labeled themselves by national origin. For example, while the country's Swedish immigrant population numbered only about 50,000 in 2000, about four million people described their ancestry as Swedish (Blanck 2009).

Identity is easier to turn on and off than the rest of ethnicity and is likely to endure longer after ethnic practices are forgotten. Identity can even be recalled suddenly. An LGE of long-ago Italian American ancestry could feel momentarily Italian if an athlete with an Italian name breaks a record, and someone of past Polish ancestry might feel that way about a media celebration of *kielbasa*.

An ethnic identity can also be re-established if it useful economically, socially, or politically. Such occasions are rarer these days, including in politics, where a big-city 'balanced ticket' no longer consists of European-origin ethnics, but instead consists of a black, a Latino, and perhaps an Asian candidate in addition to a white one.

Discrimination continues to evoke identity feelings, but with racial discrimination, particularly towards African Americans, remaining pervasive, ethnic discriminatory incidents are slowly becoming extinct in most places. Some stereotypes remain, such as the *mafioso* one associated with Italian Americans, and Polish jokes may still be told privately, but openly hostile ones have been excised from mainstream popular culture. The now almost-instant protest against the public mentions of racial, ethnic, and religious slurs and stereotypes has only hastened this and other excisions.

Research about ethnic identity can be combined with study of ethnic practices, as long as researchers make sure that they talk also with people who no longer participate in any practices. Whether and how often people feel ethnic, and what occasions bring it on, is the primary research topic, but since most LGEs will have several identity options, which one or ones are invoked and when also needs to be studied. If ethnicity is an enjoyable leisure-time activity, some LGEs might find ways to exercise all their options.

Even so, researchers must always bear in mind that ethnicity is only one facet of identity, and probably always was, except when it was attached to an important role. Current such roles include doing ethnic work, engaging in ethnic activism, and teaching or researching ethnicity. But for many ethnics it was generally a minor identity facet unless they were being stereotyped or discriminated against.

Disappearing European Ethnicity

The preceding mixture of hypothesis, observation, and occasional research findings suggests that, to follow Alba's metaphor, darkness is enveloping late-generation European ethnicity. Most LGEs are already or will soon be like all other Americans, the descendants of long-ago—and often forgotten—immigrants. As already noted, their ethnic identity or identities will be remembered and perhaps even felt and expressed when the situation demands it, but even these situations will eventually disappear.

After all, what the European immigrants took with them to America over a century ago, and even what their children and grandchildren maintained, reconstructed, or invented, is not relevant for life in the twenty-first century. Only the so-called motherhood values, such as the importance of family, the virtue of hard work, honesty, and the like, which every immigrant population thought it had invented and brought to America, remain—and these values are clearly not ethnic.

Ethnic institutions and organizations may survive longer, particularly commercial ones, notably those serving tourist curiosity about their and others' past ethnicities. However, once established, such organizations can be run and staffed by people without a related ethnic bone in their body.[3] Preserving organizations should also survive, at least if they can be perpetuated with little money (or by people with lots of money). They could even remain when all others are gone.[4]

In short, sufficient late-generation European ethnicity will exist long enough to deserve continued attention. Despite all the drawbacks of generational analysis, the ethnic paths followed and abandoned by each generation should be investigated, to determine what patterns and lines, now of decline and disappearance rather than acculturation and assimilation, can be found.

Even more important, what is held on to until the very end needs study. Such research should be conducted especially among the very late generations, for example among Scandinavians, Germans, and other Northern Europeans still living in or near places in which their immigrant ancestors settled. Nonetheless, researchers should also look for once socially and spatially isolated ethnic enclaves, which, or fragments of which, have remained in acculturated form (e.g. Hannan 2005). These enclaves may provide case studies of the long-term processes that drive the rise and fall of ethnic communities and their populations.

The Possibilities of Replenishment

Although congressional legislation terminated the turn of last century European immigration in 1924, the new waves of immigrants that arrived after 1965 have included people from the same countries, and in some cases even from the same region. Thus, in 2000, the U.S. census reported that the country's population included nearly half a million foreign-born from both Italy and Poland, over 300,000 from Russia, nearly as many from Ukraine, about 150,000 each from Greece and Romania, and around 100,000 each from Hungary, the Czech Republic, and Holland.

Although these recent immigrant newcomers and their children deserve far more research attention than they have so far received, for the purpose of this paper, two research questions have priority. One is whether and how any of these newcomers have replenished the ethnic structures and cultures of the earlier immigration, particularly whether they have they revived, strengthened, or taken over and reprogrammed LGE organizations and institutions. The second question is whether the newcomers have motivated, encouraged, or pressured their LGE predecessors to return to at least some of the old ways (Jimenez 2009).

The likelihood that either kind of replenishment has taken place is small; in fact, conflict between old and new is as likely as cooperation (Erdmans 1995). The newcomers often differ from the LGEs in age, class, and other ways, so that they have almost nothing in common, other than perhaps nominal national origin.[5] In addition, the countries left by the newest immigrants are very different from those remembered by the LGEs. As one of Erdmans' (1995, 180) Polish newcomers to Chicago put it: "Everyone here's having polka parties. In Poland, no one polkas."

Also, the newcomers do not live in the America of the LGEs, nor in the same neighborhoods even if they have settled in the same cities. In addition, their organizational activities, private practices, and identity expressions will differ from those remaining among the LGEs.

Consequently, it is also doubtful that the new immigrants have persuaded the LGEs to reverse their acculturation and re-embrace old ethnic activities, practices, and identities. However, researchers should also find out if the LGEs have persuaded any newcomers to move out of the immigrant enclaves and other structures that they have established, thereby hastening their acculturation and assimilation. Perhaps the children of these newcomers are already learning about symbolic ways of being ethnic.

The Case of Asian and Latino Newcomers

Last but not least, researchers can ask, as many are already doing, whether the descendants of the Asian, Latino, and other non-European immigrants who have arrived here since 1965 will follow the same acculturative and assimilatory processes and patterns as the Europeans who arrived between 1870 and 1924.

It is worth remembering that acculturation and assimilation are terms invented by immigration researchers and other social scientists to describe universal social processes of adaptation and incorporation. Whether undertaken by immigrants getting settled here or by graduate students transitioning to assistant professorships, both have to acculturate in order to function in their new surroundings.

Assimilation also requires informal or formal entry permits from organizations or other groups being entered, which is harder than acculturating, for example, for immigrants seeking entry into a weak labor market, or into social organizations that deem them ineligible. Dark-skinned immigrants are barred from many opportunities for assimilation by racial discrimination.

The post-1965 immigration waves that have now continued for nearly fifty years differ significantly in race, class, and geographic origins from the Europeans who are now LGEs. For example, they include all the skin colors into which white America divides phenotypes. A significant proportion are professionals, technicians, and skilled blue-collar workers, while many of today's poor immigrants, especially from the western hemisphere, are undocumented and therefore frequently persecuted and prosecuted.

Furthermore, the current waves of newcomers may have grown up with exported American popular culture and other American practices. As a result, they may end up acculturating more quickly and completely than the ancestors of the LGEs.

Consequently, it is likely that the descendants of many if not most Asian and Latino Americans will eventually follow the same paths as the LGEs. Asians are becoming English-only speakers as quickly as third-generation Europeans (Alba et al. 2002) and are taking to American schooling more successfully than many native-born students (Louie 2004; Kasinitz et al. 2008).

Second-generation Asian and Latino Americans are already marrying whites at unprecedented rates, and then children and grandchildren will be "whitened" or deracialized in much the same way as the Europeans (Gans 2012).

Thus, decades hence, many descendants of the last half-century's immigration will be behaving, thinking, and feeling much like today's LGEs. However, all or at least most other things must remain equal, particularly that they will be needed by and therefore allowed into the mainstream economy and the mainstream middle classes in much the same way as the ancestors of current LGEs.

Conclusion

I need to repeat that in the absence of significant research on the fourth and later generations, one can only hypothesize. Moreover, while it is possible that European ethnicity would eventually disappear, it can also reappear. In a global economy, patterns of immigration are no longer as predictable as in the past. While another large European immigration to America seems unlikely, a combination of European economic disasters and pressure from politically influential white Americans who want to enlarge the white population could someday bring a new set of Europeans to America. But this time, they would not be brought in steerage.

Acknowledgments

Richard Alba made helpful comments on an earlier draft of this paper.

Notes

Reprinted from *Ethic and Racial Studies*, vol. 37, no. 5, 2014, by permission of Taylor & Francis Group.

1. Alba (1990) found that almost 85 percent of the immigrants in the Albany New York region that he surveyed were intermarried.

2. Travellers to Spain or Latin America occasionally encounter Catholics and others who light candles on Friday nights as a family tradition, unaware that they may be carrying on Jewish practices of their Spanish ancestors who were forcibly converted many hundreds of years ago.

3. Informal fieldwork suggests that the cooks in many Manhattan ethnic restaurants, whatever their ethnic menus, are currently Mexican or other Latino immigrants.

4. Endowed tenured professorships in ethnic studies, especially ethnic history, may outlast every other ethnic institution.

5. Remember that the boundaries of many of today's European nations differ from those existing at the turn of the last century, and some had only recently become nations when their emigrants left for the United States.

References

Alba, R. 1985. *Italian Americans: Into the Twilight of Ethnicity.* Englewood Cliffs, NJ: Prentice Hall.

Alba, R. 1990. *Ethnic Identity: The Transformation of White America.* New Haven, CT: Yale University Press.

Alba, R., J. Logan, A. Lutz, and B. Stults. 2002. Only English by the Third Generation: Loss and Preservation of the Mother Tongue among the Grandchildren of Contemporary Immigrants. *Demography* 39 (3): 467–484. doi:10.1353/dem.2002.0023.

Blanck, D. 2009. "Swedish Immigration to North America." Rock Island, IL: Augustana College. Accessed July 29. http://www.augustana.edu/xl4897.xml

Erdmans, M. 1995. Immigrants and Ethnics: Conflict and Identity in Chicago Polonia. *Sociological Quarterly* 36 (1): 175–195. doi: 10.1111/j.1533-8525.1995.tb02326.x.

Gans, H. 1979. Symbolic Ethnicity. *Ethnic and Racial Studies* 2 (1): 1–20. doi:10.1080/01419870.1979.9993248.

Gans, H. 2012. 'Whitening' and the Changing American Racial Hierarchy. *Du Bois Review* 9 (2): 267–279. doi:30.1017/S1742058X12000288.

Hannan, K. 2005. Refashioning Ethnicity in Czech-Moravian Texas. *Journal of American Ethnic History* 26 (1): 31–60.

Jimenez, T. 2009. *Replenished Ethnicity: Mexican-Americans, Immigration and Identity.* Berkeley, CA: University of California Press.

Kasinitz, P., J. Mollenkopf, M. Waters, and J. Holdaway. 2008. *Inheriting the City: The Children of the Immigrants Come of Age.* Cambridge, MA: Harvard University Press.

Kelly, M. 1996. Ethnic Conversions: Family, Community, Women, and Kinwork. *Ethnic Studies Review* 19 (1): 81–100.

Louie, V. 2004. *Compelled to Excel: Immigration, Education and Opportunity among Chinese Americans.* Stanford, CA: Stanford University Press.

Schnell, S. 2003. Creating Narratives of Place and Identity in 'Little Sweden, USA.'" *Geographical Review* 93 (1): 1–29.

Swidler, A. 1986. Culture in Action: Symbols and Strategies. *American Sociological Review* 51 (2): 273–285. doi: 10.2307/2095521.

Waters, M. 1990. *Ethnic Options: Choosing Identities in America.* Berkeley, CA: University of California Press.

Wood, R. 1998. Touristic Ethnicity: A Brief Itinerary. *Ethnic and Racial Studies* 21 (2): 218–241. doi: 10.1080/014198798329991.

CHAPTER 17

The End of Late-Generation European Ethnicity in America?

American immigration scholars have paid little attention to the possibility that ethnicity could someday end, although it has been doing so since the first immigrants arrived in this country and became colonials and later Americans. In the process they eventually also became what I will call native-borns, who think of themselves solely as Americans.

Currently, the ending process has been going on among the descendants of the European immigration that took place between the 1870s and 1924: the people described here as late-generation ethnics (LGEs hereafter). By now, many and perhaps most are the product of several generations of ethnic intermarriage; have little memory, if any, of their immigrant origins; and have not made any use of the ethnic social structures and cultures of their ancestors. Some will retain what I call a terminal identity for a yet unknown period.

What holds for the users of ethnic structures and cultures also holds for the suppliers, the various organizations, agencies, commercial firms, and other social bodies that supplied the practices, symbols, and other social raw materials for LGEs and earlier generations. A few will survive as long as some constituents, audiences, and customers still come, and then find new opportunities or also close up shop.

Ending Theories

The first modern assimilation theorists were busy studying the changes in the lives of immigrants and of the next generation. Thus, they had no reason to think about whether what came to be called ethnicity would ever end. However, they apparently all assumed that the people they were studying would eventually become Americans, and in the process suggested several possible ending theories, although almost entirely by implication.

One theory, associated particularly with Robert Park, was amalgamation, which suggested that the immigrants would, through intermarriage, join or fuse with the by now long-term native-borns (e.g., Park 1914). That theory survives in today's notion that the immigrants and their descendants have helped to transform the previously dominant Anglo-Saxon Protestant mainstream even as it transformed them.

A second theory, which originated in the eighteenth century, proposed that eventually the descendants of the newcomers and earlier native-borns would melt into a single exceptional American who embodied all the positive qualities of all the people, or at least of all whites who had come to America since it became a nation. In its most famous formulation, by the playwright Israel Zangwill (1909), these populations were immersed in a melting pot that eradicated all the distinguishing characteristics of those who found themselves in the metaphorical pot.

The third theory, by Warner and Srole (1945), indirectly forecast an end to ethnicity. In developing their generational model of assimilation, the two sociologists created a timetable consisting of three criteria, the first of which was "the time it takes for an entire group to disappear" (Warner and Srole 1945, 289).[1]

The flowering of empirical social science research and publication opportunities after the Second World War increased the number of researchers with an investment in ethnicity and no incentive to consider its ending. Then came the so-called ethnic revival of the 1960s and the beginning of the post-1965 immigration. Many researchers turned their attention to the latest arrivals and from then on, but with some notable exceptions (e.g., Alba 1990; Steinberg 2001; Waters 1990), the later-generation descendants of the European immigration were virtually ignored. Nonetheless, even before the end of the twentieth century, it seemed likely that the LGEs themselves had disappeared or would eventually do so. Languages and cultures have always become extinct, although we associate extinctions with pre-literal tribes, without recognizing that they also happen in developed societies.

The people whom Alba (1985) described as being in the twilight of ethnicity had inherited too many ancestries through intermarriage or no longer found ethnicity to be relevant to their lives. One generation later, their children, whom I described as entering the coming darkness of ethnicity (Gans 2014), may still have displayed an occasional interest in a symbolic or other ethnic activity or two. However, as they or their children encounter fewer and fewer like-minded others, and the suppliers of ethnicity shrink and then close their doors, their ethnicity will eventually become extinct. To be sure, later immigration waves of the same national origin will maintain their own version of that ethnicity until they too turn into LGEs and repeat the extinction process.

Still, even the total disappearance of the current LGEs may take a quite a while. Although they will no longer be visible on the national scene, a few will survive locally everywhere, perhaps even into the tenth generation, such as the Germans, Scandinavians, and others who began to arrive in the United States about 160 years ago. Subsequently, when any evidence of late-generation ethnic social and cultural life is gone, material remains of one kind or another will be preserved. Some ethnic art works, artefacts, books, and other memorabilia will be acquired by general museums and nationalized to become part of the national museum culture.

Terminal Ethnic Identity

Perhaps the most interesting final stage of late-generation ethnicity (LGE hereafter) will be an individual one. Even after LGEs have given up all other manifestations of ethnicity, some, perhaps only a small proportion, will maintain a sporadic or occasional identity. The expression of that identity will usually be only of momentary length, and also will probably be a terminal one.

I think of terminal ethnic identity as a partially self-constructed one that people can create on their own from a variety of social sources. It might be *invoked*, perhaps as a sudden remembrance of a favorite ancestor or the memory of a treasured ethnic ceremony. More often, however, terminal ethnic identity is likely to be *evoked* by events, such as meeting a co-ethnic childhood friend, or the celebration of an anniversary, whether of an ancestor or a long-ago co-ethnic leader. Since terminal identities are personal creations, the evoking incident could even be a Hollywood actor playing a co-ethnic hero in an action movie.

Whether invoked or evoked, stimuli for the terminal ethnic identity are apt to be situated in the past, and more often than not will be nostalgic. Conversely, LGEs who still bear identifiable ethnic names and are therefore so identified by strangers might be reminded of past discriminatory episodes or old stereotypes involving their ethnicities. In fact, ethnic groups that are racialized or discriminated against on religious or other grounds often develop a defensive identity that persists into and beyond LGE. It can survive the ending of most other expressions of LGE, and can lead to continuing reminders of possible discriminatory threats.

Not only is the terminal ethnic identity socially constructed out of old materials, but it has to be socially shared to some extent; that is, individual terminal identities must make sense to co-ethnics, and perhaps also to others. If it were purely individual, persons mentioning it would be looked at askance and thought of, or even shunned, as eccentrics.

In 1991, Bakalian described an early version of the terminal ethnic identity when she wrote:

> For American-born generations, Armenian is a preference and Armenianness is a state of mind. . . . One can say he or she is an Armenian without speaking Armenian, marrying an Armenian, doing business with Armenians, belonging to an Armenian church, joining Armenian voluntary associations or participating in the events and activities sponsored by such organizations. (Bakalian 1991, as quoted in Nagel 1994, 154.)

Studying the End of LGE

Endings are not easy to study, since they are only apparent ex post facto once the object of study has disappeared. Endings are also not cheerful objects of study, unless they are the endings of evils, like wars or poverty. Perhaps that is one reason why sociology has neglected the topic; even the sociology of death seems to have vanished from the discipline's research agenda. In fact, there may be an unwritten scholarly taboo against considering the end of what one has been studying and the field or sub-field in which one has made a career. But then almost no one wants to think about going out of business.

These obstacles notwithstanding, the end of LGE can be studied, since it is likely to occur eventually in many of the places where ethnic populations, practices, institutions, and organizations are in the process of disappearing.[2] Interviews, including of panels, as well as ethnographic and community study methods would enable researchers to observe the terminal stages of ethnicity and its various components. Interviews in communities in which LGE is known to be declining could be done to learn whether, when, and how the individual, familial, and communal ending process begins. In which generation does it begin and end, and what sets off the decline: intermarriage, the birth of children, upward or residential mobility, or what? Which LGEs leave their ethnicity behind earliest and who is slowest and why? What ethnic components are given up first and which persevere the longest? Or does ethnicity end without anyone paying special attention or even noticing it?

Similar kinds of questions could be asked at the organizational and communal level. In addition, one would want to know whether organizations and cultures look for ways to postpone endings, and whether they find or invent special rituals to mark endings when they are near or actually come. Also, one can ask which LGEs maintain some organizational or cultural connections until the end, the most loyal ethnics, or the loneliest ones who meet their social needs in organizations. Do the last people on the ethnic ship seek to save themselves, and how; do the survivors mourn, and do their activities resemble other kinds of mourning?

Even if no traces of ethnicity are left, researchers should look for evidence of what might be called post-terminal behavior. They could investigate the possible presence of LGEs in activities and organizations of co-ethnics who arrived after 1965; they should also consider the possibility that some LGEs join or invent pan-ethnic groups, such as all-Scandinavian or all-Slavic ones.[3] Commercial enterprises are more flexible than social or cultural organizations, and can easily reinvent themselves as pan-ethnic. If Scandinavian restaurants exist in the community, researchers can find out if they were once Danish or Swedish or Norwegian. The same strategy can be followed in studying pan-ethnic fairs and festivals, although in many communities, LGE and pan-ethnic festivals may be taken over by nonethnic commercial firms.

Studies can also be done in other commercial firms. The products of ethnic food companies are frequently absorbed into the mainstream diet long before LGE, but one can ask whether and how long originally ethnic foods survive the demise of the ethnic group menu from which they were taken. Sicilian-style pizza will surely survive until long after Sicilian American LGE has ended, although that pizza will bear no resemblance to the original ethnic product.

Firms that produce popular entertainment act in much the same way. They often introduce ethnic characters and situations while parts of immigrant culture are still alive and can be used to create the ethnic stereotypes that resonate with nonethnic audiences. However, one day a researcher will be able to check to see whether Mafia characters show up on screens even after the Italian American Mafia is long gone.

Another kind of study looks at what mainstream culture retains after the ending of various ethnic groups. For example, researchers could check museums, especially of Americana, folklore, and folk art, but even art museums dedicated to the exhibition of high art, to see whether they have chosen or retained ethnic materials for immortalization as national museum culture, and, if so, which were chosen and rejected, and why.

Research into ethnicity's endings must never forget that America often describes itself as a nation of immigrants. Consequently, descendants of the early arrivals could be asked to discuss whether and how they perceive their long-ago ethnicity and its ending. Those who belong to the Sons/Daughters of the American Revolution and similar organizations, and obtain prestige from celebrating their ancestors, would make especially interesting interviewees.

However, descendants from later and less prestigious immigrations can be interviewed as well. They might also be asked whether and how they have used the now widely available ancestral history data as well as genetic testing results to explore their past ethnicity (Waters 2014). Even people who question or reject the validity or reliability of such data might provide further insights into how ethnicities end.

Studying Terminal Ethnic Identity

Identity is one of too many slippery and difficult-to-operationalize social science concepts with which empirical researchers have to contend. It is also hard to visualize since it operates partly inside people's heads, can be turned on and off easily, and may even lie dormant in mental storage until brought out by a researcher's question.

In the absence of constant and enduring emphasis on ethnic identity, such as the defensive identity that is second nature to members of racial and ethnic groups subject to prejudice, discrimination, and physical attack, LGE identity is apt to be an ephemeral reality. Sometimes, it may even be little more than a label.

For empirical purposes, I think of ethnic identity as a felt connection to a constructed or imagined collectivity, which may or may not resemble an empirically verifiable ethnic collectivity. This conception permits investigating the quality, intensity, and duration of the feeling, the actual or imagined collectivity to which it is attached, and even the kinds of attachment to the collectivity that people construct or imagine for their identity.

As best I can tell, studies of ethnic identity generally assume that all or most ethnics possess an ethnic identity. Consequently, interviewers may ask their respondents their identity. In that case, respondents, other than the offspring of multi-intermarried ancestors, cannot easily deny that they have an ethnic identity even though privately they may think of it as a label attached to them by others.

Instead, LGEs should first be asked whether they have an ethnic identity, but even the question suggests that yes is the publicly desired answer. Telling interviewees that many or most of their generation no longer have such an identity might produce more accurate answers. Probes about the characteristics of that identity must not put ideas—or remembered stereotypes—into interviewees' heads, and they should be asked how often and how intensely they feel their identity.

Ethnic identities are expressed in actions and feelings, but LGEs probably stick almost entirely to feelings. For students of terminal identity, the nature and objects of those feelings, and what invoked or evoked situations produced them, should be a major topic of study. The primary feeling is likely to be ethnic pride. Other typical feelings are pleasure and memory, including nostalgia, but negative feelings may survive too: shame, hate, anger, and remembered injustices among them. The objects towards which such feelings are directed can be legion, enabling researchers to code for types, whether of individuals or collectivities, whether real or imagined, and ancestral or national, among others.

Terminal ethnic identities also need to be studied, but unless researchers chance upon people about to give up those identities, they have to be studied ex post facto. Research in neighborhoods and other places once identified as ethnic might find people who could be asked whether, when, and how they gave up their ethnic identities.[4]

Since researchers distinguish between people's identities and their identification by others, those studying terminal ethnic identities should also check the existence of terminal identifications. LGEs may be identified as ethnics by others after they themselves have stopped invoking or evoking their ethnic identity, but the identification by others may evoke a momentary revival of that identity.

These others can be individuals or organizations, including census, research, and public agencies or commercial firms with interests in or curiosity about LGEs. As students of census research know, questions about ethnicity and even question wording can bring out such momentary revivals, although probably of ethnic labels as often as of ethnic identities.

The Post-1965 Immigration Waves

The above observations and hypotheses should also apply, all other things being equal, to the descendants of the several post-1965 immigration waves when they become LGEs. The stages and processes operating among today's LGEs should be duplicated among the newer immigrants, even though the America into which they are being absorbed differs from that of the earlier European immigrants.

However, since the children of the post-1965 waves are likely to be intermarried earlier than their predecessors, the institutions and practices that their ancestors brought with them may die out faster. Thus, the conditions associated with LGE may begin earlier than it did among the long-ago European immigrants.

These hunches will not apply to future LGEs whom whites have racialized. Although they may have also shed most of their ethnicity, they will retain a racial identity—and a defensive one—as long as they are identified by whites as nonwhites. Whether they are demonized or treated as model minorities, intensive and extensive othering, especially that involving discrimination, will keep defensive racial identities alive. In addition, as the Back to Africa, Black Power, African culture, and other African American movements suggest, racial demonization may also revive old or create new ethnic identities as well as institutions, practices, and symbols.

How long racialized ethnics maintain their racial identity depends largely on the decisions of the white population, at least as long it dominates the country's racial framing process. These decisions are likely to be affected by their feelings about particular nonwhite minorities. Conversely, if current demographic trends—and racial definitions—continue and whites actually become a minority population in mid-century America, they may themselves develop the overt racial identity that they have so far not often sought, wanted, or needed.[5] In that case, America's racial hierarchy—and perhaps its entire racial vocabulary—may change in now unpredictable ways.

Still, whites may continue to "other" nonwhites, and more intensely than before even as they themselves become a racial minority. In that case, whites will probably be more focused on their whiteness, and their ability to hold on to their share of white economic, political, and cultural power.

Even before the post-1965 waves have turned into LGEs, new waves of immigration will have arrived and will continue to arrive. In a global economy and polity, where later waves will come from cannot be predicted. For all we know now, at some point they may once again include large numbers of white Europeans.

Some General Questions

The apparent end of late-generation European ethnicity offers the opportunity to raise four research questions about ethnicity in general.

One question is whether and how the final ethnic melting predicted long ago will take place. Will post-LGEs blend into a single mainstream, or into several, and, if so, how will these differ from each other, culturally, structurally, and of course normatively? More important, will the concept of mainstream still make sense, since white Protestant Americans stopped constituting the major or even sole mainstream long ago? Most important, can the existence and nature of mainstreams be ascertained empirically?

A second question deserving of study pertains to the boundary-setting function of ethnicity and its aftermath (Brubaker 2014; Jenkins 2014). Will ethnicity, particularly white ethnicity, still be used for boundary making or will it be entirely replaced by race, and indirectly by class? One could even ask whether class will finally become a more overt boundary maker. This possibility might be hastened if America continues to become economically yet more unequal, and if America can find an acceptable visible indicator of class position.

Third, the end of LGE justifies asking why turn-of-the-nineteenth-century European ethnicity lasted as long as it did; or to put it another way, why did European national-origin identifications and identities persist through several native-born generations? One might want to ask first, why did America attach national-origin labels to people whose immigrant ancestors often did not know about or wish to be connected with their European country of origin? This research question is all the more interesting because official and unofficial labeling of the post-1965 immigration have largely replaced national origins with continental ones, Latin American, Asian, and African being the most prominent.[6] Undoubtedly, today's immigrants still identify with their national origins, but the second and later generations will either use the continental labels or just call themselves Americans. Whether symbolic attachment to a continent is deemed to constitute ethnicity is a subject for future study.

The fourth question is comparative: do the observations and hypotheses about the end of ethnicity in America apply to Europe and other countries on the planet? Ethnicity here and elsewhere are very different even if they are described with the same term. For comparative purposes, the most important difference may be between countries that encourage their immigrants to assimilate and become native-borns, and those that seek to keep them separate, inferior, and subject to discrimination.

Ethnicity and Religion

Ethnicity is secular and bears no intrinsic relation to religion except in countries with state religion is able to control some of the population's secular activities and practices. However, even where state and church are separate, ethnicity and religion are connected in various direct and indirect ways. Consequently, a comprehensive look at the end of LGE should include side glances at religion.[7] Such glances are best taken by sociologists of religion. Therefore, this paper will limit itself to four relevant end-related phenomena: existential change, the distinctiveness of some immigrant religions, worship in immigrant languages, and the Americanization of originally ethnic or foreign religions.

Existential Change

Probably the first assimilatory religious moves by immigrants were involuntary, demanded by the necessity to survive in a new country. The best example may be Orthodox Jewish immigrants having to give up the observance of the Sabbath because they had to work Saturdays in order to keep their jobs. Some Jewish immigrants were able to find jobs in their ethnic enclaves, where they could continue to practice their religions; others returned to their countries of origin for the same reason. The majority bowed to the economic imperative, and the observant among them went to the synagogue on Friday night.

Immigrant Religions

Most of the 1870–1924 European immigrants were Catholics and Jews, and since they were mainly peasants and small-town people, their religious beliefs, practices, and organizations reflected the localities and regions from which they came. Consequently, these diverged in some respects from the Catholicism and Judaism of America's native-borns. Thus, Southern Italian immigrants who had been used to their region's Marian Catholicism, which gave special emphasis to the Virgin Mary, had to get used to the dominant American Catholicism.

Worship in Immigrant Languages

American places of worship in areas where the turn-of-the-twentieth-century immigrants settled often provided foreign language services for varying periods, depending on how quickly worshippers were willing and able to understand English.

Americanization of Originally Foreign Religions

Since all American religions other than those of Native Americans originated elsewhere, most, with some notable exceptions, assimilated in ways that are remarkably similar to ethnic assimilation processes (Gans 1994). Generalizing too broadly, over the centuries, these places of worship have come ever nearer to a basic Protestant congregational model, in which attendance is voluntary and the congregation slowly takes at least some decision-making power away from the central religious bureaucracy and from the professional religious who control it.

End of ethnicity studies should therefore pay some attention to the demise of ethnic places of worship, whether they provide immigrant or American forms of worship. Such research would also provide an opportunity to compare ethnicity and religion.

Ethnicity and religion are both institutions with organized belief systems, but religion appeals to more intensely held beliefs and values. As a result, one would imagine that immigrant religions would persist longer than ethnicities, but in fact, most seem to have disappeared more quickly. Marian Catholicism may not have survived for more than two generations and the forms of Balkan Orthodox Catholicism and some Central European Protestant denominations not much longer.

Several hypotheses about the brevity of their survival can be suggested. First, not only the religions that immigrants brought with them, but also those that they encountered in America, were centralized bureaucracies with monopoly power. As a result, they were able to decide when to undertake the formal Americanization of local places of worship. Further, unlike secular ethnic institutions, religions also have to construct and maintain buildings and meet staff payrolls. Thus, endings are hastened if and when funds, including congregants' donations, become scarce or unavailable. Secular ethnic organizations can survive on much lower budgets. In addition, religious worship is place-based and when congregants want and can afford to become residentially mobile, places of worship must often move, too. True, old buildings can usually be sold to new arrivals in the old neighborhood, but moving to neighborhoods that are not immigrant or second-generation ethnic enclaves also speeds up religious assimilation.

By the time they had become LGEs, religious worship had become increasingly voluntary even in religions that demanded regular attendance. Historians could study whether and how ethnics persuaded their places of worship to start resembling the Protestant churches of the native-born, although the development of what might be called late-generation religiosity should be studied by sociologists of religion.

Those unwilling to assimilate had to isolate themselves in communities with guarded borders, the Chassidim and Amish being the most prominent successful examples. Moreover, even when worshippers have switched to Americanized religion, professional religious can keep immigrant theologies and rituals alive for themselves in institutions that serve only them. Marian Catholicism still survives, but in places such as seminaries.

Today, religion itself seems to be on the decline all over the so-called modern world, losing not only worshippers but also believers. The decline is slower in America than in Europe, but while orthodox, fundamentalist, and evangelical religions continue to flourish, liberal religions or denominations are shrinking. The American decline of religion seems to take two major forms. One is the departure from organized religion only, with belief in the deity and some at-home religious practices continuing. Others head for various kinds of spiritualism. The second form of decline is more drastic: a literal ending of religion, with rising numbers of those surrendering their religious beliefs beginning to call themselves agnostics or atheists. So far the numbers in both forms of decline remain small. Thus, national surveys report that while about 20 percent of Americans are religiously unaffiliated, some are still believers in a deity.[8] However, most of the unaffiliated, and about 15 percent of Americans altogether, say that they are no longer religious (Pew Research: Religion and Public Life Project 2012). They are sometimes called non-theists. The number of non-theist Jews is a little higher (22 percent), but it is also increasing, with a third of Jews born after 1980 indicating that they are not religious (Keysar 2010; Pew Research: Religion and Public Life Project 2013). In fact, researchers have created a special term for people who consider themselves to be Jewish even if non-religious: "Jews of No Religion." Most of these respondents describe themselves as Jewish by ancestry, but not by ethnicity; in fact they are less ethnic than religious believers (Phillips 2010).[9] The 2013 Pew study of American Jews gave respondents a list of items thought essential to being Jewish, but only one, eating traditional Jewish foods, was in any sense ethnic, and only 9 percent of respondents considered that essential (Pew Research: Religion and Public Life Project 2013, Appendix B, Q.E5g,169). What respondents considered most essential was remembrance of the Holocaust, with 60 percent offering this response (Pew Research: Religion and Public Life Project 2013, Appendix B, Q.E5a, 167). These data suggest the possibility that Jews of No Religion are mainly Jews by Identity, and especially by defensive identity. If and when anti-Semitism and the threat of anti-Semitism are eliminated, they could become Jews by Terminal Identity.

Coda

Everything we study and write is time bound. Therefore, while thinking about the possible end of ethnicity in America, it is worth considering that if and when global warming begins to approach human boiling points, huge numbers of people escaping life-threatening heat and deadly flooding are likely to head for this country. The newcomers are apt to be called invaders rather than immigrants, and will be received very differently than past immigrants. The sociologists of that time may look back nostalgically to the days when their ancestors were studying the end of ethnicity.

Notes

Reprinted from *Ethnic and Racial Studies*, vol. 38, no. 3, 2015, by permission of Taylor & Francis Group.

1. Warner and Srole thought of disappearance as being fully accepted by the white Anglo-Saxon Protestant, the dominant native-borns of the town that they studied. They did not discuss whether the accepted groups would retain some ethnic characteristics.

2. They can also be studied retroactively, and probably best in America's small towns, where tiny ethnic groups disappeared long before they could become LGEs, either because there were too few people for a functioning community or the young people left town. Also, the native-born may have demanded speedier Americanization than those in the cities.

3. In the 1960s, second- and third-generation descendants of the European immigration created a short-lived social movement that opposed the federal war on poverty's emphasis on African Americans. For political reasons, they downplayed their national origins and became known as white ethnics.

4. Place-based studies could also revive the old Chicago School concept of areas of ethnic settlement, beginning with the first or immigrant area, but aiming to trace the nth and last such areas. The last ones might be fruitful places for studying the endings of ethnicity and ethnic identity.

5. Actually, whites have always maintained a racial identity whenever they lived with or amid African Americans, especially in the South.

6. To be sure, these are all racialized populations but initially so were the Southern and Eastern Europeans who were labeled by national origins.

7. One could even ask whether, when, and how ethnicity becomes a kind of religion and religion, a kind of ethnicity.

8. The number who describe themselves as affiliated must be taken with a large grain of salt, since their claimed attendance at religious services may be as much as double that of actual attendance (Hadaway and Marler 2005).

9. While it is reasonable to assume that a large proportion of this population consists of LGEs, empirical research to test this assumption is needed.

References

Alba, R. 1985. *Into the Twilight of Ethnicity*. Englewood Cliffs, NJ: Prentice Hall.

Alba, R. 1990. *Ethnic Identity: The Transformation of White America*. New Haven, CT: Yale University Press.

Bakalian, A. 1991. "From Being to Feeling Armenian: Assimilation and Identity among Armenian Americans." Paper presented at the Annual Meeting, American Sociological Association, Cincinnati, OH, August 23.

Brubaker, R. 2014. Beyond Ethnicity. *Ethnic and Racial Studies* 37 (5): 804–808. doi:10. 1080/01419870.2013.871311.

Gans, H. 1994. Symbolic Ethnicity and Symbolic Religiosity: Toward a Comparison of Ethnic and Religious Acculturation. *Ethnic and Racial Studies* 17 (4): 577–592. doi:10. 1080/01419870.1994.9993841.

Gans, H. 2014. The Coming Darkness of Late-generation European American Ethnicity. *Ethnic and Racial Studies* 37 (5): 757–765. doi:10.1080/01419870.2013.827796.

Hadaway, C., and P. Marler. 2005. How Many Americans Attend Worship Each Week? An Alternative Approach to Measurement. *Journal for the Scientific Study of Religion* 44 (3): 307–322. doi:10.1111/j.1468-5906.2005.00288.x.

Jenkins, R. 2014. Time to Move beyond Boundary Making. *Ethnic and Racial Studies* 37 (5): 809–813. doi:10.1080/01419870.2013.871308.

Keysar, A. 2010. Secular Americans and Secular Jewish Americans: Similarities and Differences. *Contemporary Jewry* 30 (I): 29–44. doi:10.1007/s12397-009-9018-7.

Nagel, J. 1994. Constructing Ethnicity: Creating and Recreating Ethnic Identity and Culture. *Social Problems* 41 (1): 152–176. doi: 10.2307/3096847.

Park, R. 1914. Racial Assimilation in Secondary Groups. *American Journal of Sociology* 19 (5): 606–623. doi:Io.1086/212297.

Pew Research: Religion and Public Life Project. 2012, 'Nones' on the Rise. October 12.

Pew Research: Religion and Public Life Project. 2013. A Portrait of Jewish Americans. October 1.

Phillips, B. 2010. Accounting for Jewish Secularism: Is a New Cultural Identity Emerging? *Contemporary Jewry* 30 (1): 63–85. doi:10.1007/s12397-009-9020-0.

Steinberg, S. 2001. *The Ethnic Myth: Race, Ethnicity, and Class in America.* 3rd ed. Boston, MA: Beacon Press.

Warner, W., and L. Srole. 1945. *The Social Systems of American Ethnic Groups.* New Haven, CT: Yale University Press.

Waters, M. 1990. *Ethnic Options: Choosing Identities in America.* Berkeley, CA: University of California Press.

Waters, M. 2014. Ethnic Identities in the Future: The Possible Effects of Mass Immigration and Genetic Testing. *Ethnic and Racial Studies* 37 (5): 766–769. doi:10.1080/01419870.2013.871054.

Zangwill, Israel. 1909. *The Melting Pot.* New York, NY: Macmillan.

Working in Six Research Areas

A Multi-Field Sociological Career

Every year, Columbia's sociology faculty members participate in a first-year colloquium in which they introduce themselves and their work to the new graduate students. My presentation in recent years has featured an analysis of research careers in sociology, beginning with a distinction between solo-field and multi-field researchers.

"Solos," I argue, typically choose one field in their discipline, sometimes as early as graduate school, and even though they may teach courses in several fields, they devote their research to that one field, often for their entire careers.

Most sociologists, like most researchers in other fields, are solos. They are also the mainstays of normal science; in addition, they often expand and sometimes transform their fields.

"Multis" are, as the term implies, researchers who work in several fields. Some do so in several but closely related fields, others in unrelated fields; yet others conduct cross-field research that contributes to the entire discipline. Given that disciplines are organized for the solo majority, multis may sometimes be marginal figures, although at the same time they are often better known precisely because they are working in several fields.

This article describes one multi-field career: mine. Although it is mainly an autobiographical essay, it aims to be sufficiently sociological to identify the macrosociological and other forces and agents that helped me at various stages. In addition, I hope my story will offer some guidance and inspiration to young sociologists whose interests and temperaments lead them in a multi-field direction. Believing that the discipline can use more of us, this account of my life in sociology may demonstrate that a career can be made outside the solo mainstream.

My Career—An Overview

My academic career has been unusual temporally. I spent my untenured years mainly as a researcher who taught one or two courses a year, thus giving me maximal opportunity to publish. From there I proceeded directly—a full 12 years after receiving my PhD—to a tenured full professorship. Moreover, before becoming an academic, I briefly worked as a city planner. Although most of my research has been sociological, my PhD is in social planning, and I have always described myself as having been trained both in sociology and planning.

I was born in 1927, into an urban middle-class German Jewish family. We were able to leave Nazi Germany early in 1939, waited in England for the American visa for which my parents had applied years earlier, and arrived in the United States in September 1940. We came without any money into a country still suffering from the Depression, and my parents worked at menial jobs until World War II gave a boost to the domestic economy and they obtained white-collar work.

Like other immigrants, I tried to learn as much about my new country as possible and, discovering in high school that I enjoyed writing, thought I would become a journalist. Once in college, I discovered that the writing I enjoyed doing most was called sociology, so that even before graduate school I thought I would like to become a sociologist. However, I also wanted to remain a writer, and like some other professors, I ended up a writer-researcher who made his living teaching. I was fortunate also that the research and writing that interested me most did not require large grants and the proposal writing needed to obtain them.

Serendipity—and necessity—played a role in my career even before it began. My father decided that German refugees would have better job opportunities in Chicago than in New York, where most refugees had settled. We ended up in Woodlawn, a then mostly Irish low-income neighborhood of Chicago that happened, however, to be immediately adjacent to the University of Chicago. Because I had to live at home, I wound up at what I still think of as the neighborhood university, which was then and is even now often thought to be the most serious in the United States. One quarter's savings, a one-quarter scholarship, and later the GI Bill enabled me to obtain both a bachelor's and a master's degree at Chicago.

In the 1940s, those of us interested in teaching expected to wind up as high school teachers. For this reason, and also because my college social science courses had made me a believer in a unified social science, I enrolled not in sociology but in an interdisciplinary MA program in the social sciences. The program was so new that it had not yet developed a long list of requirements, and although most of my courses were in sociology, I also took courses, generally of my own choice, in several other social sciences. I did not know it then but I was already training myself for a multi-field career.

Chicago was full of brilliant professors, four of which were most important to me as a student. One was Earl Johnson, a sociologist who had studied with Robert Park and John Dewey but who saw himself as a disciple of the latter and, like Dewey, was deeply involved in public policy issues. A second was Everett Hughes, who trained me in fieldwork, taught us to think comparatively, and, in his quiet way, regularly came up with amazing insights. A third was David Riesman, a role model for multi-field sociologists if there ever was one, someone who treated even undergraduate students as his equals and encouraged them to pursue their personal research interests. But I probably learned the most from Martin Meyerson, a social scientist and planner who helped me learn how to combine sociology and planning. In addition, Meyerson supervised my MA thesis and, later, my PhD dissertation.

I also studied with W. Lloyd Warner who, in a discipline that then shunned the work of Karl Marx and was just beginning to translate Max Weber, was nearly alone in researching social class. I benefited greatly from fellow students; in sociology they included, among others, Howard Becker, Eliot Freidson, Erring Goffman, Joseph Gusfield, Louis Kriesberg, and Lee Rainwater. But there were many, many others, teachers, teaching assistants, colleagues, and of course authors who taught me how to think and analyze in social science ways. One author must receive mention: Karl Mannheim, whose *Ideology and Utopia* (1936) and its chapter on the sociology of knowledge provided me with the initial epistemological grounding for my subsequent work.

My GI Bill money ran out in 1950, and after receiving my MA that year I worked as—and in the process learned to be—a professional planner.

Planning was then still a young field so that learning the basics did not require a degree, and besides, I worked mainly as a social researcher in planning.

Although I was not interested in urban design (or physical planning), I wanted to do what I considered to be socially useful research and to use it to help shape public policy. By 1953, I realized that I did not belong in the bureaucratic organizations in which planners had to operate, and because academic opportunities were beginning to surface, I returned to graduate school. I had a difficult choice: full scholarship and full-time job offers from both Columbia's Sociology Department and the University of Pennsylvania's Planning Department, and I finally chose the latter. As a Chicago student, I had read Merton's writings on functionalism, mainly because they attended to the consequences of social action, essential knowledge for anyone interested in public policy. Subsequently, I sent Merton my MA thesis, and he invited me to study with him at Columbia. The Sociology Department had too many PhD students already, however, and I felt I would not receive sufficient individual attention. Moreover, I continued to be unhappy about sociology's reluctance to confront policy and political issues.

A PhD in sociology from Columbia would probably have trumped a PhD in planning from the University of Pennsylvania in the job market, but the Penn department was small and would give me a chance to work once more with Martin Meyerson, specifically on his ambitious research project to bring social science to bear on planning decisions. As luck would have it, I was Penn's first and only PhD student in planning, and because no PhD-level courses were yet being taught, I was once again free to choose my own courses across the social sciences. In sociology, I still remember especially my courses with Digby Baltzell and Marvin Bressler.

I received my PhD in 1957 and an assistant professorship in planning at Pennsylvania as well, but as already noted, I spent the next dozen years as a researcher there and elsewhere in research institutes, although always teaching a course on the side. I did not plan it this way, but research money was beginning to flow generously so that I could concentrate on research and writing. Furthermore, I was already becoming a prolific writer and one who also published outside the academy, which resulted in a fruitful exchange for me and my employers. Through my writing, I provided visibility and publicity for them; in exchange they gave me time to do my own work and to participate in the antipoverty and other public policy activities of the 1960s, which I describe below.

In 1969, with three published books and about 75 academic and non-academic articles in my curriculum vitae, I decided it was time to move into full-time teaching. I was also ready to become a sociologist, but after I was denied tenure at Columbia for what I have been told were political reasons, I accepted a professorship in planning at the Massachusetts Institute of Technology. I soon realized, however, that a social planner like me did not belong in what was then a purely physical planning program, and in 1971, after Columbia's post-1968 trauma had ended, I joined its Sociology Department, where I have been ever since.

I did not give up social planning, however, but just found a new and sociologically acceptable term for it: social policy. My major lecture course was called Urban Sociology and Social Policy, and I also led graduate seminars on social policy. I have always most enjoyed helping students undertake empirical and policy research, and as often as possible I have taught graduate and undergraduate research seminars and in the fields that have most interested me. Although I became an emeritus in 2007, I still teach the course on Field Research Methods I have given since 1975. The rest of the time I write.

My Six Research Fields

No one ever told me to find a single research field and then to stay with it. Perhaps no one yet thought this way in the post-World War II years, or else I was far away from the disciplinary mainstream where, I have been told, such suggestions are made. However, thus unencumbered, I have always followed my research nose, the issues coming up in the world outside, and the questions that I wanted to answer through research and felt competent to address.

Nevertheless, looking back on the research and writing I have done so far, I see my work as falling into six fields:

1. Community Studies—and Urban Sociology
2. Public Policy
3. Ethnicity—and Race
4. Popular Culture, the Media, and the News Media
5. Democracy
6. Public Sociology

Six fields may seem like a large number, but some of my research and writing straddles fields, and almost all the fields are related. Moreover, some—and in a few cases much—of my work in each of the first five fields is about inequality and equality, economic, political, social, and cultural. The last field is the exception: It arrived on my intellectual doorstep when the 2004 president of the American Sociological Association (ASA), Michael Burawoy, resurrected a term I had used when I was president of the association in 1988—but more about that below.

However, the six fields have something else in common: I became interested in some aspect of each before I entered graduate school, and in some cases even earlier. Perhaps they all go back to a poor immigrant's initial curiosity about the United States. The incentive and other structures shaping the academy and sociology since I began graduate school have played a role as well.

Although I believe my empirical research itself to have been value-free—or rather to apply the values shared by empirical researchers—the topics I have chosen for study, the ways I framed them, and the implications I have drawn from my findings have reflected my values. I have never hidden the role of such values and, when relevant, have always indicated that I see myself as a left-liberal on many issues.

Conversely, I do not think of myself as an intentional follower of any sociological or other school, instead letting the topics of my research and their framing guide me toward whatever concepts and theories seem relevant to the analysis. Like everyone else, I was of course concurrently shaped by all the usual sources of influence, but identifying them is a task for someone else. This is an autobiographical essay (for earlier autobiographical essays, see Gans 1990b, 2003b).

The remainder of this article discusses each of the six fields: how I came to them or they to me, how they are connected, both to each other and to my life, and what I tried to contribute to them. The discussion follows the above order, but in my actual work, I moved between fields, and I still do. In retrospect, some of my colleagues must have thought that I parachuted in and out of fields, and I have often wondered how the solos among whom I landed felt about it and me. They could not have been too unhappy because ultimately I received lifetime awards in several fields in which I have worked, and in 2006, the ASA's highest one, the Career of Distinguished Scholarship award.

1. Community Studies and Urban Sociology

Some people think of me primarily as an urban sociologist, but my initial field is more accurately described as community studies. This field came to me: As a student in Everett Hughes's classic field methods course, I had to choose a Chicago census tract and study an institution in it. As a result, I produced a small community study, and then another one doing preliminary work for Morris Janowitz's study of the community press (Janowitz 1952).

Equally important, I was turned on by field methods, more properly called participant observation and now also called ethnography. Like all other research methods, it has its shortcomings, and it is suitable only for some research questions, but I still think it is the most scientific of the available sociological research methods because it brings researchers into close and continuing contact with the people they are studying and the groups and institutions in which they are embedded.

As I suggest in detail in discussing Field 5 (Democracy), I was also interested in politics, especially political participation. David Riesman, although on the Chicago faculty, was then in New Haven working on what would become *The Lonely Crowd* (Riesman et al. 1951). He was also interested in political participation, and because we came at it from different angles, we corresponded about it extensively. Fortunately for me, he was as compulsive a letter writer as I.

For my MA thesis, I decided to study political participation in a local community. David Riesman told me to contact Martin Meyerson, a young professor in Chicago's Planning Department, to help me find a suitable community for study, and led me to the new town of Park Forest, Illinois. It later became famous as the research site for *Organization Man* (Whyte 1956).

Park Forest was a planned new town, then 1.5 years old, and as I watched it become a community, I decided that I would someday move into another new town as its first resident and watch that process from the very beginning. The research also made me a sociological expert on new towns, maybe then the first and only in the world, but a few years later, I was offered a position with a Chicago architectural planning firm that was planning three new mining towns in northern Minnesota and northern Michigan. Because the houses had to attract and recruit workers, I interviewed area miners who were building their own houses about their design-related preferences and priorities and sent my findings back to the Chicago architects designing the houses for the three towns. Subsequently, I put some of my new town research findings to good use in helping to plan the new town of Columbia, Maryland (Gans 1964b).

THE LEVITTOWNERS

In 1956, while I was studying at Penn, William Levitt, the builder of two previous Levittowns, announced that he would build his third in New Jersey, about 20 miles from Philadelphia. I bought a house there (I was buyer number 25), arrived in October 1958, conducted three years of fieldwork and in-depth interviewing, and published the findings a half dozen years later (Gans 1967).

Community studies are an intensely stimulating genre because the fieldworkers not only obtain answers to their initial questions but, by being there day to day, also learn a great deal about a humongous number of subjects—findings that are both broadening and that come in handy for decades after. The Levittown study showed me how a set of strangers come together to create a functioning community, but I also learned about the origins and operations of a variety of community, neighborhood, and block institutions, formal and informal, as well as about most of the topics covered in introductory sociology courses.

I also observed the extent to which class and class conflict saturated community life, and much of *The Levittowners* was in fact a case study of young lower middle- and working-class Americans. In addition, I studied whether and how people's lives changed in the move from the city and discovered that, beyond achieving many of the goals for which they moved to the suburbs in the first place, the changes were much fewer than commonly believed. That also suggested the limited effects of space and the built environment on people's lives, a theme about which I am still writing (e.g., Gans 2002).

David Riesman liked to argue that one of sociology's functions was to debunk what, thanks to John Kenneth Galbraith, we now call the conventional wisdom. Levittown was a fertile site, rich in empirical data to debunk the stereotypes that demonized the new postwar suburbs. I found that Levittown was not a sterile, conformity-ridden, and homogeneous aggregation of unhappy young urbanites forced by government to move to the suburbs. My debunking helped to evoke nonscholarly interest in the book and reviews in some general media and, because few sociologists studied suburbs, turned me into a suburban expert for quote-hunting journalists. In addition, Levittown supplied some raw materials for a critical and often reprinted analysis of Louis Wirth's *Urbanism as a Way of Life* (Gans 1962b).

THE URBAN VILLAGERS

When Levitt had to postpone the start of Levittown, New Jersey, for a year, he and serendipity provided me with an extremely lucky break: the invitation to do a fieldwork study in the West End of Boston. The invitation came from the National Institute of Mental Health (NIMH), and specifically from Dr. Leonard Duhl, a social psychiatrist who funded several of NIMH's sociological studies in those days, but David Riesman, who would play a continuing role in my career for many years, had recommended me.

NIMH was supporting a larger study, by the psychiatrist Erich Lindemann, of how people react to disaster, and the West Enders were about to face one: the loss of their neighborhood to slum clearance. The main study was a before-after displacement interview study with a 500-person sample, and my role was to provide the interview study with a sociological analysis of the community and institutions the West Enders were about to lose.

In October 1957, my then wife and I moved into a fifth floor but comfortable tenement apartment in the West End. Following the lead of Helen and Robert Lynd's work in Muncie, Indiana (Lynd & Lynd 1929), and particularly William F. Whyte's (1943) study in the North End, the neighborhood immediately adjacent to the West End, I examined the everyday life of the area, mainly the working-class Italian Americans who constituted its most numerous population, as well as the institutions that served, underserved, and controlled them and the other West Enders.

However, when I wrote up my findings, I also added observations and reflections on a variety of theoretical and other issues, including several that had preoccupied me in graduate school. Among the book's main themes were the structural and cultural differences between the poor, the working class, and the middle classes; in addition, I argued that class position was more important than ethnicity in understanding the West Enders. The last two chapters of the book described the then-forthcoming destruction of the West End, debunked the claim that it was a slum, and offered a critical analysis of the slum clearance program, with recommendations for how to reform it so as not to victimize the people whom it displaced.

To my great surprise, *The Urban Villagers* (1962a) became a success, selling over 180,000 copies, especially, I am told, as a supplementary text in a variety of sociology courses. I still meet people who tell me that the book inspired them to become sociologists. My critical analysis of the West End's destruction, beginning with an article in the planners' professional journal (Gans 1959), initially made me an outcast among mainstream planners and others who favored urban renewal. However, as a result of Jane Jacobs's (1961) influential general critique of planning and the recognition that urban renewal brought about Negro removal, liberals and even some planners began to oppose the renewal program. Consequently, by the mid-1960s, I was frequently invited to testify, consult, talk, and write about urban renewal and participate in antirenewal planning and related activities (e.g., Gans 1965a).

2. Public Policy

My formal involvement in public policy began in 1950 when I started to work as, and to become, a planner, but informally it began much earlier. Growing up as a Jewish child in Nazi Germany and spending the start of World War II in England must have started the process, but it took a particular turn during my adolescence when I learned, in a distinctive fashion, to think about issues of equality and democracy.

In the early 1940s, I spent two summers at Jewish camp near Chicago that helped the local truck farmers harvest their crops as part of the war effort. The camp itself was first and foremost an educational venture in labor or democratic socialist Zionism. There, I first learned about the Israeli kibbutzim, the agricultural collective settlements in which all property was commonly owned and which were governed by direct democracy, the entire community meeting weekly to make the needed decisions.

Much impressed, I thought of moving to Israel after high school to spend my life on a kibbutz. Indeed, during my college years, I was part of a study group that intended to go to Israel for a year to study the kibbutzim before deciding to move there. Although I was never able to do more than visit some of these communities, my youthful library research about them initiated a lifelong interest in egalitarian policies.

My interest in and knowledge of public policy were enriched and, equally significant, legitimated when, as a graduate student, I took Social

Science 2400, the University of Chicago's mandatory year-long course that aimed to teach us how the social sciences could help the newly founded United Nations make the world a more prosperous, democratic, and in other respects better place for everyone.

My first academic public policy project was my dissertation at the University of Pennsylvania, one of the three planned volumes in the Meyerson project to use social science concepts and methods in planning. My study was entitled "Recreation Planning for Leisure Behavior: A User-Oriented Approach," which argued among other things that public recreation planning needed to pay more attention to the usage patterns of its users and the avoidance practices of the nonusers. However, I also wrote about the suppliers of recreation: the social movements that lobbied for more parks and public playgrounds and proposed a recreation planning program that responded to the wishes, values, and interests of users, suppliers, and the larger community. My topic was framed broadly enough to enable me to include findings on leisure behavior and connect them to recreation planning. That gave me a chance also to bring in popular culture and the mass media, subjects that were more interesting to me than recreation planning.

In addition, the dissertation, which came to nearly 800 pages, also devoted itself to theorizing the social science-planning interface that Meyerson, my fellow PhD student John Dyckman, and I were attempting to develop. My theorizing and other parts of the dissertation are summarized in Gans (1968a, chapters 6–9).

When I received my PhD in planning in 1957, I was fully credentialed to work in public policy, but my initial contribution was my 1959 critique of slum clearance, mentioned above. However, then serendipity and the early signs of dramatic changes in American society intervened and sent me in an additional direction.

The Urban Villagers was published about the same time as Michael Harrington's *The Other America* (Harrington 1962), which helped to inspire the War on Poverty. Not long after my book appeared and received favorable reviews, I began to be viewed as a sociologist of urban poverty—or at least someone who could make sociological presentations on poverty. Although I insisted that most of the West Enders I wrote about were earning moderate incomes, I met enough poor ones to satisfy the sudden demand for knowledge on the subject. In addition, I could talk about antipoverty policy.

Consequently, I spent part of my time in the 1960s writing and talking about poverty. The writing was mostly for non-academic publications. The talking took place in a variety of committees, workshops, conferences, and seminars in which a number of us analyzed federal proposals and tried to develop alternative ones that we thought had a better chance of helping poor people to escape poverty.

In many of the meetings, I sat with the young professionals, organizers, activists, and political staffers, several working for one of the Kennedys, who actually invented the programs associated with the War on Poverty. But I was hardly the only sociologist. S.M. Miller was perhaps the most active sociological convener of policy discussions, and Frances Piven and Richard Cloward were the most active in developing new antipoverty policies. Among many others were Lee Rainwater, as well as Peter Marris and Frank Riesman. Through a policy committee affiliated with the Congress of Racial Equality (CORE), then the most liberal of the civil rights organizations, we also worked with the black leadership around Martin Luther King, including James Farmer, Bayard Rustin, George Wiley, and, among the policy-oriented academics, Kenneth Clark and Hylan Lews.

The antipoverty policy analysts were not always in agreement; some, with Michael Harrington in the leadership, called for jobs and full employment as the policy centerpiece; others, most vocally Frances Piven and Richard Cloward and the welfare rights movement that they helped to found and lead, believed that broader and more generous welfare benefits for poor families, regardless of the number of parents, were more urgent.

I never thought of it as a dichotomous policy issue, and the basic theme of much of my writing and talking about poverty proposed that poverty could not be eliminated until enough secure and decently paid jobs were available for the poor who could work. Income supports had to be made available to the rest, including the mothers who should stay home to raise their children until they began to attend whatever pre-kindergarten schooling was available to them.

In those days, we still believed in the possibility of full employment, although I had resonated to the automation scare of the 1960s and began to suggest that new technology (still mostly on the horizon) would increasingly affect work time, either increasing joblessness or reducing work hours (Gans 1964a).

Twenty years later, I received a German Marshall Fund fellowship to go to Europe and study early experiments with reductions in the workweek and worksharing to increase the total number of jobs (Gans 1990c). Although Western European workweek reductions have not yet created as many jobs as expected and are now being revoked in response to employer demands, I still think that they will someday be necessary everywhere, including in the United States.

My concurrent activities in antipoverty policy and antirenewal activities led, among other things, to an invitation in 1966 from Senator Ribicoff of Connecticut to testify before his Committee on the Crisis of the Cities. That gave me an opportunity to describe that crisis as a by-product of economic and racial inequality and to try to connect antipoverty and urban policy (Gans 1966b). A few years later I became a consultant for the National Advisory Commission on Civil Disorders, for which I wrote a memo on the *ghetto* rebellions and subsequently drafted chapter 9 of the Kerner Report (Gans 1968b).

STRUGGLING AGAINST INEQUALITY

At the start of the 1970s, the programs of what many activists had since the mid-1960s called the Skirmish on Poverty were, with some notable exceptions, about to go on the chopping block. I reacted in two ways. The first was, strangely enough, optimistic, for I chose to see the decline in poverty brought about by Lyndon Johnson's War on Poverty, the economic growth that improved the lives of the working and middle classes, and the socio-cultural trends set in motion by the hippies, yippies, and other radical young people as a sign of a forthcoming equality revolution. My conclusion was much too hopeful, but I assembled a set of essays, some which had earlier appeared in the *New York Times Magazine*, on that theme and titled them *More Equality* (Gans 1973).

Several of the other social scientists working on antipoverty policy were also egalitarians, and although we did not then stress it in our writing, many of us believed that the reduction of poverty had to be accompanied by a drastic shrinkage of the economic and other gaps between the poor and the nonpoor. That gap was modest in comparison to today's much grosser inequality, but gross enough to us even then. We also began to speculate that poor people suffered not only from poverty but also from the social and psychological effects of inequality, an idea that has by now received some empirical verification.

My second reaction to the end of the War on Poverty was an article entitled "The Positive Functions of Poverty," which appeared in the *American*

Journal of Sociology (Gans 1972). The article argued that poverty persisted in part because it was functional, i.e., useful, for the more affluent classes. The body of the article identified 15 such functions, including supplying a labor force ready to do the society's dirty work at low wages; providing neighborhoods that could be torn down as slums; and, because the poor tend not to vote, making the actual electorate economically more conservative than it would otherwise be.

Because the article's tone was, despite my best efforts, ironic, it was at first dismissed as a satire, but over the years it has been reprinted more than two dozen times, including in anthologies used in English writing courses. In retrospect, I suppose I was saying—even if unintentionally—that we are all implicated in the persistence of poverty. The article had a second agenda: to present a radical functional analysis so as to rebut the charge that functionalism was inherently conservative.

THE CULTURE OF POVERTY AND THE UNDERCLASS

One of the people in the then tiny circle of social scientists concerned with poverty that I met at the start of the 1960s was a dynamic young Labor Department official named Daniel Patrick Moynihan. He had a PhD as well as experience in New York state politics, and in 1965 he became famous as the author of "The Negro Family: The Case for National Action," now commonly known as the Moynihan Report.

Like its author, the Moynihan Report was both liberal and conservative. Its liberal parts advocated greater equality and discussed the negative effects of joblessness, but the chapter discussing the report's title argued that single parenthood and other problems of the black family were major causes of the perpetuation of black poverty. Needless to say, that chapter received most of the political and media attention.

Commonweal, the liberal Catholic weekly, asked me to comment on the report, and I wrote a carefully balanced review (Gans 1965b) that attempted, between the lines, to persuade the author to rethink his analysis of the black family. Afterward, Moynihan invited me first to the planning conference for the 1966 White House Conference to Fulfill These Rights and then to an eighteen-month long seminar on poverty sponsored by the American Academy of Arts and Sciences. The seminar, which met monthly, discussed most of the major empirical and policy issues of the period, but I now remember it mainly as an endless debate with Oscar Lewis over the culture of poverty.

A majority of the seminar members, including me, were critical of Lewis's analysis because he provided little empirical evidence for it. Some of us were also concerned that the political opponents of antipoverty policy, including academics, were using Lewis's concept to blame the poor for their own poverty and that Lewis did not protest their misuse of his work. Eventually, several of us wrote papers critical of the culture of poverty for the book that came out of the seminar (Moynihan 1969).

The culture of poverty continued to be the major blaming concept for another decade, but in the late 1970s, it was replaced by a much more graphic one: underclass, which unlike Lewis's concept made the black poor its major villain. Like the popular version of the culture of poverty, it viewed the poor as lazy, stupid, impulsive, promiscuous, abusive, criminal, and given to family breakdown and other pathologies, a list that had not changed significantly for many centuries. Myrdal (1963) introduced the term as a color-blind concept to describe a new social stratum generated by the ever more capital-intensive economy that was likely to be permanently stuck at the bottom of, and even under, the existing class hierarchy. About a dozen years later, Myrdal's term was racialized and redefined to blame the poor, especially the black poor, after the 1970s *ghetto* disorders, the spread of crack cocaine, and the increase in street crime.

Having seen Lewis's originally scholarly concept turned into a political weapon against the poor and noticing that Myrdal's underclass was following the same path, I became curious about the process by which this took place and especially of the roles that social scientists and journalists played in it. In 1989, I received a Russell Sage Foundation Visiting Scholarship to do the research, fortunately for me at the same time as Michael Katz, the historian of poverty who had just published a book on *The Undeserving Poor* (Katz 1989). My book, *The War Against the Poor* (Gans 1995), identified the mixture of journalistic and social science inputs that had transformed Myrdal's term and the foundations and other institutions that then put it into wide play in the popular press and elsewhere.

I have not done any significant research or writing on poverty and antipoverty policy since this book was published, but I have continued to pursue public policy questions. My most recent book, *Imagining America in 2033* (Gans 2008), although subtitled "a Utopian narrative," is also a book about desirable and feasible future public policy. I used the book, and its futurist standpoint, to further explore policies I had written about earlier and to suggest scenarios by which they might be implemented. However,

I also wrote about several—for me—new policy areas: the larger economy, war and peace, energy and global warming, the family, and education, among others.

Although the book is new, my plan to write it was not. That was hatched when I first read Edward Bellamy's influential but also highly implausible Utopia *Looking Backward* (Bellamy 1888) in high school or college and thought I would like someday to attempt a more plausible Utopia. I first tried to write the book in the early 1970s, perhaps partially in despair about what the Nixon administration was doing to the United States at the time, but I still had too many empirical projects to begin or finish first.

Even my interest in the future is not recent. Although I know that prediction and merely projecting trends is dangerous and should be avoided by social scientists, I was also trained to think about long-term planning. Although I am not a futurist, my list of publications includes nearly a dozen articles with the word future in the title, beginning as far back as the mid-1950s.

CONNECTING POLICY AND POLITICS

Growing up in Nazi Germany meant that politics was always in the air, and this probably stimulated an early interest in the politics of my new country. Going to the University of Chicago in the 1940s made me and others the constant target of conversion and recruitment attempts by Stalinist and Trotskyist student activists, which added ideology to my ongoing political education. However, my campus experiences convinced me early on that I was most comfortable with social democratic or left-liberal political values, and that has never changed.

Living in a poor neighborhood in Chicago and under the city's already well-functioning political machine, I learned early on that money makes the world go 'round, and politics helps to allocate and distribute it. As a planner, I also learned that policy and politics are forever intertwined, and over the years my regular but marginal involvements in various kinds of political organizations have given me a political education that has often been useful in my policy work.

Toward the end of my student days, I did some political work for my local congressman and joined the local branch of Americans for Democratic Action (ADA), the then influential liberal organization. While studying at Penn, I became active in its Philadelphia branch. In the 1960s, I was elected to the national ADA board and participated in an effort to push the board in an egalitarian direction on domestic economic policy. Along with some other social scientists, I also served on the board of the League for Industrial Democracy (LID), a small but influential democratic-socialist organization that was bitterly anticommunist and thus intensely hawkish on the Vietnam War. The LID was considerably more constructive on civil rights and racial equality, which gave me a chance to work with Bayard Rustin, Michael Harrington, and the young people around them, particularly on A. Phillip Randolph's "Freedom Budget" before I resigned in protest against the LID's support of the war.

The LID was very much Old Left, and most of my fellow board members were bitterly opposed to the New Left. I was not and had in fact become friendly early on with the leaders of the Students for a Democratic Society (SDS), including Tom Hayden and my now Columbia colleague Todd Gitlin. I served mainly as an occasional and informal kibitzer-adviser on public policy and on the uses of sociology to several New Left organizations (Gans 1965c, 1966a) and thereby added a distinctive course to my political education. I took what turned out to be a much longer course when several of the so-called New York Intellectuals (many of whom I had met when I was still a graduate student and again as a regular contributor to *Commentary*, the then politically liberal Jewish magazine) began to turn neoconservative.

These and other political activities and experiences have influenced both my policy-related research and my teaching. Politics changes all the time, and policy analysis must confront these changes. Although the academy still often tries to be above politics, students, even in basic sociology courses, must obtain as much instruction about the political process, past and present, as we can give them.

3. Ethnicity and Race

The census tract that I chose in Everett Hughes's 1947 fieldwork course included a section of the Jewish area in Hyde Park, the neighborhood in which the University of Chicago is located, and part of my final report included findings about the Jewish community. My choice was not accidental; like other Jewish adolescents, I had spent part of my teens exploring my Jewish identity (to use today's language), and first research projects are almost always motivated in part by personal curiosities.

W. Lloyd Warner was once more an influence, in this case with his book on ethnicity in Yankee City (Warner & Srole 1945). Later, I became very interested in the two authors' analysis of social and cultural assimilation. My interest in assimilation was so strong that originally I thought about writing my master's thesis on the treatment of assimilation in the Yiddish theater. Instead, I later studied several Jewish night club entertainers, watching them guilt-trip their assimilating audiences for deserting the culture of their immigrant parents (e.g., Gans 1953).

Then, at the start of my thesis fieldwork in Park Forest, I learned that some of the Jewish residents were actively trying to establish a synagogue and Sunday school. These institutions were intended to persuade their children, who were growing up with Christian peers and wanted to celebrate Christmas, to instead celebrate Chanukah. In fact, watching a group of strangers trying to create Jewish institutions in Park Forest first gave me the idea that later led to my study of Levittown, New Jersey.

Nathan Glazer, whom I had met through David Riesman when they were working together on *The Lonely Crowd*, was then editing a sociological section in *Commentary*. When I told him what I was doing, he asked me to write an article about my Park Forest findings. The resulting article (Gans 1951) gave me my first, and totally unexpected, minutes of recognition. It also emboldened me to undertake a two-article analysis of the larger Jewish community in the United States (Gans 1956a,b) and what I saw as its assimilating and thus changing culture. In the second of those articles, I suggested in a footnote (1956b, p. 561) that Jews and other ethnic groups were undergoing a "more or less straight line of cultural and social assimilation," as a result of which I have often been credited with and blamed for inventing a "straight-line theory" of ethnicity.

By the 1970s, ethnicity was a rapidly growing sociological field. Reading the new literature about non-Jewish ethnic groups—and doing the informal fieldwork in New York City's multi-ethnic community that becomes second nature to every fieldworker living in that city—I began to suspect that my observations about American Jewry in the 1950s might hold true for the second and third generations of other ethnic groups. I had already noticed in Park Forest that the Jewish parents I was studying were more interested in feeling Jewish—and using Jewish cultural and religious objects and symbols to do so—than in participating in the organized Jewish community or practicing the ethnic and religious laws and customs of their ancestors. At the time, I called this phenomenon symbolic Judaism, but in the 1970s I elaborated on it and renamed it symbolic ethnicity (Gans 1979b). Since then, sociologists studying other ethnic groups have found the concept relevant, and I suspect it will be applicable to the descendants of the continuing post-1965 immigration as well.

In the 1980s, students of ethnicity had begun to recognize that unlike the poor and white (or at least swarthy) European immigrants of the 1880–1924 wave about which they had been generalizing, the new immigrants were predominantly nonwhite and multiclass and included a significant number of professionals.

The field of ethnicity had by now been renamed immigration, and many of the younger researchers, themselves members of the post-1965 wave, argued that the then hegemonic acculturation and assimilation model did not apply to a multiclass and multiracial immigrant population. Some members of my cohort of researchers disagreed, arguing that while racial and class discrimination would get in the way of social assimilation into the white community, the children of the new immigrants would nevertheless assimilate culturally (or acculturate) and absorb the mainstream American cultures of their time much like their predecessors of the old European immigration (e.g., Gans 1999b, but the definitive statement is Alba & Nee 2003). Conversely, I have also argued that some children of poor immigrants might acculturate so completely that they would reject immigrant jobs that in bad times might result in their downward economic mobility. I called this phenomenon second-generation decline (Gans 1992b); Portes & Zhou (1993) called it downward assimilation, and our pessimistic assessment has stimulated a considerable amount of significant research.

Partly as a result of the arrival of Asian American and Latino graduate students at Columbia University, I began to teach and write once more about race (e.g., Gans 1999c, 2005).[1] However, I continue to argue, as I did in *The Urban Villagers*, that the analysis of the subject remains incomplete until the role of class is factored in.

4. The Media and the News Media

My work in the media, which began with the entertainment media and popular culture but then moved into the news media, actually started immediately after we arrived in Chicago. The landlady in the Woodlawn rooming house where we lived the first year had stored a year's worth of *Chicago Tribune* Sunday comics in her basement, and I spent endless and entranced hours going through them. German popular culture for children was dominated by movies, but by 1935 the Nazis had banned American films and so completely politicized German movies that we stopped going to the movies. America's Sunday comics offered me a means for satisfying my immigrant curiosity about my new country, and I suppose indirectly it led to my various activities in the media field.

At the University of Chicago, I discovered a fledgling communications program that was buried in the Library School and run by its dean, Bernard Berelson. The University of Pennsylvania, like other schools, offered only a couple of communications courses, but after receiving my PhD I taught a course on mass communications and popular culture. I also joined interested colleagues to lobby for a mass communications program, which eventually became a reality as the Annenberg School of Communication. Many years later, at Columbia, I joined another lobbying group that helped to bring about the Journalism School's PhD program in communications.

In 1949, I wrote a term paper entitled "Popular Culture and High Culture" for a University of Chicago graduate seminar taught by Elihu Katz and David Riesman. I later turned it into a short article, then several ever longer ones, and finally into a book (Gans 1974). *Popular Culture and High Culture* described five "taste publics" and "taste cultures" stratified by class and laid out the aesthetic values and cultural choices of these publics in various media and arts. However, as the book's subtitle pointed out ("an analysis and evaluation of taste"), I was concerned not only with the analysis of taste but also with its evaluation. I criticized the advocates of high culture who claimed that only its aesthetic values were acceptable and argued for cultural democracy on the grounds that people's aesthetic values and cultural choices reflected their level of education and socioeconomic position. Until people had access to the income and schooling of the professional cultural elite, they could not even be asked to choose high culture.

My defense of popular culture earned me a number of angry reviews, especially from critics in the humanities. A decade later, my book was literally swamped by Pierre Bourdieu's *Distinction* (1984), which came to roughly the same empirical conclusion but was based on a subtler and more wide-ranging analysis and ended up on the side of high culture. However, I gather my book continues to be useful for stimulating discussion in undergraduate media and culture courses.

But I was always pursuing empirical research as well. It began with the studies of Jewish entertainers, mentioned above, which were followed later by an article about Hollywood movies (Gans 1957) in which, as in my dissertation, I once more made the case for the users and analyzed the indirect role of the eventual audience in the movie-making process. That year, I also paid a brief visit to Hollywood with the idea of undertaking an ethnographic study of the making of a movie. I am still sorry that I never got to carry out such a study.

In the summer of 1957 and just before moving into the West End, I went to Great Britain to try to discover why an overwhelming majority of the British movie audience, like most other Europeans, preferred American movies over domestic ones (Gans 1962c). I discovered that British movies were made by and for the educated upper middle class, in which the lower classes were often villains or targets of humor. As a result, the then largely working-class audiences flocked to American movies, whose heroes looked classless to those British moviegoers.

My other media activity was an active if pre-professional practice as a fledgling journalist and essayist. I wrote features and news stories for and then coedited the high school paper, served as a stringer for Chicago's City News Bureau, contributed regularly to a *Chicago Daily News* sports column—an early form of blogging—and was a working journalist for part of my military service. I also wrote for the college humor magazine at Chicago. My specialty was short satires, a genre that I continued to pursue over the years. Some were published in various not-so-mass media, and a few I have included in two of my books of essays (Gans 1968a, 1999a).

Since my graduate student years, I have also written for nonacademic publications. I will discuss that work, which is now called public sociology, in the final section of this paper.

My serious interest in news media research began in 1962, during the Soviet-American nuclear crisis over Cuba, when I was finishing my field work in Levittown. Although I wondered whether its completion would be preempted by a nuclear holocaust, I also became curious why the news media appeared to egg on those calling for war. I decided that if they and I survived, I would undertake an ethnographic study of some newsrooms to satisfy my curiosity.

First I had to finish writing *The Levittowners*, which took much longer than *The Urban Villagers*. However, I was also able to work on a related news media study before I could begin my own. After John F. Kennedy's assassination, Paul Lazarsfeld obtained funding to study how network television, then still inventing its news programming, covered the assassination, and I saw this as my opportunity to gain entry for my future study. As the most senior interviewer for the Lazarsfeld study, I was assigned to interview anchormen and top executives, although when I started my own study, I had no trouble gaining entry even in news organizations in which I knew no one.

When I finally began my fieldwork in 1966, my project had grown into a more general analysis of how the national news media go about deciding what is news, and I spent many months in the last half of the 1960s in the newsrooms of two newsweeklies and two television network evening news programs. That gave me a chance to compare print and electronic news media, although the similarities, most imposed by a basic journalistic method that has not changed much in the past century, were much greater than the differences resulting from technology.

I also discovered that the news sources, and indirectly the audience, play as great a role in the determination of newsworthiness as the journalists and that between the pressure of deadlines and the imperatives of the journalistic method, the journalists have less autonomy than is commonly thought. My research included a content analysis of the news programs and magazines, and the resulting chapter on journalistic values has received more attention over the years than the structural analyses in the rest of the book.

Although I may have been the first sociologist to do extended fieldwork in the news media, by the time *Deciding What's News* was finally published (Gans 1979a), others had also undertaken ethnographic studies, notably Gitlin (1980) and Tuchman (1980). Unfortunately, our and concurrent other work on the news media did not evoke new interest in media sociology, and while journalists are still writing books about the news media, no American sociologist has yet published a book-length ethnography on today's news media.

In 2003, I published a second book on the news media, *Democracy and the News* (Gans 2003a), which asked what journalists could, could not, and should do to strengthen American democracy. I was fortunate to receive a year's fellowship in Everette Dennis's Gannett Center for Media Studies and later another year at the Freedom Forum Media Studies Center. Although my study involved no fieldwork, I met with many journalists, political writers, and news executives there. My research suggested that while the news media are necessary for democracy, they are not sufficient to preserve it, and journalists can do much less on its behalf than they believe they do.

5. Democracy

Democracy and the News was also a sequel to *Middle American Individualism* (Gans 1988), which despite its title was actually about the future of liberal democracy. Written during the Reagan era, the book analyzed the differences between the popular individualism of working-and lower middle-class America and the individualism of corporate America, suggesting that middle America did not favor corporate individualism and sought instead to retain the New Deal and the Great Society and the welfare state that these federal programs had brought about.

However, my concern with democracy originated during my adolescence when, as I noted earlier, I discovered the direct democracy of the Israeli kibbutzim. In graduate school, I became interested in what role citizens could and should play in representative democracy, and my master's thesis research on political participation in Park Forest also dealt with this subject.

The empirical data to support the argument in *Middle American Individualism* came from polls and surveys, not from ethnography, but the book was a change of direction in other respects as well. For one thing, it was a return to the participation issues I had grappled with in my master's thesis; for another, it was a reaction to the various and often successful attacks on liberal democracy since the 1960s. However, the last and longest chapter was an exercise in what might be called political policy making: a set of proposals for the future of liberal democracy.

For that chapter, I resurrected the notion, from my dissertation, of user-friendliness and argued that if the users, i.e., the citizenry, did not want to come to politics and government, perhaps a user-friendly government, with bureaucracies that would serve and even come to the citizenry when the latter needed it, might initiate a greater interest in politics. I advocated the establishment of new citizen lobbies to represent the citizenry, thereby ending the corporate monopoly on lobbying; subtler polling that enabled politicians to get a more complete understanding of their constituencies; and pluralistic news media that better informed and represented the variety of interests in the so-called mass audience.

The penultimate and longest chapter of my new book, *Imagining America in 2033* (Gans 2008), takes one more stab at this topic, this time looking at it in terms of political and other processes that could, over the coming decades, make American democracy more representative. At its analytic level, the book argues that the long-term erosion of jobs, work time, and thus purchasing power will force government to rescue both the consumers and the economy that depends on them. While the fierce political battle to bring about this rescue is taking place, government might have to become more representative.

Force never operates without agency, however. For example, that political battle could require the citizen lobbies I wrote about in my earlier books to become significant political players. Other essential changes proposed in the book include a basic but broad education in politics for everyone, as well as the democratization of the Senate and other political institutions, which will eventually require amending the Constitution.

6. Public Sociology

In 1987, I was elected president of the ASA, and as a result of this gratifying honor, I became involved in one more field. My first impulse in choosing the theme for the 1988 annual meeting was to do the conventional thing: pick one of my fields that could benefit from an annual meeting's programmatic input and publicity. However, I remembered that, as the 1973 president of the Eastern Sociological Society, I gave an address on equality that fell flat and decided that as ASA president I would choose a theme that would or should appeal to the entire discipline: sociology itself.

My theme was "Sociology in America: The Discipline and the Public," and my program committee and I scheduled a set of thematic sessions on how sociology was serving and could better serve the public. My presidential address (Gans 1989) offered my own observations and recommendations. The edited volume then required of ASA presidents (Gans 1990a) included the most relevant of the meeting papers and some others.

As always, most of what we produced in the thematic sessions and the book sank quietly into disciplinary history, but one of the words I used in passing in my presidential address surfaced again 15 years later. Proposing that we recruit colleagues able and willing to make their research and writing salient for both their colleagues and at least the educated public, I suggested that they might be called public sociologists. I added that public sociologists had to be able to write in clear English and avoid the pitfalls of undue professionalism such as narrowness. Those so inclined should use their findings and insights to consider becoming social critics as well.

Michael Burawoy used public sociology again in his theme "For Public Sociology," for the 2004 annual meetings (Burawoy 2005), and thanks to his analytic skills, programming talent, energy, and outreach, a social movement for public sociology has developed in the discipline.

Even if the term public sociology was new in 1988, the practice was not; a number of American sociologists had written for the general public, and some of them had reached it very successfully. The list includes W.E.B. DuBois, Robert and Helen Lynd, and in the second half of the twentieth century Daniel Bell, Nathan Glazer, C. Wright Mills, Robert Nisbet, David Riesman, Alan Wolfe, and many others.

I have sought to write both for the discipline and the general public from the beginning of my career, and, having started my writing as a journalist, I never thought much about doing anything else. Also, when I was in graduate school, both at Chicago and Penn, no one urged us to write in the technical journal style I call sociologese. More important, as there were few tenure track jobs back then, choosing between publishing or perishing was not yet required, and publishing in mainstream journals or with academic presses had not yet become essential routes to tenure. Besides, most of the ethnographers who were our role models in graduate school were able to report their findings and insights in clear English even as they were writing for their disciplines.

Writing for the general public became more urgent in the 1960s, when my policy- and politics–oriented colleagues and I were eager to reach the public with our critical analyses of and proposals for public policy. For me, the incentive to do public sociology has never ended, originally because I thought sociological findings and ideas could counter the conservative attacks on antipoverty policy and the poor, and then because there were other policy and political issues to which sociology could make a contribution. But even as a student, I already thought that many of sociology's insights were significant enough to be shared with the general public.

My own outreach as a public sociologist has been mainly through my books, almost all of which have been published by trade presses. Except from the late 1960s to the mid-1970s when my articles appeared on the *New York Times* op-ed page and in its Sunday Magazine, my shorter work has been published mostly in smaller magazines and journals of opinion. These have included *Commonweal, Chronicle Review, Dissent, The Nation, The New Republic,* and *Social Policy*—for which I also reviewed more than 30 films during the 1970s.

In addition, like many other sociologists, I have long served as a regular supplier of quotes and sociological angles for telephoning journalists. However, perhaps unlike most others, I have also been writing to journalists when I thought a little sociological analysis could add to their reporting or when they made unfair or inaccurate comments about the discipline. As the author of articles and books on the news media, I felt qualified to write such letters. While most journalists do not respond, over the years I have maintained a periodic correspondence—now of course by email—with a number of them, including columnists and reporters in the major national news media.

PUBLIC SOCIOLOGY AND THE DISCIPLINE

Public sociology can take many forms, but the need for sociologists to write books and articles for the general public is more urgent than ever. Given that the discipline's future depends directly and indirectly on public support, public sociology will contribute to its survival and growth.

Trying to reach the general public should help to make sociology more relevant and useful to at least some sectors of that public and of the larger society. We should especially aim to be relevant and useful to the people who most need social, economic, and political support—as well as more equality. If we can contribute sociological findings and insights to help achieve world peace and more global equality, so much the better. At the same time, we have to resist pandering and avoid overdramatizing our findings and hyping our work to appeal to media gatekeepers.

Still, we must make sure that our ability to contribute matches our good intentions to do so. Actually, aiming to produce first-rate public sociology may even help to produce more high-quality sociology. Despite the rigor of peer review, the journalistic and other gatekeepers who ultimately decide whether our sociology should become public are in some respects more demanding than our peers. They would of course like us to come up with headline-making findings, but at the least they will reject work that is merely a sociological reframing of already common knowledge.

A relevant and useful sociology—and public sociology—could also give the discipline a leg up in the increasing competition between the social sciences. When I was a graduate student, we talked, somewhat pretentiously to be sure, of sociology as the queen of the social sciences, reifying it for its ability to theorize and study empirically any subject we chose. Today, that queen has lost her throne if she ever had one, for other social sciences feel free to investigate topics we thought were purely sociological.

Economists with an empirical bent analyze the same national and other large databases that were once virtually wholly-owned sociological property. They and psychologists regularly run laboratory experiments on subjects once monopolized by sociologists, and anthropologists are finally doing fieldwork in the United States, thereby providing competition for sociological fieldworkers.

Last but not least there are book-writing journalists, some with at least undergraduate training in sociology and social science research methods. Although journalists working for daily and weekly media must meet deadlines that leave too little time for research, many book writers have as much if not more time for research than academic researchers. They have a better nose than we for the currently topical, and they are faster than we are in doing and publishing their work. And their prose will probably always be more lively than ours.

FOR SOCIOLOGY

I am not overly worried by the competition and believe in fact that the discipline may ultimately benefit from it. Moreover, sociology retains a number of distinctive strengths that, if properly exploited, enable it to keep pace with at least its academic competitors. Let me mention just five.

First, we continue to be the irreverent and philosophically daring social science. Second, despite the cultural turn that the discipline copied from the humanities, we still provide distinctive relational and structural analyses. Third, sociology has long specialized in going backstage. In an ever more scripted public sphere, we can therefore demonstrate the nakedness of various emperors and empresses better than the other social sciences. We also remain more active and effective debunkers.

Fourth, although all the social sciences depend to some extent on funding from the country's dominant institutions and other elites, sociologists continue to take an empirically grounded, bottoms-up perspective more often than other social scientists, subaltern theorizers notwithstanding. Sociologists also study ordinary people more often, although we still concentrate on the poor and the victims and need to do more research among and on the affluent as well as the victimizers.

Fifth, we come closest to the people we study. Sociology conducts a larger number of interview and fieldwork studies than its competitors, even if such studies are not always as attentive to macrosociological factors as they should be. I do not mean to denigrate theorizing, historical studies, surveys, database analyses, or quantitative research, but sociology's emphasis on qualitative empirical work has distinguished it from the other social sciences, even anthropology.

If sociologists can develop these strengths further in the coming years, public and other kinds of sociology will surely flourish.[2]

Disclosure Statement

The author is not aware of any affiliations, memberships, funding, or financial holdings that might be perceived as affecting the objectivity of this review.

Notes

Reprinted from *Annual Review of Sociology*, vol. 35, 2009, by permission of Annual Reviews.

1. I was inspired particularly by the Asian American and Latina students whose dissertations I sponsored or cosponsored, notably Margaret Chin, Jennifer Lee, Sara Lee, Ayumi Takenaka, Norma Fuentes, and Cynthia Duarte.

2. For brevity, articles reprinted in one of my essay collections [*People and Plans* (1968a); *People, Plans and Policies* (1992); and *Making Sense of America* (1999a)] are cited only in them.

References

Alba, R., Nee, V. 2003. *Remaking the American Mainstream*. Cambridge, MA: Harvard University Press.

Bellamy, E. 1888. *Looking Backward*. Boston, MA: Houghton Mifflin.

Bourdieu, P. 1984. *Distinction*. Cambridge, MA: Harvard University Press.

Burawoy, M. 2005. For public sociology. *Am. Sociol. Rev.* 70(1):4–24.

Gans, HJ. 1951. Park Forest: birth of a Jewish community. *Commentary* 11(4):330–39 (edited version in Gans 1999a, chapter 8).

Gans, HJ. 1953. The 'Yinglish' music of Mickey Katz: a study in American-Jewish popular culture. *American Quarterly* 5:213–18.

Gans, HJ. 1956a. American Jewry: present and future. *Commentary* 21(5):422–30.

Gans, HJ. 1956b. The future of American Jewry. *Commentary* 21(6):555–63.

Gans, HJ. 1957. The creator-audience relationship in the mass media: an analysis of movie making. In *Mass Culture: The Popular Arts in America*, ed. B Rosenberg, D White, pp. 315–24. Glencoe, IL: Free Press.

Gans, HJ. 1959 (1968). The human implications of current redevelopment and relocation planning. See Gans 1968a, chapter 15.

Gans, HJ. 1962a (1982). *The Urban Villagers.* Glencoe, IL: Free Press. Revised and expanded ed.

Gans, HJ. 1962b (1968). Urbanism and suburbanism as ways of life: a re-evaluation of definitions. See Gans 1968a, chapter 4.

Gans, HJ. 1962c. Hollywood films on British screens: an analysis of the functions of American popular culture abroad. *Soc. Probl.* 9:324–28.

Gans, HJ. 1964a. Some proposals for government policy in an automating society. *The Corresp.* 30(Jan.–Feb.):74–82.

Gans, HJ. 1964b (1968). Planning for the everyday life and problems of the average suburban and new town resident. See Gans 1968a, chapter 14.

Gans, HJ. 1965a (1968). The failure of urban renewal: a critique and some proposals. See Gans 1968a, chapter 18.

Gans, HJ. 1965b (1968). The Negro family: reflections on the 'Moynihan Report.' See Gans 1968a, chapter 20.

Gans, HJ. 1965c. The new radicalism: sect or political action movement. *Studies on Left* 5(Summer): 126–31.

Grans, HJ. 1966a. A rational approach to radicalism. *Studies on Left* 6(Jan.–Feb.): 37–46.

Gans, HJ. 1966b (1968). The federal role in solving America's urban problems. See Gans 1968a, chapter 19.

Gans, HJ. 1967 (1982). *The Levittowners: How People Live and Politic in Suburbia.* New York: Pantheon Books. 2nd ed., New York: Columbia University Press.

Gans, HJ. 1968a. *People and Plans.* New York: Basic Books.

Gans, HJ. 1968b (1992). Comparing the immigrant and Negro experience. See Gans 1992a, chapter 18.

Gans, HJ. 1972 (1999). The positive functions of poverty. See Gans 1999a, chapter 4.

Gans, HJ. 1973. *More Equality.* New York: Pantheon.

Gans, HJ. 1974 (1999). *Popular Culture and High Culture.* New York: Basic Books. Revised and updated ed.

Gans, HJ. 1979a (2004). *Deciding What's News.* New York: Pantheon. 25th anniv. ed., Evanston, IL: Northwestern University Press.

Gans, HJ. 1979b (1999). Symbolic ethnicity: the future of ethnic groups and cultures in America. See Gans 1999a, chapter 9.

Gans, HJ. 1988. *Middle American Individualism.* New York: Free Press.

Gans, HJ. 1989 (1999). Sociology in America: the discipline and the public. See Gans 1999a, chapter 12.

Gans, HJ, ed. 1990a. *Sociology in America.* Newbury Park, CA: Sage.

Gans, HJ. 1990b (1999). An autobiographical account. See Gans 1999a, appendix A.

Gans, HJ. 1990c (1992). Planning for worksharing: toward egalitarian worktime reduction. See Gans 1992a, chapter 16.

Gans, HJ. 1992a. *People, Plans and Policies.* New York: Columbia University Press.

Gans, HJ. 1992b (1999). Second-generation decline: scenarios for the economic and ethnic futures of the post-1965 American immigrants. See Gans 1999a, chapter 10.

Gans, HJ. 1995. *The War Against the Poor.* New York: Basic Books.

Gans, HJ. 1999a. *Making Sense of America.* Lanham, MD: Rowman & Littlefield.

Gans, HJ. 1999b. Toward a reconsideration of 'assimilation' and 'pluralism;' the interplay of acculturation and ethnic retention. See Gans 1999a, chapter 11.

Gans, HJ. 1999c. The possibility of a new racial hierarchy in the 21st-century United States. In *Cultural Territories of Race: Black and White Boundaries*, ed. M Lamont, pp. 371–90. Chicago, IL, University of Chicago Press.

Gans, HJ. 2002. The sociology of space: a user centered view. *City Community* 1(4):329–39.

Gans, HJ. 2003 a. *Democracy and the News.* New York: Oxford University Press.

Gans, HJ. 2003b. My years in antipoverty research and policy. In *Our Studies, Ourselves,* ed. B Giassner, R Hertz, pp. 90–102. New York: Oxford University Press.

Gans, HJ. 2005. Race as class. *Contexts* 4(4): 17–21.

Gans, HJ. 2008. *Imagining America in 2033.* Ann Arbor, MI: University of Michigan Press.

Gitlin, T. 1980. *The Whole World Is Watching.* Berkeley, CA: University of California Press.

Harrington, M. 1962. *The Other America.* New York: Macmillan.

Jacobs, J. 1961. *The Death and Life of Great American Cities.* New York: Random House.

Janowitz, M. 1952. *The Community Press in an Urban Setting.* Glencoe, IL: Free Press.

Katz, M. 1989. *The Undeserving Poor.* New York: Pantheon.

Lynd, RS., Lynd, HM. 1929. *Middletown in Transition: A Study in Cultural Conflicts.* New York: Harcourt Brace.

Mannheim, K. 1936. *Ideology and Utopia.* New York: Harcourt Brace.

Moynihan, D, ed. 1969. *On Understanding Poverty.* New York: Basic Books.

Myrdal, G. 1963. *Challenge to Affluence.* New York: Pantheon.

Portes, A., Zhou, M. 1993. The new second generation. *Annals of the American Academy of Political and Social Science* 530:74–96.

Riesman, D., Glazer, N., Denney, R. 1951. *The Lonely Crowd.* New Haven, CT: Yale University Press.

Tuchman, G. 1980. *Making News.* New York: Free Press.

Warner, W., Srole, L. 1945. *The Social Systems of American Ethnic Groups.* New Haven, CT: Yale University Press.

Whyte, W.F. 1943. *Street Corner Society.* Chicago, IL: University of Chicago Press.

Whyte, W.H. 1956. *The Organization Man.* New York: Simon & Schuster.